ATLAS OF
RUSSIAN HISTORY

ATLAS OF
RUSSIAN HISTORY

Martin Gilbert
Fellow of Merton College, Oxford

Cartographic consultant **ARTHUR BANKS**

DORSET PRESS

1984 Dorset Press

This edition published by Dorset Press, a division of MARBORO BOOKS Corp., by arrangement with the proprietor.
Originally published as *Russian History Atlas*.

Russian History Atlas was first published in Great Britain in 1972.

Library of Congress Catalog Card Number: 72-80174

ISBN 0-88029-018-8

Printed in the United States of America

Contents

Preface

I have designed this Atlas in the hope that it is possible to present—
within the span of 146 maps—a survey of Russian history from the
earliest times to the present day. In drafting each map, I drew upon
material from a wide range of published works—books, articles, atlases
and single sheet maps—each of which I have listed in the bibliography.

On the maps themselves I have included much factual material not
normally associated with historical geography, such as the text of one of
Stalin's few surviving personal communications—the postcard to his sister-
in-law (printed on map 54), and Lenin's telegram to the Bolsheviks in
Sweden (printed on map 87). I have drafted each map individually, in such
a way as to enable the maximum factual information to be included
without making use of a separate page of text; and I have compiled the
index in order that it may serve as a means of using the Atlas as if it were a
volume of narrative.

I wish to acknowledge the help of many colleagues and friends. In 1962
I began research into Russian history under the supervision of Dr George
Katkov, whose insatiable curiosity about elusive historical facts, and whose
enthusiasm in tracking them down, have influenced all my subsequent
work. I also benefitted from the teaching and encouragement of Mr David
Footman, Mr Max Hayward, Dr Harry Willetts and the late Mr Guy Wint.
When I was preparing the first sketches for this Atlas, the maps I had
drawn and the facts I had incoporrated on them were scrutinized by three
friends—Mr Michael Glenny, Mr Dennis O'Flaherty and Dr Harry
Shukman—to each of whom I am most grateful for many detailed
suggestions, and for giving up much time to help me. At the outset of my
research I received valuable bibliographical advice from Dr J. L. I.
Simmons, and suggestions for specific maps from Mr Norman Davies,
Dr Ronald Hingley, Mr John B. Kingston and Mr Ewald Uustalu.
Jane Cousins helped me with bibliographical and historical research;
Mr Arthur Banks transcribed my sketches into clear, printable maps, and
Kate Fleming kept a vigilant eye on the cartography. Susie Sacher helped
me to compile the index: Sarah Graham, as well as undertaking all the

secretarial work, made many important suggestions, factual and cartographic.

I should welcome any suggestions for new maps which could be incorporated in subsequent editions, and any note of errors or obscurities.

Note on Transliteration

I have tried to adopt a uniform system of transliteration from the Russian. But where a place is familiar to English readers in an anglicized form, I have used the familiar form (thus Archangel, not Arkhangelsk; Caucasus, not Kavkaz; Moscow, not Moskva). Towns in the frontier area between eastern Europe and Russia are in general given their Russian transliteration: I have given alternate spellings in the index. In the case of the Polish towns of Belzec, Bialystok and Przemysl, I have retained the Polish forms (rather than the less familiar Russian, Belzhets, Belostok and Peremyshl.)

List of Maps

Section One

ANCIENT AND EARLY MODERN RUSSIA

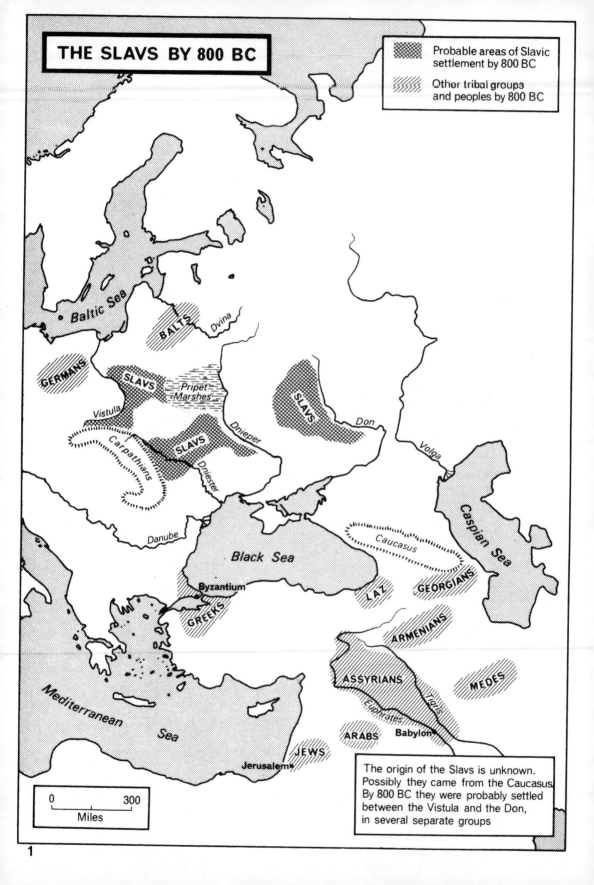

THE SLAVS BY 800 BC

Probable areas of Slavic settlement by 800 BC

Other tribal groups and peoples by 800 BC

Baltic Sea

BALTS

Dvina

GERMANS

SLAVS

Pripet Marshes

SLAVS

Vistula

Don

Volga

Carpathians

SLAVS

Dnieper

Dniester

Caspian Sea

Danube

Caucasus

Black Sea

Byzantium

LAZ

GEORGIANS

GREEKS

ARMENIANS

ASSYRIANS

MEDES

Mediterranean Sea

Euphrates

Tigris

ARABS

Babylon

JEWS

Jerusalem

The origin of the Slavs is unknown. Possibly they came from the Caucasus. By 800 BC they were probably settled between the Vistula and the Don, in several separate groups

0	300

Miles

1

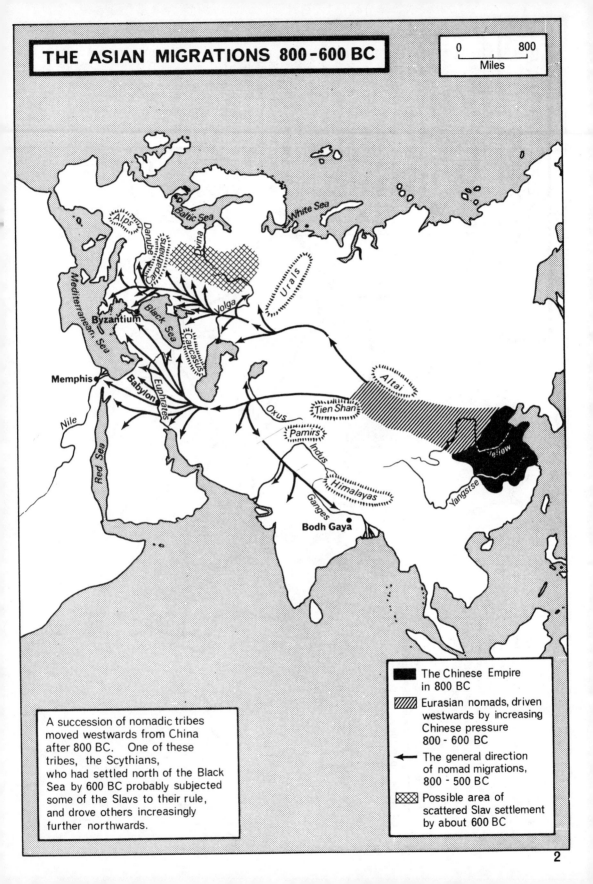

THE ASIAN MIGRATIONS 800-600 BC

0   800
Miles

Alps

Baltic Sea

White Sea

Danube

Carpathians

Dvina

Urals

Volga

Mediterranean Sea

Byzantium

Black Sea

Caucasus

Altai

Memphis

Babylon

Euphrates

Oxus

Tien Shan

Nile

Pamirs

Yellow

Red Sea

Indus

Himalayas

Ganges

Yangstse

Bodh Gaya

A succession of nomadic tribes
moved westwards from China
after 800 BC. One of these
tribes, the Scythians,
who had settled north of the Black
Sea by 600 BC probably subjected
some of the Slavs to their rule,
and drove others increasingly
further northwards.

■ The Chinese Empire
in 800 BC

▨ Eurasian nomads, driven
westwards by increasing
Chinese pressure
800 - 600 BC

← The general direction
of nomad migrations,
800 - 500 BC

▨ Possible area of
scattered Slav settlement
by about 600 BC

2

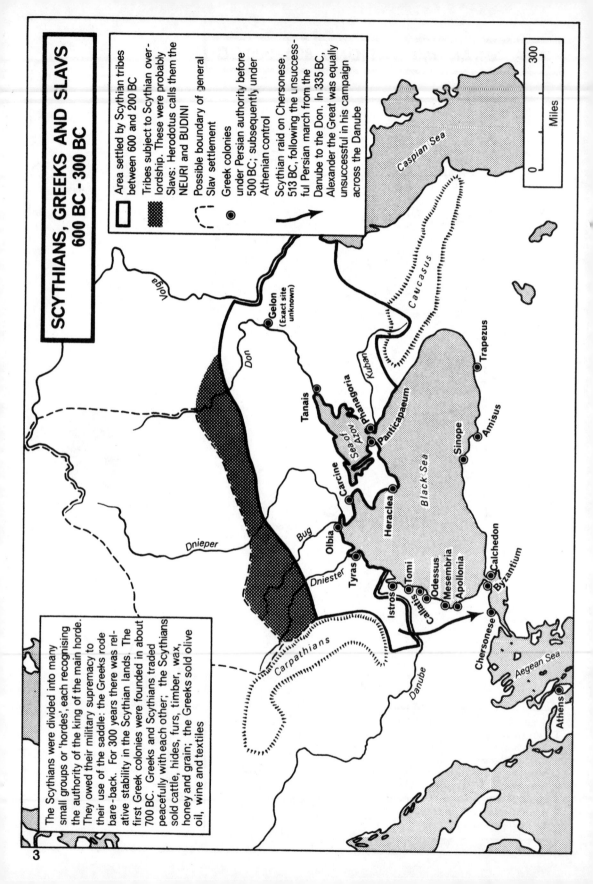

SCYTHIANS, GREEKS AND SLAVS
600 BC - 300 BC

Area settled by Scythian tribes between 600 and 200 BC

Tribes subject to Scythian over-lordship. These were probably Slavs: Herodotus calls them the NEURI and BUDINI

Possible boundary of general Slav settlement

● Greek colonies under Persian authority before 500 BC; subsequently under Athenian control

→ Scythian raid on Chersonese, 513 BC, following the unsuccess-ful Persian march from the Danube to the Don. In 335 BC, Alexander the Great was equally unsuccessful in his campaign across the Danube

The Scythians were divided into many small groups or 'hordes', each recognising the authority of the king of the main horde. They owed their military supremacy to their use of the saddle: the Greeks rode bare-back. For 300 years there was rel-ative stability in the Scythian lands. The first Greek colonies were founded in about 700 BC. Greeks and Scythians traded peacefully with each other; the Scythians sold cattle, hides, furs, timber, wax, honey and grain; the Greeks sold olive oil, wine and textiles

300
Miles
0

Caspian Sea

Volga

Don

Gelon (Exact site unknown)

Tanais

Caucasus

Kuban

Sea of Azov

Phanagoria

Panticapaeum

Trapezus

Amisus

Sinope

Black Sea

Carcine

Heraclea

Dnieper

Bug

Olbia

Dniester

Tyras

Istros

Callatis

Tomi

Odessus

Mesembria

Apollonia

Calchedon

Byzantium

Carpathians

Danube

Chersonese

Aegean Sea

Athens

3

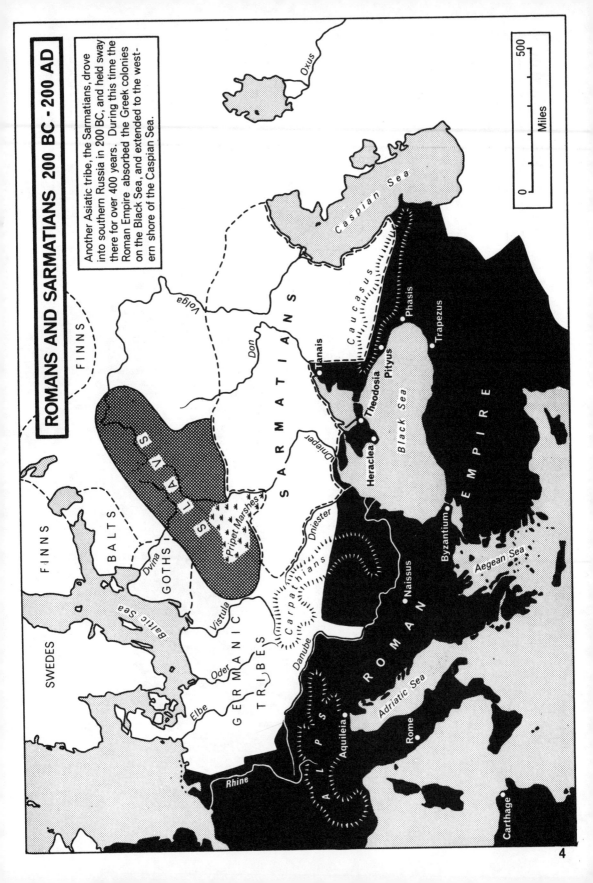

ROMANS AND SARMATIANS 200 BC - 200 AD

Another Asiatic tribe, the Sarmatians, drove into southern Russia in 200 BC, and held sway there for over 400 years. During this time the Roman Empire absorbed the Greek colonies on the Black Sea, and extended to the western shore of the Caspian Sea.

500

Miles

0

Oxus

Caspian Sea

Volga

FINNS

Don

Caucasus

Phasis

Trapezus

Tanais

Pityus

Theodosia

Black Sea

Heraclea

Dnieper

S A R M A T I A N S

SLAVS

Pripet Marshes

Dniester

Byzantium

Aegean Sea

Carpathians

Naissus

R O M A N   E M P I R E

FINNS

BALTS

GOTHS

Dvina

SWEDES

Baltic Sea

Vistula

Oder

G E R M A N I C   T R I B E S

Elbe

Danube

A L P S

Rhine

Aquileia

Rome

Adriatic Sea

Carthage

4

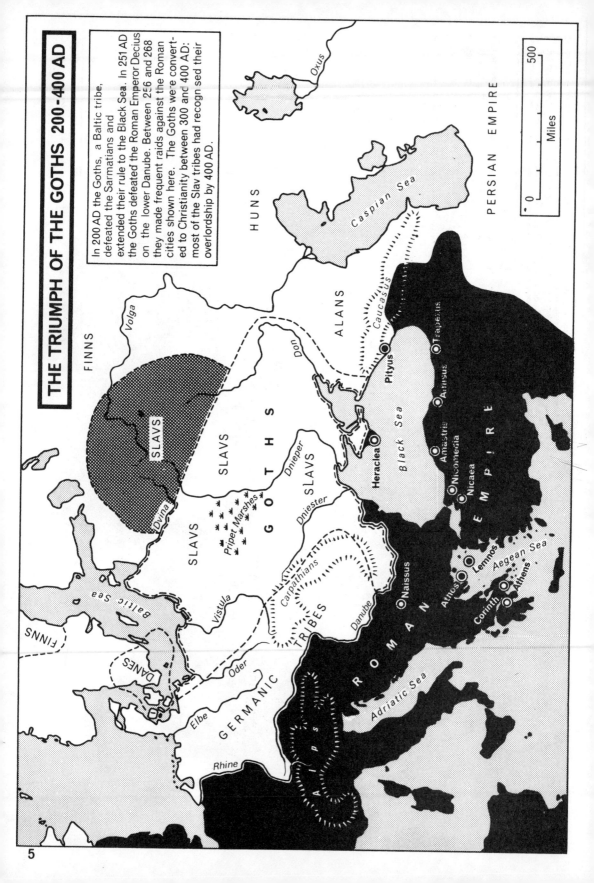

THE TRIUMPH OF THE GOTHS 200-400 AD

In 200 AD the Goths, a Baltic tribe, defeated the Sarmatians and extended their rule to the Black Sea. In 251 AD the Goths defeated the Roman Emperor Decius on the lower Danube. Between 256 and 268 they made frequent raids against the Roman cities shown here. The Goths were converted to Christianity between 300 and 400 AD: most of the Slav tribes had recognised their overlordship by 400 AD.

500

Miles

0

PERSIAN EMPIRE

Oxus

Caspian Sea

HUNS

ALANS

Caucasus

FINNS

Volga

Don

Pityus

Trapezus

Amisus

Amastris

Black Sea

Nicomedia

Nicaea

Heraclea

SLAVS

SLAVS

Dnieper

SLAVS

G O T H S

SLAVS

Dniester

Pripet Marshes

Dvina

FINNS

Baltic Sea

DANES

Vistula

Oder

Elbe

GERMANIC

Carpathians

TRIBES

Danube

Rhine

A L P S

R O M A N

E M P I R E

Naissus

Athos

Corinth

Athens

Lemnos

Aegean Sea

Adriatic Sea

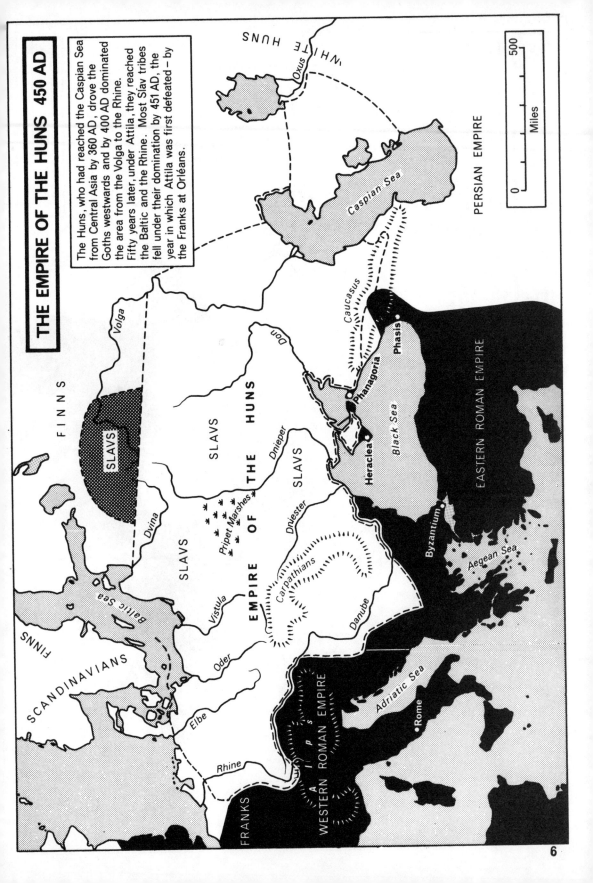

THE EMPIRE OF THE HUNS 450 AD

The Huns, who had reached the Caspian Sea from Central Asia by 360 AD, drove the Goths westwards and by 400 AD dominated the area from the Volga to the Rhine. Fifty years later, under Attila, they reached the Baltic and the Rhine. Most Slav tribes fell under their domination by 451 AD, the year in which Attila was first defeated – by the Franks at Orléans.

WHITE HUNS

PERSIAN EMPIRE

Oxus

Caspian Sea

Caucasus

FINNS

SLAVS

Volga

Don

Dvina

Dnieper

Dniester

Pripet Marshes

SLAVS

SLAVS

SLAVS

EMPIRE OF THE HUNS

Phanagoria

Phasis

Heraclea

Black Sea

EASTERN ROMAN EMPIRE

Byzantium

Aegean Sea

Baltic Sea

Vistula

Oder

Elbe

Carpathians

Danube

Rhine

FINNS

SCANDINAVIANS

FRANKS

A l p s

WESTERN ROMAN EMPIRE

Adriatic Sea

Rome

Miles
0   500

6

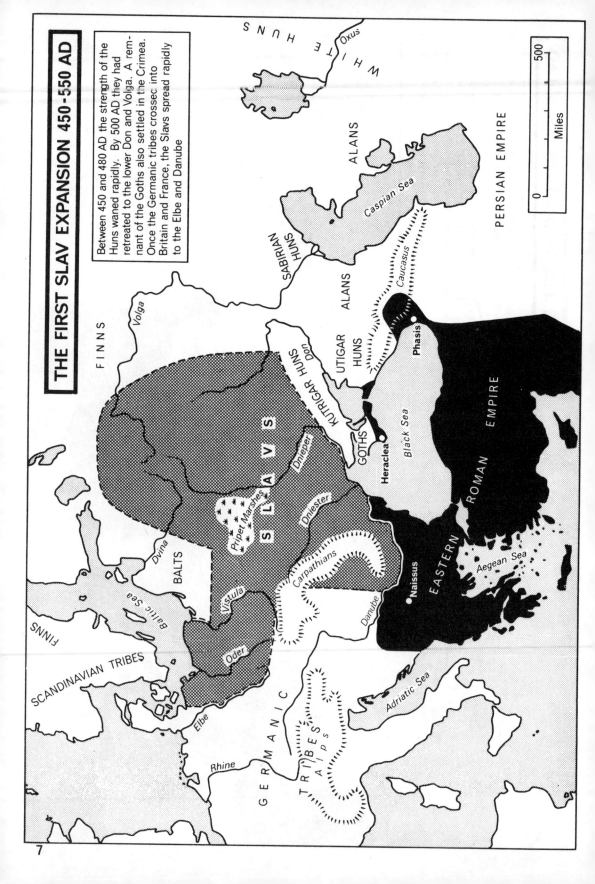

THE FIRST SLAV EXPANSION 450-550 AD

Between 450 and 480 AD the strength of the Huns waned rapidly. By 500 AD they had retreated to the lower Don and Volga. A remnant of the Goths also settled in the Crimea. Once the Germanic tribes crossed into Britain and France, the Slavs spread rapidly to the Elbe and Danube

WHITE HUNS

Oxus

ALANS

Caspian Sea

PERSIAN EMPIRE

0   500
Miles

FINNS

Volga

SABIRIAN HUNS

ALANS

UTIGAR HUNS

KUTRIGAR HUNS

Don

Caucasus

Phasis

Black Sea

GOTHS

Heraclea

EASTERN ROMAN EMPIRE

Aegean Sea

Dnieper

Dniester

Pripet Marshes

S L A V S

Carpathians

Danube

Naissus

Dvina

BALTS

Vistula

Baltic Sea

FINNS

SCANDINAVIAN TRIBES

Oder

Elbe

G E R M A N I C   T R I B E S

Alps

Rhine

Adriatic Sea

7

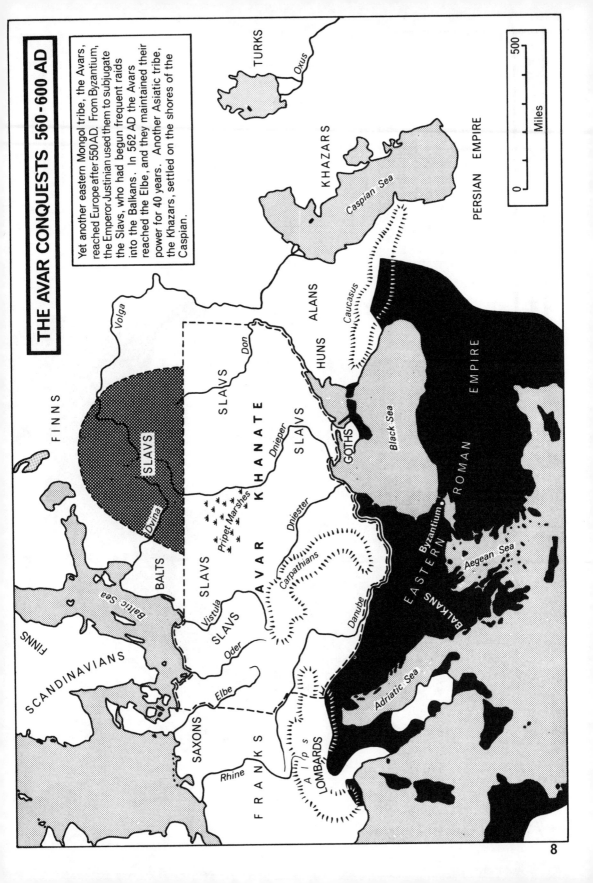

THE AVAR CONQUESTS 560-600 AD

Yet another eastern Mongol tribe, the Avars, reached Europe after 550AD. From Byzantium, the Emperor Justinian used them to subjugate the Slavs, who had begun frequent raids into the Balkans. In 562 AD the Avars reached the Elbe, and they maintained their power for 40 years. Another Asiatic tribe, the Khazars, settled on the shores of the Caspian.

500

0

Miles

TURKS

Oxus

KHAZARS

Caspian Sea

PERSIAN EMPIRE

FINNS

Volga

SLAVS

SLAVS

Don

Caucasus

HUNS   ALANS

Dnieper

AVAR KHANATE

SLAVS

Pripet Marshes

GOTHS

Black Sea

E A S T E R N

BALTS

SLAVS

Dniester

Vistula

Carpathians

Dvina

SLAVS

R O M A N   E M P I R E

Baltic Sea

FINNS

SLAVS

Oder

Danube

Byzantium

Aegean Sea

SCANDINAVIANS

B A L K A N S

SAXONS

Elbe

A l p s

LOMBARDS

Adriatic Sea

F R A N K S

Rhine

8

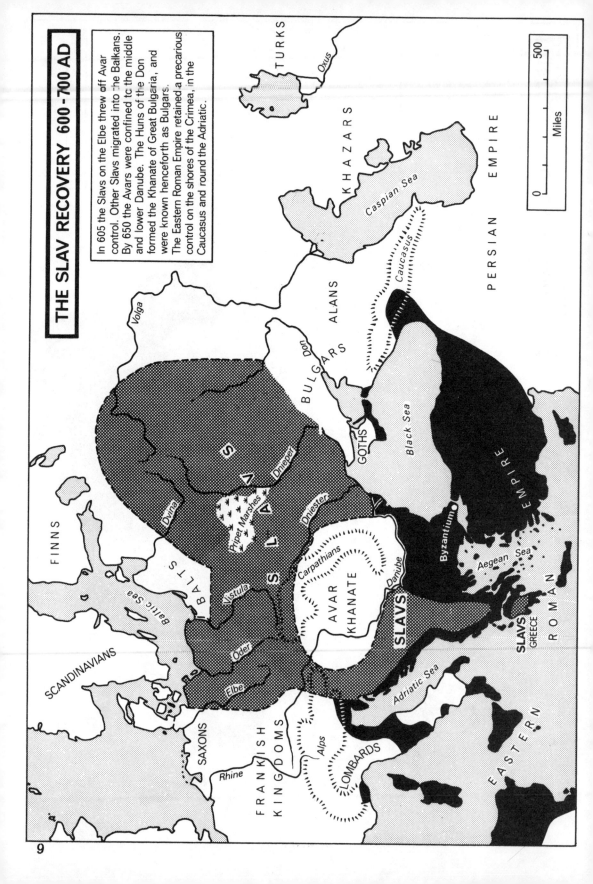

THE SLAV RECOVERY 600 - 700 AD

In 605 the Slavs on the Elbe threw off Avar control. Other Slavs migrated into the Balkans. By 650 the Avars were confined to the middle and lower Danube. The Huns of the Don formed the Khanate of Great Bulgaria, and were known henceforth as Bulgars. The Eastern Roman Empire retained a precarious control on the shores of the Crimea, in the Caucasus and round the Adriatic.

TURKS

Oxus

KHAZARS

Caspian Sea

PERSIAN EMPIRE

Volga

ALANS

Caucasus

BULGARS

Don

FINNS

S L A V S

Dnieper

GOTHS

Black Sea

Dvina

Pripet Marshes

Dniester

BALTS

Carpathians

Danube

Byzantium

Aegean Sea

Vistula

AVAR KHANATE

SLAVS

EASTERN ROMAN EMPIRE

Baltic Sea

Oder

SLAVS
GREECE

SCANDINAVIANS

Elbe

Adriatic Sea

SAXONS

FRANKISH KINGDOMS

Alps

LOMBARDS

Rhine

0   500

Miles

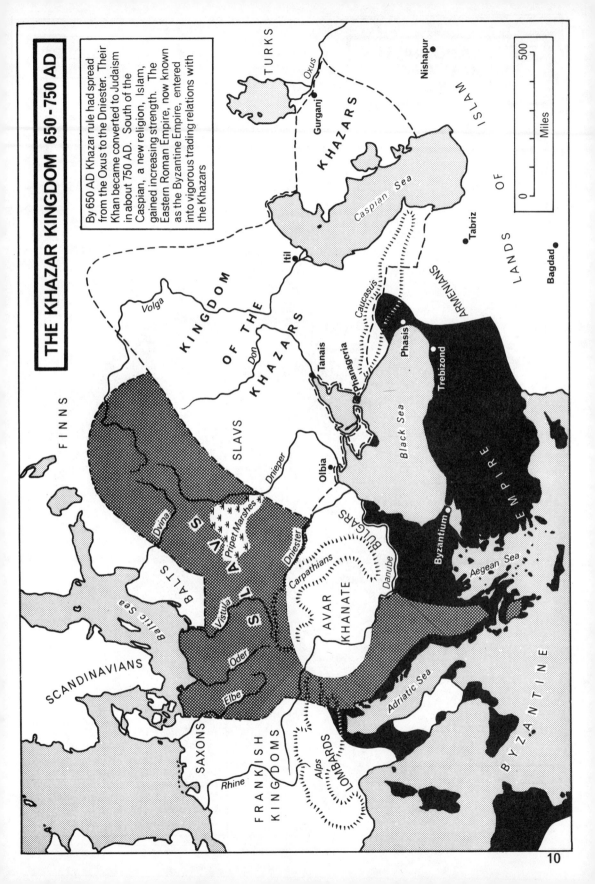

THE KHAZAR KINGDOM 650-750 AD

By 650 AD Khazar rule had spread from the Oxus to the Dniester. Their Khan became converted to Judaism in about 750 AD. South of the Caspian, Islam, a new religion, gained increasing strength. The Eastern Roman Empire, now known as the Byzantine Empire, entered into vigorous trading relations with the Khazars

500

0

Miles

TURKS

Nishapur

Oxus

KHAZARS

Gurganj

Caspian Sea

LANDS

Itil

Tabriz

OF

KINGDOM

Volga

Bagdad

ISLAM

Don

OF

THE

ARMENIANS

Caucasus

KHAZARS

Phasis

Tanais

Phanagoria

Trebizond

SLAVS

Dnieper

Black Sea

Olbia

FINNS

Dvina

S

Pripet Marshes

V

Dniester

BULGARS

Byzantium

EMPIRE

BALTS

Vistula

A

Carpathians

Danube

Aegean Sea

Baltic Sea

S

AVAR

KHANATE

SCANDINAVIANS

Oder

Elbe

Adriatic Sea

Alps

BYZANTINE

SAXONS

LOMBARDS

FRANKISH KINGDOMS

Rhine

THE SCANDINAVIAN MIGRATIONS 800 – 1000 AD

0   400
Miles

VINLAND
(Site unknown)
St. Lawrence

GREENLAND

NORTH
ATLANTIC
OCEAN

ICELAND

North
Pole

FAROE
ISLANDS

Iona

Lindisfarne
Jarrow
ENGLAND

Lisbon
SPAIN
Seville
FRANCE
Pamplona
Paris
Valence

Rome

Mediterranean Sea

Novgorod
Ladoga

Kiev
Dnieper

Olbia

KHAZARIA
Tanais

Volga

Constantinople
Black Sea

BYZANTIUM

Itil

Semender

Caspian Sea

ARMENIA
Antioch
Edessa
SYRIA

Baku

Red Sea

Persian Gulf

PERSIA

Gümüsh
Tepe

The Vikings, or Norsemen, sailed in successive waves from Scandinavia from 793 AD, when they landed at Lindisfarne, to 1098 when they reached Armenia. One line of Norse penetration and settlement was through the Slav lands, from Novgorod to Kiev, along the river trade routes which linked Scandinavia with Constantinople

■ The Scandinavian homelands in 800 AD
← Principal Scandinavian migrations 800-1000 AD

11

THE SLAVS AND THE NORSEMEN BY 880 AD

Slav settlement by 880 AD
SERB Principal Slav tribes
BALTS Other tribes
'Kievan Rus', ruled by the Norsemen (Varangarians), who took tribute from the neighbouring Slavs, and protected them against Khazar and Pecheneg attacks

NORSE
SWEDES
FINNS
DANES
Visby
Baltic Sea
BALTS
SLOVIANIANS
Novgorod
CHEREMESIANS
Volga
OBODRICHI
VIATCHIANS
MORDVINS
POLOCHANE
Smolensk
KRIVICHIANS
GERMANS
POLES
MAZOVIANS
Pripet Marshes
RADIMICHIANS
Elbe
SILESIANS
SEVERIANS
Don
CZECHS
DEREVLIANS
Kiev
KHAZARS
MORAVIANS
POLIANIANS
SLOVAKS
VOLHYNIANS
Danube
SLOVENES
MAGYARS
PECHENEGS
Venice
VLACHS
Tmutorokan
CROATS
Black Sea
Caucasus
Adriatic Sea
SERBS
Preslav
ARMENIANS
BULGARS
Constantinople
Ægean Sea
Athens
GREEKS

The Norse settlers between Novgorod and Kiev quickly dominated the local Slavs, over whom they established political control. Known as "Varangarians", these Norse overlords moulded the Slavs into a coherent federation, "Kievan Rus". Originally Norse speaking, Kievan Rus, or Russia, saw a close mingling of Scandinavian and Slav culture; and the emergence of a strong Kievan, or Russian national consciousness. The first Varangarian ruler, Rurik, led an expedition against Constantinople in 860 AD. His successor Oleg established his capital at Kiev in about 880 AD.

0 — 300
Miles

12

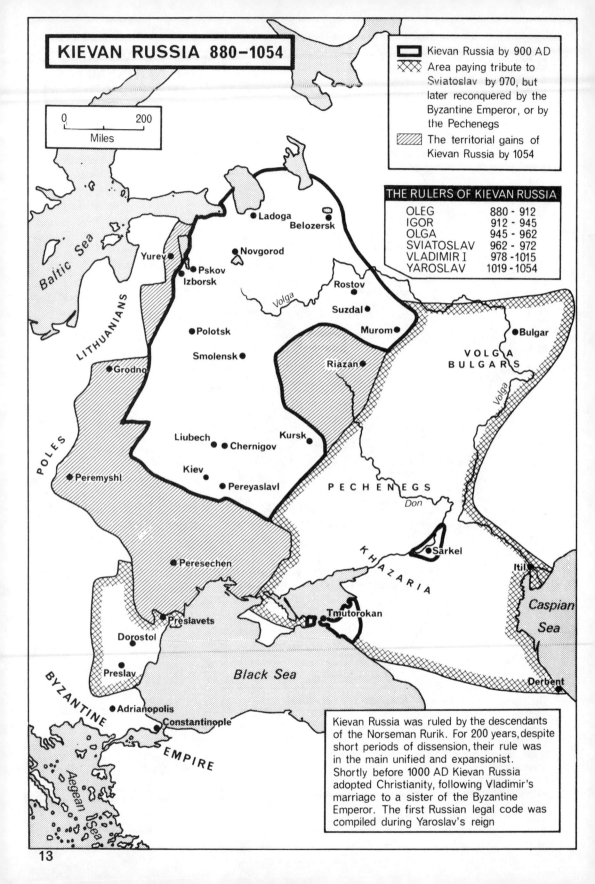

KIEVAN RUSSIA 880–1054

0   200
Miles

Kievan Russia by 900 AD

Area paying tribute to Sviatoslav by 970, but later reconquered by the Byzantine Emperor, or by the Pechenegs

The territorial gains of Kievan Russia by 1054

THE RULERS OF KIEVAN RUSSIA

OLEG	880 - 912
IGOR	912 - 945
OLGA	945 - 962
SVIATOSLAV	962 - 972
VLADIMIR I	978 - 1015
YAROSLAV	1019 - 1054

Baltic Sea

Ladoga
Belozersk
Yurev
Novgorod
Pskov
Izborsk
Rostov
Volga
Suzdal
Murom
Bulgar
Polotsk
VOLGA
BULGARS
Smolensk
Riazan
Volga
LITHUANIANS
Grodno

Liubech
Kursk
Chernigov
Kiev
Pereyaslavl
PECHENEGS
Don

POLES
Peremyshl

Peresechen
KHAZARIA
Sarkel
Itil
Caspian
Sea

Preslavets
Tmutorokan
Dorostol
Black Sea
Preslav
Derbent
BYZANTINE
Adrianopolis
Constantinople
EMPIRE

Aegean Sea

Kievan Russia was ruled by the descendants of the Norseman Rurik. For 200 years, despite short periods of dissension, their rule was in the main unified and expansionist. Shortly before 1000 AD Kievan Russia adopted Christianity, following Vladimir's marriage to a sister of the Byzantine Emperor. The first Russian legal code was compiled during Yaroslav's reign

13

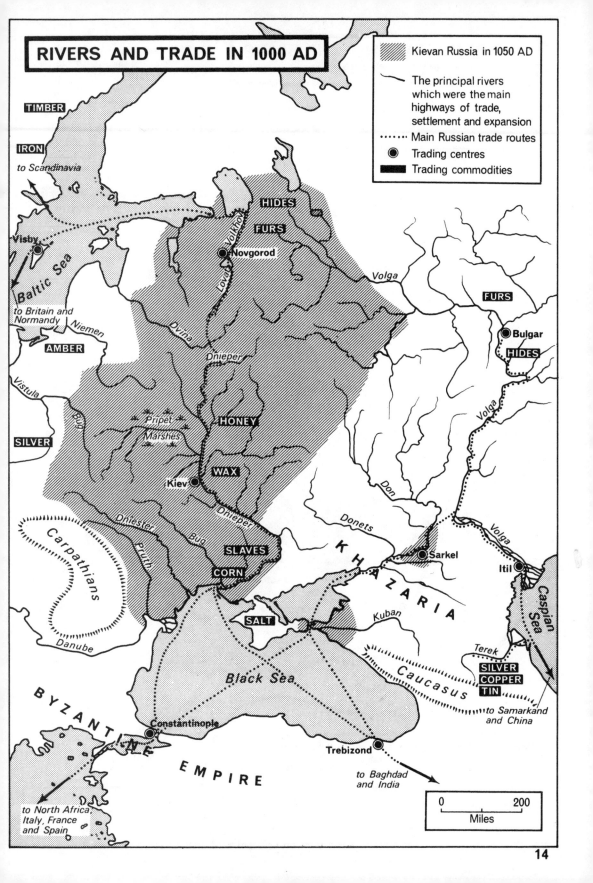

RIVERS AND TRADE IN 1000 AD

Kievan Russia in 1050 AD

The principal rivers which were the main highways of trade, settlement and expansion

Main Russian trade routes

Trading centres

Trading commodities

TIMBER

IRON
to Scandinavia

HIDES

FURS

Visby

Baltic Sea

Novgorod

Lovat

Volkhov

Volga

FURS

to Britain and Normandy

Niemen

Dvina

Bulgar

HIDES

AMBER

Dnieper

Vistula

Bug

Pripet Marshes

HONEY

Volga

SILVER

WAX

Kiev

Dnieper

Don

Donets

Volga

Carpathians

Dniester

Pruth

Bug

SLAVES

CORN

KHAZARIA

Sarkel

Itil

Danube

SALT

Kuban

Caspian Sea

Black Sea

Caucasus

Terek

SILVER
COPPER
TIN

to Samarkand and China

BYZANTINE

Constantinople

Trebizond

to Baghdad and India

EMPIRE

to North Africa, Italy, France and Spain

0	200

Miles

CHRISTIANITY AND THE SLAVS BY 1000 AD

The spread of Christianity led to the division of the Slav world. The Croats (in 700 AD) and the Poles (in 999 AD) were converted to Roman Catholicism. The Serbs (in 700 AD), Bulgars (865 AD) and Russians (988 AD) were converted to Eastern (Orthodox) Catholicism. This led in particular to strong antipathy between Russians and Poles, and also between Serbs and Croats

NORSE

SWEDES

North Sea

Baltic Sea

SAXONS

GERMANS

Oder

POLES

•Novgorod

•Smolensk

RUSSIANS

•Kiev

Volga

Don

Caspian Sea

•Paris

FRANKS

Rhine

Danube

Carpathians

MAGYARS

Dniester

ALANS

Caucasus

Alps

Milan•

CROATS

Adriatic Sea

SERBS

Black Sea

Constantinople

Tiflis

ARMENIANS

•Tabriz

Rome•

BULGARS

•Ochrid

GREEKS

Tarsus

Tigris

Kairouan•

Athens

Mediterranean Sea

•Aleppo

•Bagdad

Euphrates

Pyrenees

Alexandria

Jerusalem•

Dead Sea

Nile

Red Sea

The spread of Eastern, or Orthodox, Catholicism, under Constantinople's authority by 1000 AD

Western, or Roman, Catholicism

Areas under Muslim, or Islamic, rule

0   400
Miles

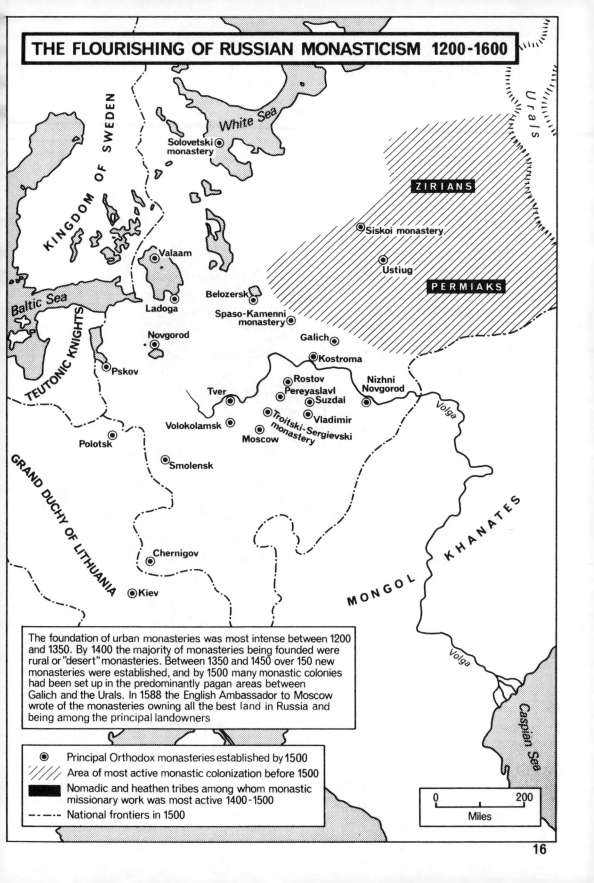

THE FLOURISHING OF RUSSIAN MONASTICISM 1200-1600

White Sea

KINGDOM OF SWEDEN

Urals

ZIRIANS

Solovetski monastery

⊙ Siskoi monastery

⊙ Valaam

Ustiug ⊙

PERMIAKS

Belozersk

Baltic Sea

Ladoga

Spaso-Kamenni monastery ⊙

TEUTONIC KNIGHTS

Novgorod

Galich ⊙

⊙ Kostroma

⊙ Pskov

Rostov ⊙

Nizhni Novgorod

Tver ⊙

Pereyaslavl ⊙

⊙ Suzdal

Volokolamsk ⊙

Troitski-Sergievski monastery ⊙

⊙ Vladimir

Polotsk ⊙

Moscow ⊙

⊙ Smolensk

MONGOL KHANATES

GRAND DUCHY OF LITHUANIA

⊙ Chernigov

Volga

⊙ Kiev

Volga

Caspian Sea

The foundation of urban monasteries was most intense between 1200 and 1350. By 1400 the majority of monasteries being founded were rural or "desert" monasteries. Between 1350 and 1450 over 150 new monasteries were established, and by 1500 many monastic colonies had been set up in the predominantly pagan areas between Galich and the Urals. In 1588 the English Ambassador to Moscow wrote of the monasteries owning all the best land in Russia and being among the principal landowners

⊙ Principal Orthodox monasteries established by 1500

/// Area of most active monastic colonization before 1500

■ Nomadic and heathen tribes among whom monastic missionary work was most active 1400-1500

–·–·– National frontiers in 1500

0   200

Miles

16

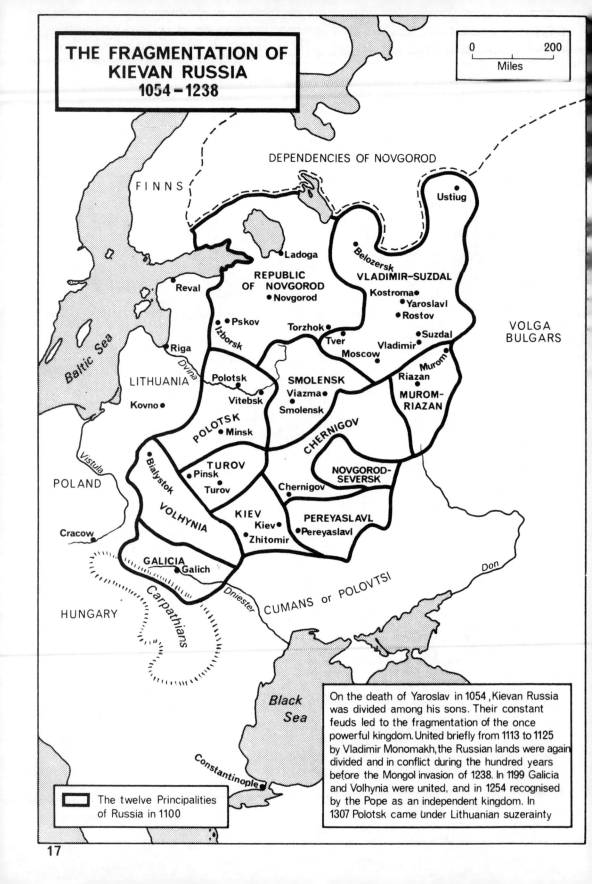

THE FRAGMENTATION OF KIEVAN RUSSIA 1054–1238

0   200
Miles

DEPENDENCIES OF NOVGOROD

FINNS

Ustiug

Ladoga

Belozersk

VLADIMIR–SUZDAL

Reval

REPUBLIC OF NOVGOROD
Novgorod

Kostroma

Yaroslavl

Rostov

Pskov

Torzhok

Tver

Suzdal

VOLGA BULGARS

Riga

Izborsk

Vladimir

Moscow

Murom

Dvina

Polotsk

SMOLENSK

Riazan

LITHUANIA

Vitebsk

Viazma

MUROM–RIAZAN

Kovno

Smolensk

POLOTSK

Minsk

CHERNIGOV

Vistula

Bialystok

TUROV

Pinsk

NOVGOROD–SEVERSK

POLAND

Turov

Chernigov

VOLHYNIA

KIEV

Kiev

PEREYASLAVL

Cracow

Zhitomir

Pereyaslavl

Don

GALICIA

Galich

Dniester

CUMANS or POLOVTSI

Carpathians

HUNGARY

Black Sea

Constantinople

The twelve Principalities
of Russia in 1100

On the death of Yaroslav in 1054, Kievan Russia
was divided among his sons. Their constant
feuds led to the fragmentation of the once
powerful kingdom. United briefly from 1113 to 1125
by Vladimir Monomakh, the Russian lands were again
divided and in conflict during the hundred years
before the Mongol invasion of 1238. In 1199 Galicia
and Volhynia were united, and in 1254 recognised
by the Pope as an independent kingdom. In
1307 Polotsk came under Lithuanian suzerainty

Baltic Sea

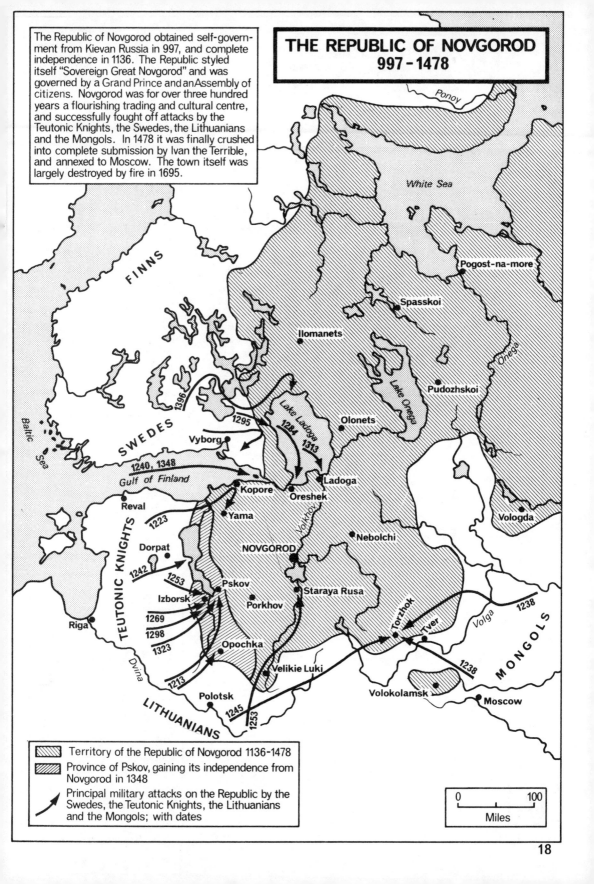

The Republic of Novgorod obtained self-government from Kievan Russia in 997, and complete
independence in 1136. The Republic styled
itself "Sovereign Great Novgorod" and was
governed by a Grand Prince and an Assembly of
citizens. Novgorod was for over three hundred
years a flourishing trading and cultural centre,
and successfully fought off attacks by the
Teutonic Knights, the Swedes, the Lithuanians
and the Mongols. In 1478 it was finally crushed
into complete submission by Ivan the Terrible,
and annexed to Moscow. The town itself was
largely destroyed by fire in 1695.

THE REPUBLIC OF NOVGOROD
997 – 1478

Ponoy

White Sea

Pogost-na-more

Spasskoi

FINNS

Ilomanets

Lake Onega

Olonets

Pudozhskoi

Onega

SWEDES

1396

1295

Lake Ladoga

1284

1313

Vyborg

Baltic
Sea

1240, 1348
Gulf of Finland

Kopore

Oreshek

Ladoga

Volkhov

Vologda

Reval

1223

Yama

Nebolchi

TEUTONIC KNIGHTS

Dorpat

NOVGOROD

1242

1253

Pskov

Staraya Rusa

Izborsk

Porkhov

Riga

1269

1298

1323

Opochka

Torzhok

Tver

Volga

1238

MONGOLS

Velikie Luki

1238

1213

Volokolamsk

Moscow

Dvina

Polotsk

1245

1253

LITHUANIANS

Territory of the Republic of Novgorod 1136-1478

Province of Pskov, gaining its independence from
Novgorod in 1348

Principal military attacks on the Republic by the
Swedes, the Teutonic Knights, the Lithuanians
and the Mongols; with dates

0   100
Miles

18

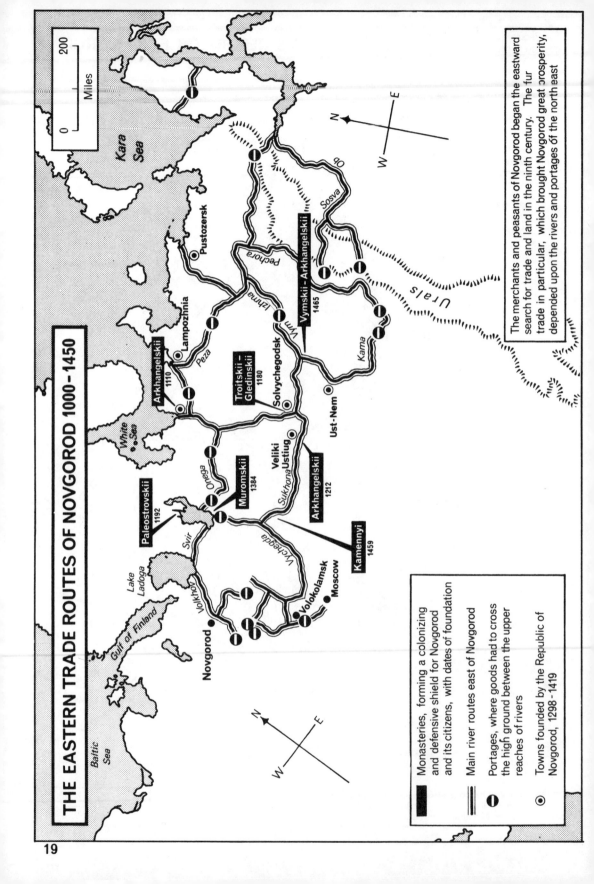

THE EASTERN TRADE ROUTES OF NOVGOROD 1000-1450

The merchants and peasants of Novgorod began the eastward search for trade and land in the ninth century. The fur trade in particular, which brought Novgorod great prosperity, depended upon the rivers and portages of the north east

Monasteries, forming a colonizing and defensive shield for Novgorod and its citizens, with dates of foundation

Main river routes east of Novgorod

Portages, where goods had to cross the high ground between the upper reaches of rivers

Towns founded by the Republic of Novgorod, 1298-1419

Kara Sea

Pustozersk

Vymskii – Arkhangelskii
1465

Arkhangelskii
1110

Lampozhnia

Troitskii – Gledinskii
1180

Solvychegodsk

White Sea

Ust-Nem

Veliki Ustiug

Arkhangelskii
1212

Paleostrovskii
1192

Muromskii
1384

Kamennyi
1459

Moscow

Volokolamsk

Novgorod

Lake Ladoga

Gulf of Finland

Baltic Sea

Peza

Izhma

Pechora

Ob

Sosva

Urals

Vym

Kama

Sukhona

Vychegda

Onega

Svir

Volkhov

0   200
Miles

19

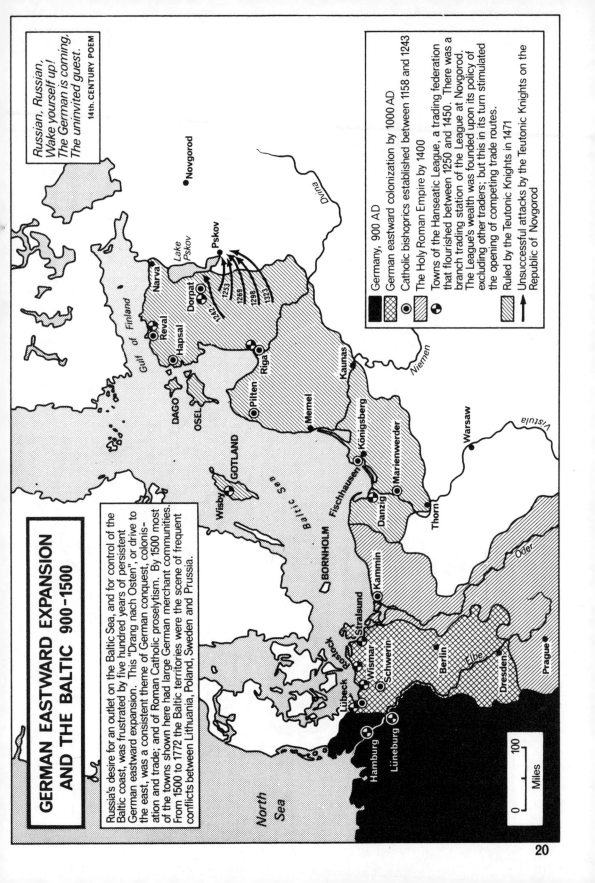

GERMAN EASTWARD EXPANSION AND THE BALTIC 900-1500

Russia's desire for an outlet on the Baltic Sea, and for control of the Baltic coast, was frustrated by five hundred years of persistent German eastward expansion. This "Drang nach Osten", or drive to the east, was a consistent theme of German conquest, colonisation and trade; and of Roman Catholic proselytism. By 1500 most of the towns shown here had large German merchant communities. From 1500 to 1772 the Baltic territories were the scene of frequent conflicts between Lithuania, Poland, Sweden and Prussia.

Russian, Russian,
Wake yourself up!
The German is coming,
The uninvited guest.

14th. CENTURY POEM

Germany, 900 AD

German eastward colonization by 1000 AD

Catholic bishoprics established between 1158 and 1243

The Holy Roman Empire by 1400

Towns of the Hanseatic League, a trading federation that flourished between 1250 and 1450. There was a branch trading station of the League at Novgorod. The League's wealth was founded upon its policy of excluding other traders; but this in its turn stimulated the opening of competing trade routes.

Ruled by the Teutonic Knights in 1471

Unsuccessful attacks by the Teutonic Knights on the Republic of Novgorod

North Sea

Baltic Sea

Gulf of Finland

Lake Pskov

Novgorod

Narva
Reval
Hapsal
Dorpat
Pskov
Riga
Pilten
DAGO
OSEL
GOTLAND
Wisby
BORNHOLM
Memel
Kaunas
Königsberg
Marienwerder
Fischhausen
Danzig
Thorn
Warsaw
Kammin
Stralsund
Wismar
Schwerin
Rostock
Lübeck
Hamburg
Lüneburg
Berlin
Dresden
Prague

Dvina
Niemen
Vistula
Oder
Elbe

1242
1253
1269
1298
1323

0   100
Miles

20

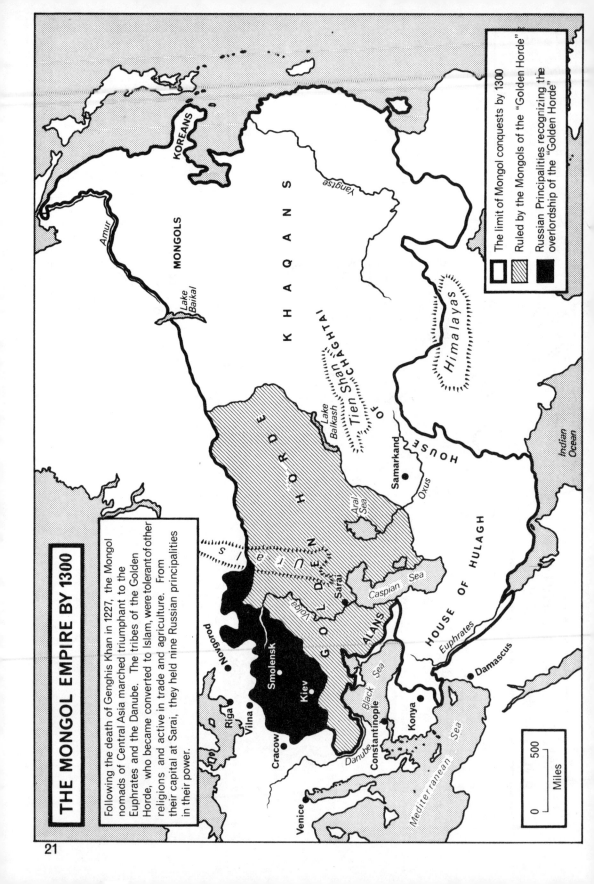

THE MONGOL EMPIRE BY 1300

Following the death of Genghis Khan in 1227, the Mongol nomads of Central Asia marched triumphant to the Euphrates and the Danube. The tribes of the Golden Horde, who became converted to Islam, were tolerant of other religions and active in trade and agriculture. From their capital at Sarai, they held nine Russian principalities in their power.

The limit of Mongol conquests by 1300

Ruled by the Mongols of the "Golden Horde"

Russian Principalities recognizing the overlordship of the "Golden Horde"

KOREANS

MONGOLS

Amur

Lake Baikal

Yangtse

KHAQANS

Himalayas

CHAGHTAI

Tien Shan

OF

HOUSE

Lake Balkash

Samarkand

Oxus

Aral Sea

Indian Ocean

GOLDEN HORDE

SIBERIA

URALS

Caspian Sea

HOUSE OF HULAGH

Sarai

Volga

Euphrates

ALANS

Damascus

Novgorod

Smolensk

Kiev

Black Sea

Konya

Riga

Vilna

Constantinople

Danube

Cracow

Mediterranean Sea

Venice

0   500
Miles

21

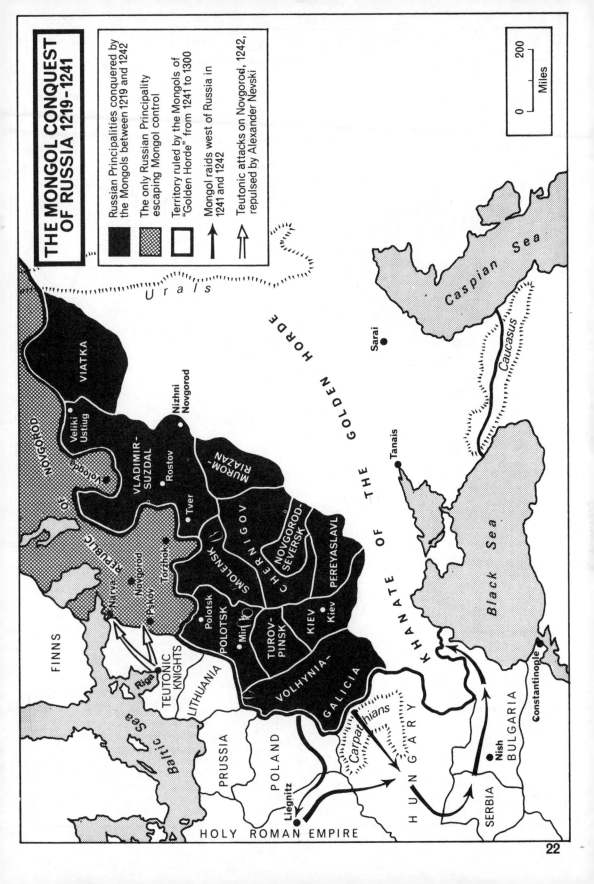

THE MONGOL CONQUEST OF RUSSIA 1219–1241

Russian Principalities conquered by the Mongols between 1219 and 1242

The only Russian Principality escaping Mongol control

Territory ruled by the Mongols of "Golden Horde" from 1241 to 1300

Mongol raids west of Russia in 1241 and 1242

Teutonic attacks on Novgorod, 1242, repulsed by Alexander Nevski

200

Miles

0

Caspian Sea

U r a l s

Sarai

Caucasus

Tanais

VIATKA

NOVGOROD

Veliki Ustiug

Vologda

Nizhni Novgorod

VLADIMIR– SUZDAL

Rostov

Tver

MUROM– RIAZAN

Black Sea

THE GOLDEN HORDE

KHANATE OF

CHERNIGOV

NOVGOROD SEVERSK

PEREYASLAVL

REPUBLIC

Narva

Novgorod

Pskov

Torzhok

SMOLENSK

Polotsk

POLOTSK

Minsk

TUROV– PINSK

KIEV

Kiev

Constantinople

FINNS

Riga

TEUTONIC KNIGHTS

LITHUANIA

VOLHYNIA–

GALICIA

Carpathians

H U N G A R Y

BULGARIA

Nish

SERBIA

Baltic Sea

PRUSSIA

POLAND

Liegnitz

HOLY ROMAN EMPIRE

THE LITHUANIAN CONQUESTS 1240-1462

Baltic Sea

ROSTOV

NOVGOROD

TVER

Riga

PSKOV

MOSCOW

TEUTONIC KNIGHTS

Polotsk

Viazma

Vitebsk

Smolensk

Kovno

Vilna

RIAZAN

TEUTONIC KNIGHTS

Minsk

Briansk

Grodno

Slonim

Warsaw

Brest-Litovsk

Turov

Pinsk

KINGDOM

Chernigov

OF

Vladimir

POLAND

Kiev

Lvov

Zhitomir

Poltava

CRIMEAN KHANATE Mongols

CRIMEAN KHANATE Mongols

Haji-bey

Sea of Azov

Black Sea

0   150

Miles

Grand Principality of Lithuania, 1240

Lithuanian conquests by 1340, including the Russian Principalities of Polotsk and Pinsk-Turov

Ruled by Lithuania in 1462

Russian Principalities unconquered by Lithuania

Shattered by Mongol invasions, and divided among themselves, the Russian Principalities fell easy victims to Lithuanian expansion after 1240.
In 1386, Lithuania and the Kingdom of Poland united under a single king. The Catholicism of this powerful kingdom was an extra cause of conflict with Russia.

THE EASTWARD SPREAD OF CATHOLICISM BY 1462

Simultaneously with the Mongol invasions from the east, Russia was subjected to the continual westward movement of Roman Catholicism. Under Swedish and Lithuanian pressure, Russian Orthodoxy was pushed back almost to Moscow. Roman Catholicism also made advances against the Orthodox Bulgars in the Balkans, and against the Muslim lands in the eastern Mediterranean.

LAPLAND
1300

NORWAY

SWEDEN

DENMARK

RUSSIA

Vyborg
1293

Reval
1219

Novgorod

Pskov

Tver

Moscow

Baltic Sea

Mitava
1271

Kaluga

Danzig
1200

Vilna
1386

Smolensk
1450

PRUSSIA

LITHUANIA

Warsaw

THE

POLAND

Kiev
1385

HOLY

Prague

GALICIA

BOHEMIA

ROMAN

Vienna

Lvov
1340

UKRAINE

EMPIRE

HUNGARY

Tana
1261

CROATIA

TRANSYLVANIA

Kaffa
1261

Black Sea

Rome

BALKANS

Constantinople
1261

Amastris
1310

Samsun
1310

Aegean Sea

Athens
1305

Edessa
1098

Antioch
1098

| | The Roman Catholic world in 1000 AD |
| | Conquered between 1000 and 1462 AD by Roman Catholic rulers, and forming part of Catholic kingdoms |

0   300
Miles

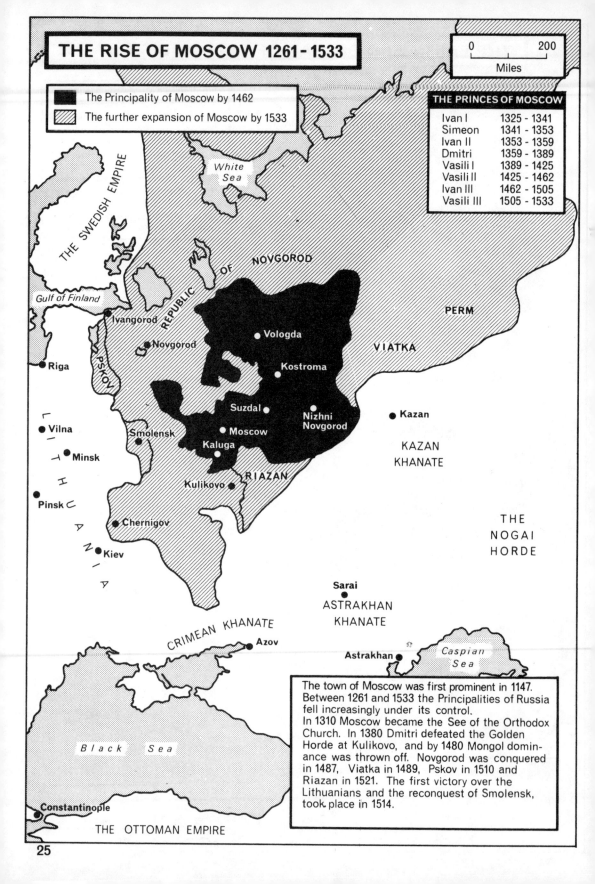

THE RISE OF MOSCOW 1261-1533

0   200
Miles

The Principality of Moscow by 1462
The further expansion of Moscow by 1533

THE PRINCES OF MOSCOW

Ivan I	1325 - 1341
Simeon	1341 - 1353
Ivan II	1353 - 1359
Dmitri	1359 - 1389
Vasili I	1389 - 1425
Vasili II	1425 - 1462
Ivan III	1462 - 1505
Vasili III	1505 - 1533

THE SWEDISH EMPIRE

White Sea

REPUBLIC OF NOVGOROD

Gulf of Finland

Ivangorod

Novgorod

PERM

Vologda

VIATKA

Riga

PSKOV

Kostroma

Suzdal

Nizhni Novgorod

Kazan

Vilna

Smolensk

Moscow

KAZAN KHANATE

Minsk

Kaluga

L I T H U A N I A

Kulikovo

RIAZAN

Pinsk

THE NOGAI HORDE

Chernigov

Kiev

Sarai

ASTRAKHAN KHANATE

CRIMEAN KHANATE

Azov

Astrakhan

Caspian Sea

Black Sea

The town of Moscow was first prominent in 1147.
Between 1261 and 1533 the Principalities of Russia
fell increasingly under its control.
In 1310 Moscow became the See of the Orthodox
Church. In 1380 Dmitri defeated the Golden
Horde at Kulikovo, and by 1480 Mongol domin-
ance was thrown off. Novgorod was conquered
in 1487, Viatka in 1489, Pskov in 1510 and
Riazan in 1521. The first victory over the
Lithuanians and the reconquest of Smolensk,
took place in 1514.

Constantinople

THE OTTOMAN EMPIRE

25

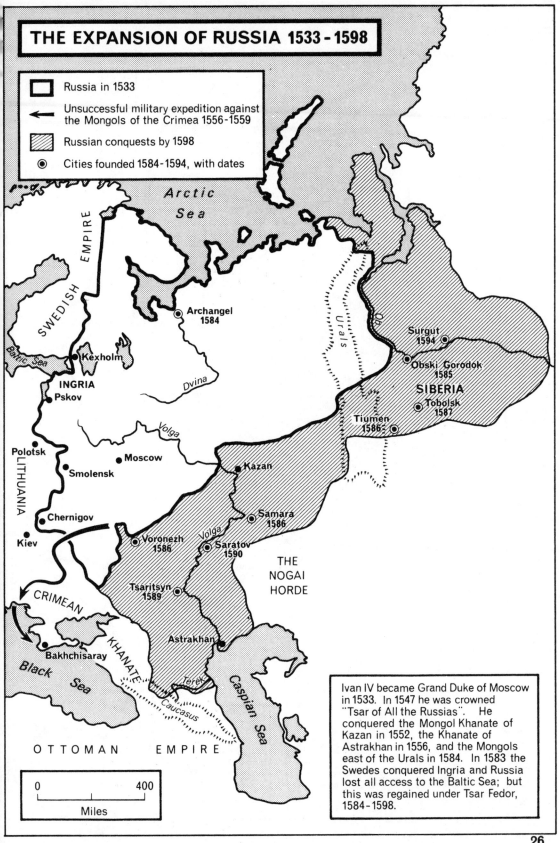

THE EXPANSION OF RUSSIA 1533 - 1598

Russia in 1533

Unsuccessful military expedition against the Mongols of the Crimea 1556-1559

Russian conquests by 1598

⊙ Cities founded 1584-1594, with dates

Arctic Sea

SWEDISH EMPIRE

Archangel 1584

Kexholm

Baltic Sea

INGRIA

Pskov

Polotsk

LITHUANIA

Smolensk

Moscow

Chernigov

Kiev

Dvina

Volga

Kazan

Urals

Ob

Surgut 1594 ⊙

Obski Gorodok 1585 ⊙

SIBERIA

Tobolsk 1587 ⊙

Tiumen 1586 ⊙

Samara 1586 ⊙

Voronezh 1586 ⊙

Saratov 1590 ⊙

Volga

THE NOGAI HORDE

Tsaritsyn 1589 ⊙

CRIMEAN KHANATE

Bakhchisaray

Black Sea

Astrakhan

Terek

Caucasus

Caspian Sea

OTTOMAN EMPIRE

0   400

Miles

Ivan IV became Grand Duke of Moscow in 1533. In 1547 he was crowned "Tsar of All the Russias". He conquered the Mongol Khanate of Kazan in 1552, the Khanate of Astrakhan in 1556, and the Mongols east of the Urals in 1584. In 1583 the Swedes conquered Ingria and Russia lost all access to the Baltic Sea; but this was regained under Tsar Fedor, 1584-1598.

MOSCOW AND THE RIVERS OF EUROPEAN RUSSIA 1460-1860

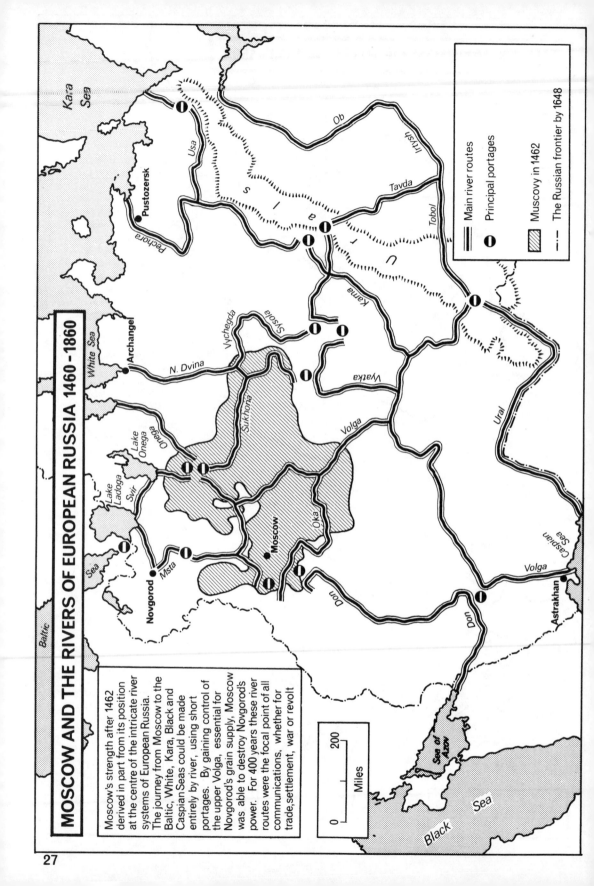

Moscow's strength after 1462 derived in part from its position at the centre of the intricate river systems of European Russia. The journey from Moscow to the Baltic, White, Kara, Black and Caspian Seas could be made entirely by river, using short portages. By gaining control of the upper Volga, essential for Novgorod's grain supply, Moscow was able to destroy Novgorod's power. For 400 years these river routes were the focal point of all communications, whether for trade, settlement, war or revolt

Legend:
- Main river routes
- Principal portages
- Muscovy in 1462
- The Russian frontier by 1648

Kara Sea · Pustozersk · Ob · Irtysh · Usa · Pechora · Tavda · Tobol · Siberia · Ural · Kama · Vychegda · Sysola · Vyatka · Archangel · N. Dvina · White Sea · Sukhona · Volga · Ural · Onega · Lake Onega · Lake Ladoga · Svir · Baltic Sea · Msta · Novgorod · Moscow · Oka · Don · Volga · Caspian Sea · Astrakhan · Don · Sea of Azov · Black Sea

0 — 200 Miles

27

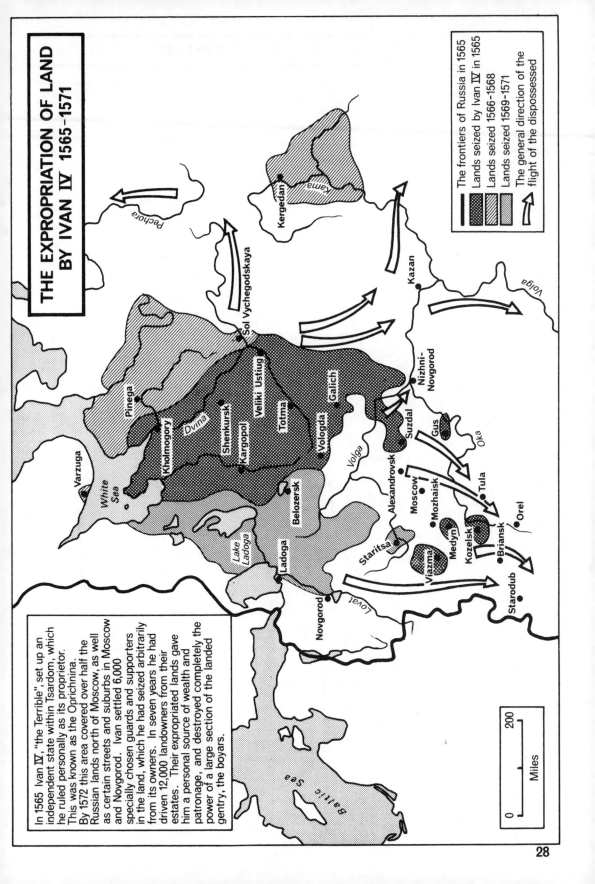

THE EXPROPRIATION OF LAND BY IVAN IV 1565-1571

In 1565 Ivan IV, "the Terrible", set up an independent state within Tsardom, which he ruled personally as its proprietor. This was known as the Oprichnina.
By 1572 this area covered over half the Russian lands north of Moscow, as well as certain streets and suburbs in Moscow and Novgorod. Ivan settled 6,000 specially chosen guards and supporters in the land, which he had seized arbitrarily from its owners. In seven years he had driven 12,000 landowners from their estates. Their expropriated lands gave him a personal source of wealth and patronage, and destroyed completely the power of a large section of the landed gentry, the boyars.

The frontiers of Russia in 1565
Lands seized by Ivan IV in 1565
Lands seized 1566-1568
Lands seized 1569-1571
The general direction of the flight of the dispossessed

0   200
Miles

Varzuga
White Sea
Pinega
Kholmogory
Dvina
Shenkursk
Kargopol
Veliki Ustiug
Totma
Vologda
Galich
Sol Vychegodskaya
Pechora
Kergedan
Kama
Kazan
Volga
Nizhni-Novgorod
Suzdal
Gus
Oka
Alexandrovsk
Moscow
Mozhaisk
Tula
Orel
Medyn
Viazma
Kozelsk
Briansk
Stratisk
Starodub
Novgorod
Lovat
Ladoga
Lake Ladoga
Belozersk
Volga
Baltic Sea

28

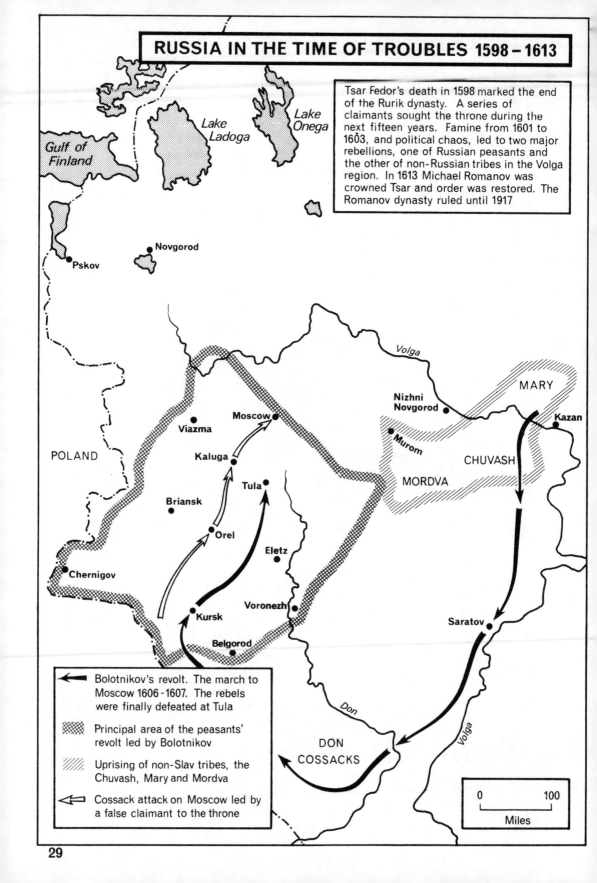

RUSSIA IN THE TIME OF TROUBLES 1598 – 1613

Tsar Fedor's death in 1598 marked the end of the Rurik dynasty. A series of claimants sought the throne during the next fifteen years. Famine from 1601 to 1603, and political chaos, led to two major rebellions, one of Russian peasants and the other of non-Russian tribes in the Volga region. In 1613 Michael Romanov was crowned Tsar and order was restored. The Romanov dynasty ruled until 1917

Gulf of Finland

Lake Ladoga

Lake Onega

Novgorod

Pskov

Volga

Nizhni Novgorod

MARY

Kazan

Moscow

Viazma

Murom

CHUVASH

Kaluga

MORDVA

POLAND

Tula

Briansk

Orel

Eletz

Chernigov

Voronezh

Saratov

Kursk

Belgorod

Don

Volga

DON
COSSACKS

Bolotnikov's revolt. The march to Moscow 1606-1607. The rebels were finally defeated at Tula

Principal area of the peasants' revolt led by Bolotnikov

Uprising of non-Slav tribes, the Chuvash, Mary and Mordva

Cossack attack on Moscow led by a false claimant to the throne

0   100

Miles

29

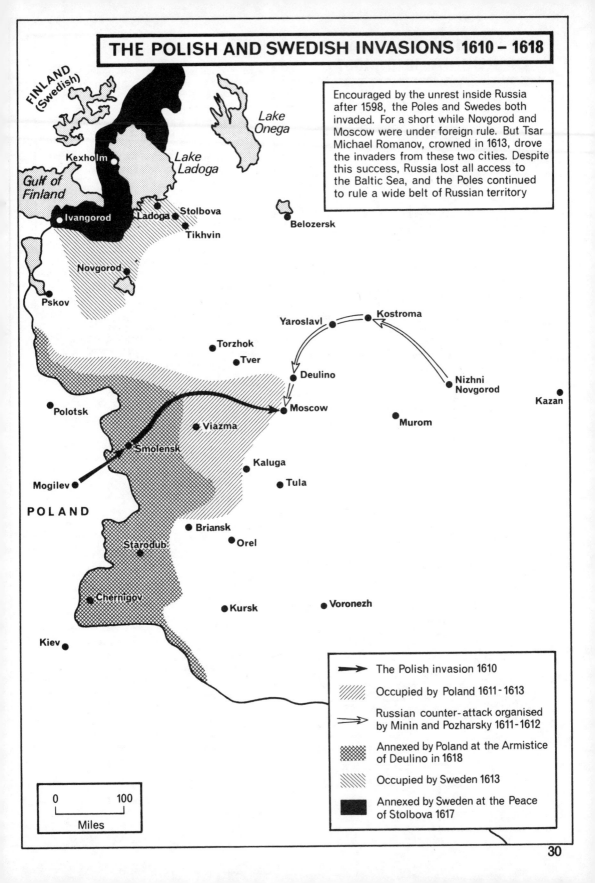

THE POLISH AND SWEDISH INVASIONS 1610 – 1618

FINLAND (Swedish)

Lake Onega

Kexholm

Lake Ladoga

Gulf of Finland

Ivangorod

Ladoga

Stolbova

Tikhvin

Belozersk

Novgorod

Pskov

Encouraged by the unrest inside Russia after 1598, the Poles and Swedes both invaded. For a short while Novgorod and Moscow were under foreign rule. But Tsar Michael Romanov, crowned in 1613, drove the invaders from these two cities. Despite this success, Russia lost all access to the Baltic Sea, and the Poles continued to rule a wide belt of Russian territory

Kostroma

Yaroslavl

Torzhok

Tver

Deulino

Nizhni Novgorod

Kazan

Polotsk

Moscow

Murom

Viazma

Smolensk

Kaluga

Mogilev

Tula

POLAND

Briansk

Starodub

Orel

Chernigov

Kursk

Voronezh

Kiev

0   100

Miles

The Polish invasion 1610

Occupied by Poland 1611-1613

Russian counter-attack organised by Minin and Pozharsky 1611-1612

Annexed by Poland at the Armistice of Deulino in 1618

Occupied by Sweden 1613

Annexed by Sweden at the Peace of Stolbova 1617

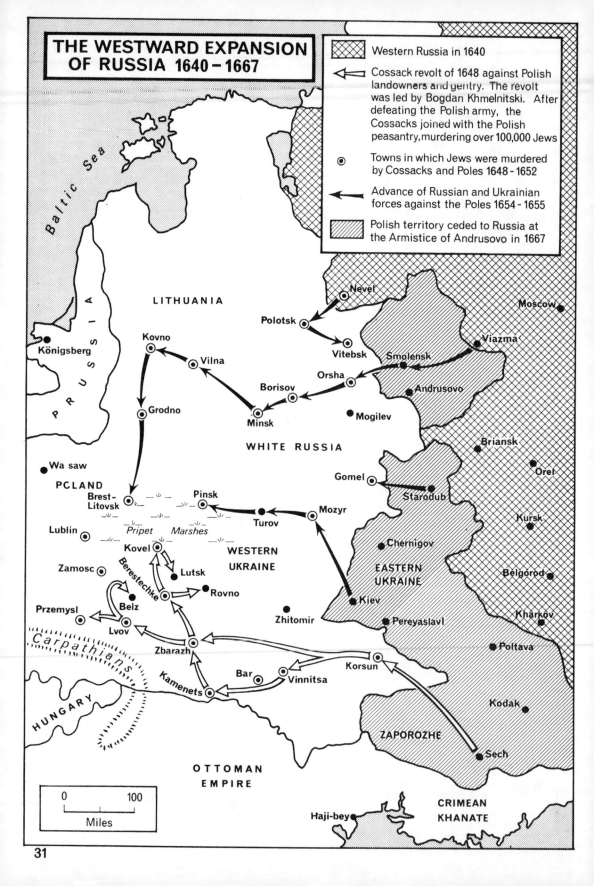

THE WESTWARD EXPANSION OF RUSSIA 1640–1667

Western Russia in 1640

Cossack revolt of 1648 against Polish landowners and gentry. The revolt was led by Bogdan Khmelnitski. After defeating the Polish army, the Cossacks joined with the Polish peasantry, murdering over 100,000 Jews

Towns in which Jews were murdered by Cossacks and Poles 1648-1652

Advance of Russian and Ukrainian forces against the Poles 1654-1655

Polish territory ceded to Russia at the Armistice of Andrusovo in 1667

Baltic Sea

PRUSSIA

Königsberg

LITHUANIA

Nevel

Moscow

Polotsk

Viazma

Kovno

Vitebsk

Smolensk

Vilna

Orsha

Andrusovo

Borisov

Grodno

Mogilev

Minsk

Briansk

WHITE RUSSIA

Wa saw

Gomel

Orel

PCLAND

Starodub

Brest-Litovsk

Pinsk

Mozyr

Kursk

Lublin

Turov

Pripet Marshes

Chernigov

Kovel

WESTERN UKRAINE

EASTERN UKRAINE

Belgorod

Zamosc

Lutsk

Berestechke

Rovno

Kiev

Przemysl

Belz

Zhitomir

Kharkov

Lvov

Pereyaslavl

Zbarazh

Poltava

Carpathians

Bar

Vinnitsa

Korsun

Kamenets

Kodak

HUNGARY

ZAPOROZHE

Sech

OTTOMAN EMPIRE

0   100

Miles

CRIMEAN KHANATE

Haji-bey

SOCIAL UNREST 1648 and 1670

In 1648 uprisings took place in many of the principal Russian towns. As a result, a new code of laws was drawn up, protecting the rights of traders and town-dwellers. In 1670 a Don Cossack, Stenka Razin, led a widespread revolt of Cossacks, peasants, small traders, minor officials and the dispossessed of the Volga, Don and Donets river valleys. The revolt was crushed in 1671 and Razin broken on the wheel in Moscow.

Kargopol

Olonets

Solvychegodsk

Veliki Ustiug

Cherdin

Solikamsk

Totma

Gdov

Novgorod

Pskov

Ostrov

Romanov

Volga

Vladimir

Ruza

Moscow

Yadrin

Simbirsk

Koslov

Penza

Samara

Tambov

Donets

Kursk

Voronezh

Saratov

Don

Tsaritsyn

DON
COSSACKS

Gurev

Sea of
Azov

Astrakhan

*Caspian
Sea*

Terski
Gorodok

Black Sea

⊙ Urban uprisings of 1648-1650

■ The peasants' revolt led by
Stenka Razin 1670 - 1671

— The Russian frontier in 1670

0   500
Miles

32

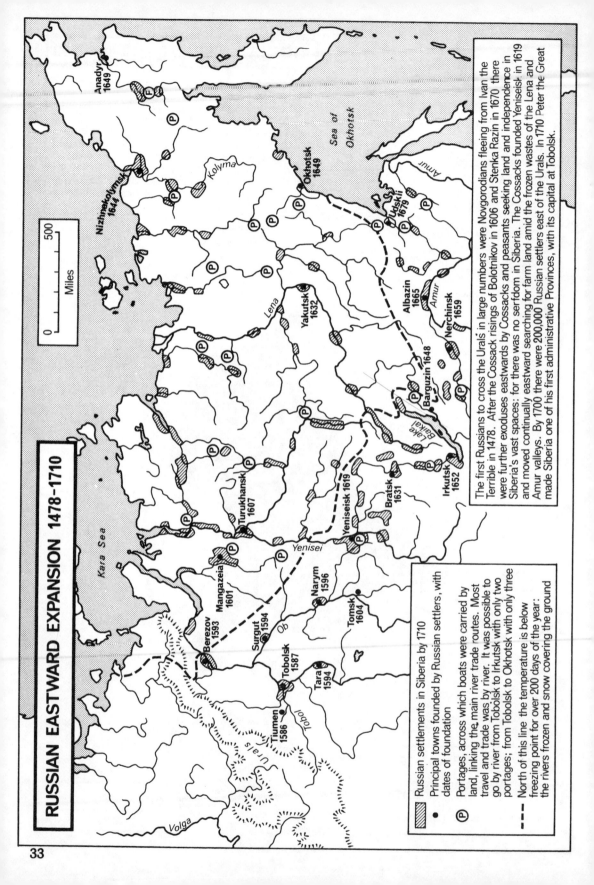

RUSSIAN EASTWARD EXPANSION 1478-1710

The first Russians to cross the Urals in large numbers were Novgorodians fleeing from Ivan the Terrible in 1478. After the Cossack risings of Bolotnikov in 1606 and Stenka Razin in 1670 there were further exoduses eastwards by Cossacks and peasants seeking land and independence in Siberia's vast spaces: for there was no serfdom in Siberia. The Cossacks founded Yeniseisk in 1619 and moved continually eastward searching for farm land amid the frozen wastes of the Lena and Amur valleys. By 1700 there were 200,000 Russian settlers east of the Urals. In 1710 Peter the Great made Siberia one of his first administrative Provinces, with its capital at Tobolsk.

Russian settlements in Siberia by 1710

Principal towns founded by Russian settlers, with dates of foundation

Ⓟ Portages, across which boats were carried by land, linking the main river trade routes. Most travel and trade was by river. It was possible to go by river from Tobolsk to Irkutsk with only two portages; from Tobolsk to Okhotsk with only three

--- North of this line the temperature is below freezing point for over 200 days of the year: the rivers frozen and snow covering the ground

Anadyr 1649

Nizhnekolymsk 1644

Kolyma

Okhotsk 1649

Sea of Okhotsk

Udskii 1679

Amur

Albazin 1665

Nerchinsk 1659

Barguzin 1648

Yakutsk 1632

Lena

Lake Baikal

Irkutsk 1652

Bratsk 1631

Turukhansk 1607

Yeniseisk 1619

Yenisei

Kara Sea

Mangazeia 1601

Narym 1596

Tomsk 1604

Berezov 1593

Surgut 1594

Ob

Tobolsk 1587

Tara 1594

Tiumen 1586

Tobol

Urals

Volga

500

Miles

0

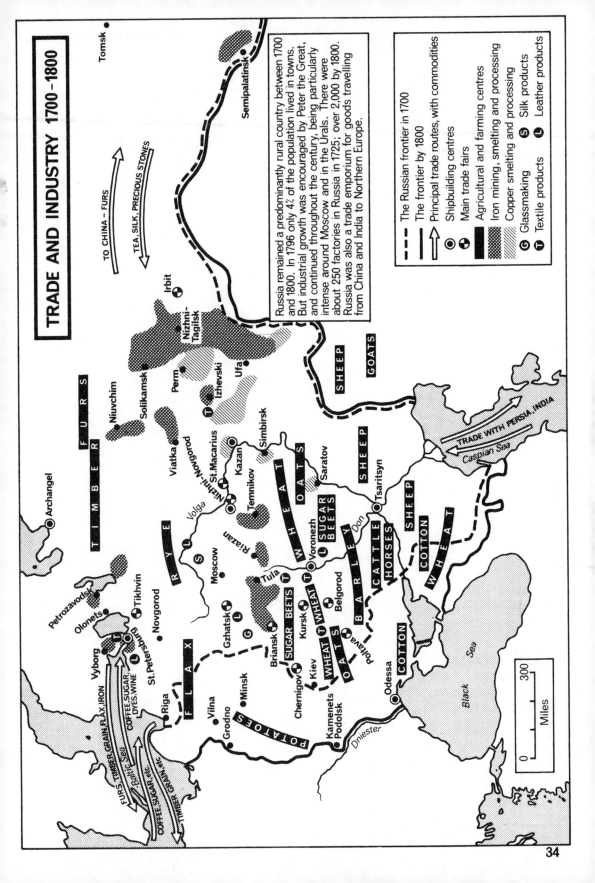

TRADE AND INDUSTRY 1700-1800

Russia remained a predominantly rural country between 1700 and 1800. In 1796 only 4% of the population lived in towns. But industrial growth was encouraged by Peter the Great, and continued throughout the century, being particularly intense around Moscow and in the Urals. There were about 250 factories in Russia in 1725; over 2,000 by 1800. Russia was also a trade emporium for goods travelling from China and India to Northern Europe.

Legend:

- ▬ ▬ The Russian frontier in 1700
- ▬ · ▬ The frontier by 1800
- ↑ Principal trade routes, with commodities
- ◉ Shipbuilding centres
- ⊕ Main trade fairs
- ⬛ Agricultural and farming centres
- ▨ Iron mining, smelting and processing
- ▩ Copper smelting and processing
- Ⓖ Glassmaking
- Ⓣ Textile products
- Ⓢ Silk products
- Ⓛ Leather products

TO CHINA – FURS

TEA, SILK, PRECIOUS STONES

TRADE WITH PERSIA, INDIA

Caspian Sea

FURS TIMBER

SHEEP

GOATS

SHEEP

SHEEP

SHEEP

WHEAT

OATS

SUGAR BEETS

BARLEY

CATTLE

HORSES

COTTON

WHEAT

COTTON

POTATOES

FLAX

RYE

SUGAR BEETS

WHEAT

OATS

Tomsk

Semipalatinsk

Irbit

Nizhni-Tagilsk

Niuvchim

Solikamsk

Perm

Izhevski

Ufa

Viatka

Simbirsk

St.Macarius

Kazan

Temnikov

Saratov

Tsaritsyn

Nizhni-Novgorod

Volga

Riazan

Don

Archangel

Moscow

Voronezh

Tula

Belgorod

Kursk

Briansk

Poltava

Petrozavodsk

Tikhvin

Olonets

Novgorod

Gzhatsk

Chernigov

Kiev

Vyborg

St. Petersburg

Riga

Vilna

Minsk

Grodno

Kamenets Podolsk

Odessa

Dniester

Black Sea

Baltic Sea

FURS, TIMBER, GRAIN, FLAX, IRON

COFFEE, SUGAR, DYES, WINE

COFFEE, SUGAR, etc.

TIMBER, GRAIN, etc.

0   300
Miles

34

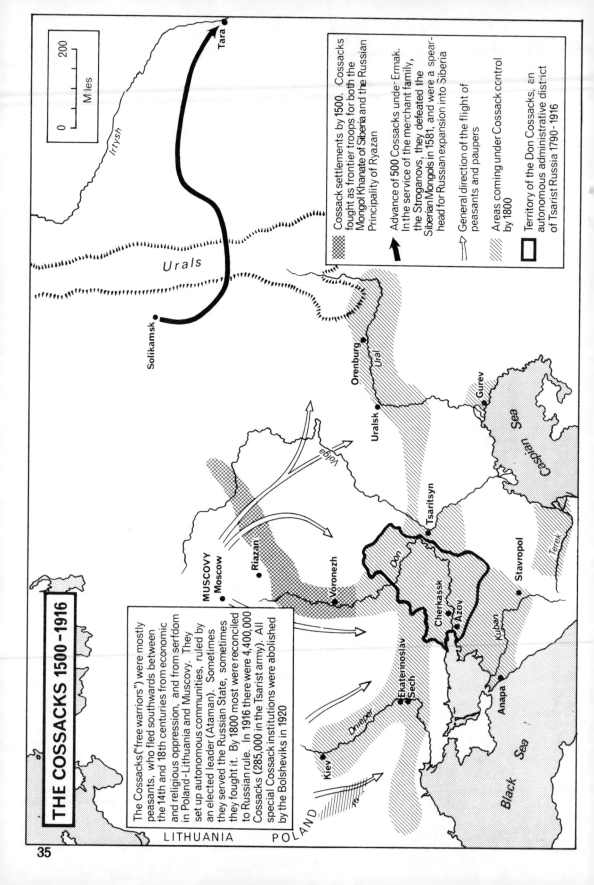

THE COSSACKS 1500–1916

The Cossacks ("free warriors") were mostly peasants, who fled southwards between the 14th and 18th centuries from economic and religious oppression, and from serfdom in Poland-Lithuania and Muscovy. They set up autonomous communities, ruled by an elected leader (Ataman). Sometimes they served the Russian State, sometimes they fought it. By 1800 most were reconciled to Russian rule. In 1916 there were 4,400,000 Cossacks (285,000 in the Tsarist army). All special Cossack institutions were abolished by the Bolsheviks in 1920

Cossack settlements by 1500. Cossacks fought as frontier troops for both the Mongol Khanate of Siberia and the Russian Principality of Ryazan

Advance of 500 Cossacks under Ermak. In the service of the merchant family, the Stroganovs, they defeated the Siberian Mongols in 1581, and were a spearhead for Russian expansion into Siberia

General direction of the flight of peasants and paupers

Areas coming under Cossack control by 1800

Territory of the Don Cossacks, an autonomous administrative district of Tsarist Russia 1790-1916

Miles
0 — 200

Irtysh

Tara

Solikamsk

Urals

Orenburg

Uralsk

Ural

Gurev

Caspian Sea

MUSCOVY
Moscow

Riazan

Voronezh

Volga

Tsaritsyn

Don

Cherkassk

Azov

Stavropol

Terek

Kuban

Ekaterinoslav
Sech

Dnieper

Kiev

Anapa

Black Sea

LITHUANIA   POLAND

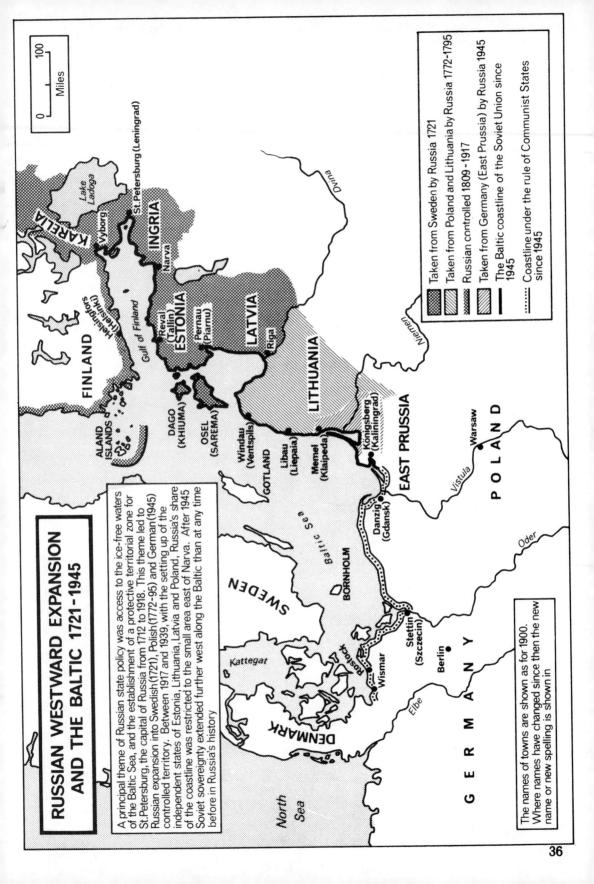

RUSSIAN WESTWARD EXPANSION AND THE BALTIC 1721-1945

A principal theme of Russian state policy was access to the ice-free waters of the Baltic Sea, and the establishment of a protective territorial zone for St.Petersburg, the capital of Russia from 1712 to 1918. This theme led to Russian expansion into Swedish(1721), Polish(1772-95) and German(1945) controlled territory. Between 1917 and 1939, with the setting up of the independent states of Estonia, Lithuania, Latvia and Poland, Russia's share of the coastline was restricted to the small area east of Narva. After 1945 Soviet sovereignty extended further west along the Baltic than at any time before in Russia's history

The names of towns are shown as for 1900. Where names have changed since then the new name or new spelling is shown in

Taken from Sweden by Russia 1721

Taken from Poland and Lithuania by Russia 1772-1795

Russian controlled 1809 - 1917

Taken from Germany (East Prussia) by Russia 1945

The Baltic coastline under the rule of the Soviet Union since 1945

Coastline under the rule of Communist States since 1945

Map labels

North Sea

Kattegat

SWEDEN

DENMARK

GERMANY

Berlin

Elbe

Oder

Rostock

Wismar

Stettin (Szczecin)

BORNHOLM

GOTLAND

Baltic Sea

Danzig (Gdansk)

Vistula

POLAND

Warsaw

EAST PRUSSIA

Niemen

Königsberg (Kaliningrad)

Memel (Klaipeda)

Libau (Liepaia)

Windau (Ventspils)

LITHUANIA

LATVIA

Riga

Dvina

OSEL (SAREMA)

DAGO (KHIUMA)

Pernau (Piarnu)

ESTONIA

Reval (Tallin)

Narva

INGRIA

St. Petersburg (Leningrad)

Vyborg

Gulf of Finland

ALAND ISLANDS

FINLAND

Helsingfors (Helsinki)

Lake Ladoga

KARELIA

Miles
100
0

36

Section Two

IMPERIAL RUSSIA

WAR AND REVOLT UNDER PETER THE GREAT 1695 – 1723

Peter the Great's reign saw a series of widespread revolts ruthlessly crushed, the successful conquest of Swedish land, and Russian access to the ice-free waters of the Baltic Sea. But Peter was unable to drive the Turk from the Crimea, or to reach the Black Sea.

1695 Unsuccessful attack on the Turks at Azov

1696 Azov captured from the Turks. Taganrog founded as a new naval base

1700 Russians defeated by the Swedes at Narva

1709 Swedes defeated by the Russians at Poltava

1710 First Russian attacks against the Swedes, leading to Baltic annexations from Sweden in 1721

1711 Unsuccessful attack against the Turks at Jassy and Braila. Azov and Taganrog returned to Turkey

1722 Successful attack against Persia largely to forestall a Turkish advance to the Persian shore of the Caspian Sea

The privileged Moscow garrison, or Streltsy, who had helped Peter's half-sister Sophia seize power in 1682, had been exiled by him to Astrakhan in 1698. They opposed his increasingly heavy taxation and in 1705 set up a Cossack-style Government and elected an Ataman. Peter refused all pleas for mercy; the revolt was crushed and its leaders were executed with great cruelty, 1706-1708.

The Bashkirs, a Muslim nomad people subject to Russia since 1557, resented Russian colonization and sought Crimean and Turkish help to assert their independence. In 1708 they attacked Russian colonists and destroyed over 300 villages from the Ural river to the Volga, killing or capturing 13,000 settlers. The revolt was not finally crushed until 1711.

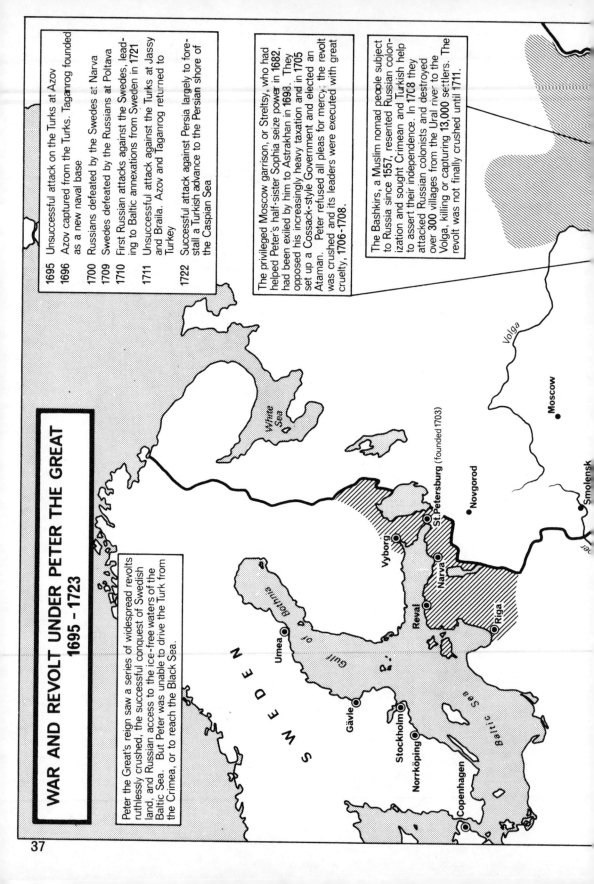

White Sea

Volga

SWEDEN

Gulf of Bothnia

Baltic Sea

Umea

Gävle

Stockholm

Norrköping

Copenhagen

Reval

Vyborg

Narva

Riga

St.Petersburg (founded 1703)

Novgorod

Moscow

Smolensk

37

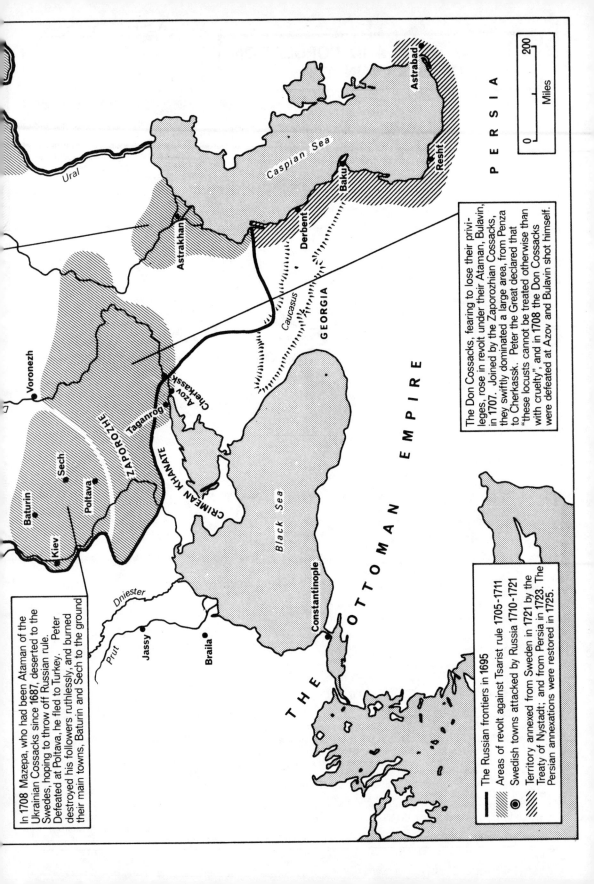

In 1708 Mazepa, who had been Ataman of the Ukrainian Cossacks since 1687, deserted to the Swedes, hoping to throw off Russian rule. Defeated at Poltava, he fled to Turkey. Peter destroyed his followers ruthlessly, and burned their main towns, Baturin and Sech to the ground

The Don Cossacks, fearing to lose their privileges, rose in revolt under their Ataman, Bulavin, in 1707. Joined by the Zaporozhian Cossacks, they swiftly dominated a large area, from Penza to Cherkassk. Peter the Great declared that "these locusts cannot be treated otherwise than with cruelty", and in 1708 the Don Cossacks were defeated at Azov and Bulavin shot himself.

——— The Russian frontiers in 1695

▨▨▨ Areas of revolt against Tsarist rule 1705-1711

◉ Swedish towns attacked by Russia 1710-1721

▨▨▨ Territory annexed from Sweden in 1721 by the Treaty of Nystadt; and from Persia in 1723. The Persian annexations were restored in 1725.

PERSIA

Caspian Sea

Astrabad

Resht

Baku

Derbent

Astrakhan

Caucasus

GEORGIA

Ural

Voronezh

ZAPOROZHE

Baturin

Sech

Poltava

Kiev

Taganrog

Azov

Cherkassk

CRIMEAN KHANATE

Black Sea

Constantinople

THE OTTOMAN EMPIRE

Dniester

Prut

Jassy

Braila

0   200
|————————————|
Miles

THE PROVINCES AND POPULATION OF RUSSIA IN 1724

0   300

Miles

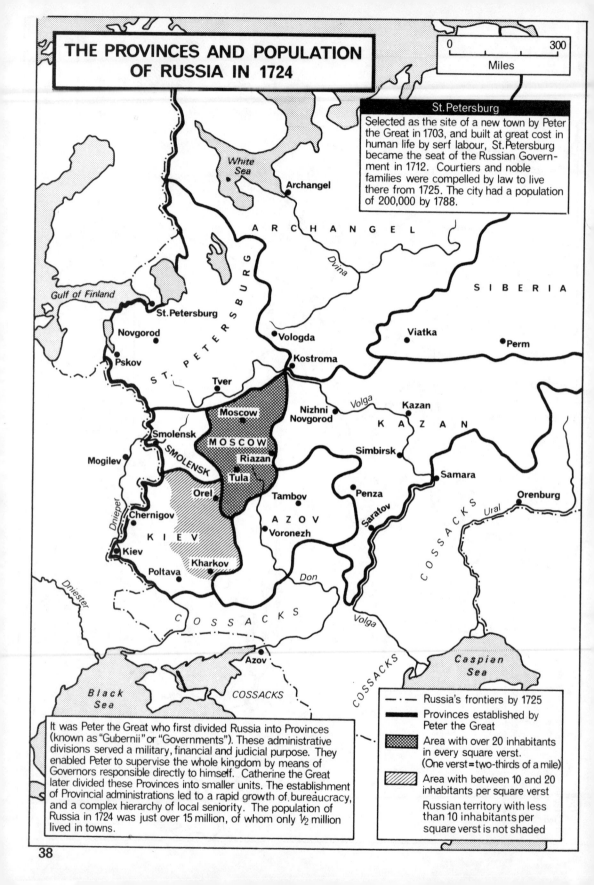

St. Petersburg

Selected as the site of a new town by Peter the Great in 1703, and built at great cost in human life by serf labour, St. Petersburg became the seat of the Russian Government in 1712. Courtiers and noble families were compelled by law to live there from 1725. The city had a population of 200,000 by 1788.

White Sea

Archangel

A R C H A N G E L

Dvina

S I B E R I A

Gulf of Finland

St. Petersburg

Novgorod

Pskov

S T.   P E T E R S B U R G

Vologda

Viatka

Perm

Kostroma

Tver

Volga

Kazan

Moscow

Nizhni Novgorod

K A Z A N

Smolensk

M O S C O W

Simbirsk

Mogilev

SMOLENSK

Riazan

Tula

Samara

Orel

Tambov

Penza

Orenburg

Chernigov

Saratov

Ural

K I E V

A Z O V

Voronezh

C O S S A C K S

Dnieper

Kiev

Poltava

Kharkov

Don

Volga

Dniester

C O S S A C K S

Azov

C O S S A C K S

Caspian Sea

Black Sea

COSSACKS

COSSACKS

It was Peter the Great who first divided Russia into Provinces (known as "Gubernii" or "Governments"). These administrative divisions served a military, financial and judicial purpose. They enabled Peter to supervise the whole kingdom by means of Governors responsible directly to himself. Catherine the Great later divided these Provinces into smaller units. The establishment of Provincial administrations led to a rapid growth of bureaucracy, and a complex hierarchy of local seniority. The population of Russia in 1724 was just over 15 million, of whom only ½ million lived in towns.

— · — Russia's frontiers by 1725

▬▬ Provinces established by Peter the Great

▓ Area with over 20 inhabitants in every square verst. (One verst = two-thirds of a mile)

▨ Area with between 10 and 20 inhabitants per square verst

Russian territory with less than 10 inhabitants per square verst is not shaded

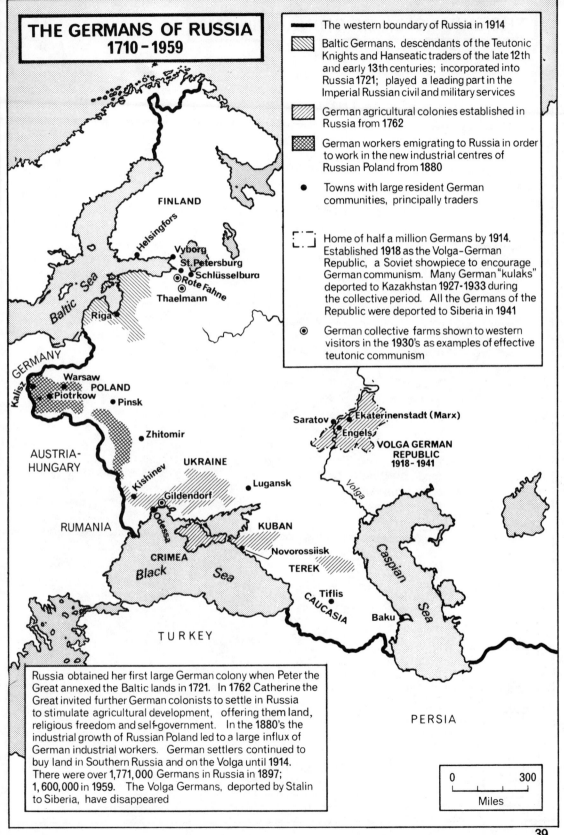

THE GERMANS OF RUSSIA
1710 - 1959

— The western boundary of Russia in 1914

Baltic Germans, descendants of the Teutonic Knights and Hanseatic traders of the late 12th and early 13th centuries; incorporated into Russia 1721; played a leading part in the Imperial Russian civil and military services

German agricultural colonies established in Russia from 1762

German workers emigrating to Russia in order to work in the new industrial centres of Russian Poland from 1880

● Towns with large resident German communities, principally traders

Home of half a million Germans by 1914. Established 1918 as the Volga-German Republic, a Soviet showpiece to encourage German communism. Many German "kulaks" deported to Kazakhstan 1927-1933 during the collective period. All the Germans of the Republic were deported to Siberia in 1941

◉ German collective farms shown to western visitors in the 1930's as examples of effective teutonic communism

FINLAND

Helsingfors

Vyborg
St. Petersburg
Schlüsselburg
◉ Rote Fahne
Thaelmann

Baltic Sea

Riga

GERMANY

Warsaw
POLAND
Piotrkow
● Pinsk

Kalisz

AUSTRIA-
HUNGARY

Zhitomir

UKRAINE

Kishinev

Gildendorf

Odessa

RUMANIA

CRIMEA
Black   Sea

● Lugansk

KUBAN

Novorossiisk

TEREK

Saratov
Ekaterinenstadt (Marx)
Engels

VOLGA GERMAN
REPUBLIC
1918 - 1941

Volga

Caspian Sea

Tiflis
CAUCASIA
Baku

TURKEY

PERSIA

Russia obtained her first large German colony when Peter the Great annexed the Baltic lands in 1721. In 1762 Catherine the Great invited further German colonists to settle in Russia to stimulate agricultural development, offering them land, religious freedom and self-government. In the 1880's the industrial growth of Russian Poland led to a large influx of German industrial workers. German settlers continued to buy land in Southern Russia and on the Volga until 1914. There were over 1,771,000 Germans in Russia in 1897; 1,600,000 in 1959. The Volga Germans, deported by Stalin to Siberia, have disappeared

0   300
Miles

39

THE EXPANSION OF CHINA 1720–1760

THE

RUSSIAN

EMPIRE

Okhotsk ⊙

Yakutsk ⊙

Tobolsk ⊙

Yeniseisk ⊙

Tomsk ⊙   Krasnoyarsk ⊙

Omsk ⊙   Nerchinsk ⊙   ■ Albazin

Irkutsk ⊙   ● Harbin

Lake
Baikal

Semipalatinsk ⊙

Ustkamenogorsk ⊙   Maimachin ■

M O N G O L S

Lake
Balkhash   ● Peking

Kulja ●   ● Hami

Urumchi   ● Nanking

DOMINIONS OF THE   Sian ●
ZUNGAR KALMUKS

Yarkand ●   C H I N A

Khotan ●

Chengtu ●

T I B E T   ● Canton

Lhasa ●

H i m a l a y a s   Yunnan ●

⊙   Cities founded by the Russians before 1720

■   The Chinese Empire in 1720, ruled by
      the Manchu Dynasty

▨   Under Chinese control by 1720, providing
      the Manchus with a reservoir of
      military power

▨   Conquered by China between 1724 and 1764

▨   Conquered by China in 1780

0   500
                    Miles

RUSSIAN EXPANSION UNDER CATHERINE THE GREAT 1762–1796

The Provinces of Russia in 1750

Territory annexed by Russia 1762-1796, giving Russia an outlet on the Black Sea, and a common frontier with Prussia and Austria

White Sea

Archangel

ARCHANGEL

FINLAND

Helsingfors

ST. PETERSBURG

Novgorod

NOVGOROD

Vologda

Viatka

Perm

ESTONIA

LIVONIA

Pskov

KAZAN

Baltic Sea

KURLAND

Tver

MOSCOW

Moscow

Kazan

Ufa

UFA

Niemen

Vilna

LITHUANIA

Minsk

SMOLENSK

NIZHNI NOVGOROD

PRUSSIA

WHITE RUSSIA

Stavropol

Samara

Warsaw

Pinsk

Orel

BELGOROD

AUSTRIA

PODLESIA

Lutsk

KIEV

Kiev

VORONEZH

Dniester

PODOLIA

Dnieper

Belgorod

ASTRAKHAN

Jassy

ZAPOROZHE

Astrakhan

Odessa

Taganrog

Kutchuk Kainardji

CRIMEA

KUBAN

Sebastopol

KABARDA

Tarki

Caspian Sea

Black Sea

THE OTTOMAN EMPIRE

Constantinople

Kars

PERSIA

0   200
Miles

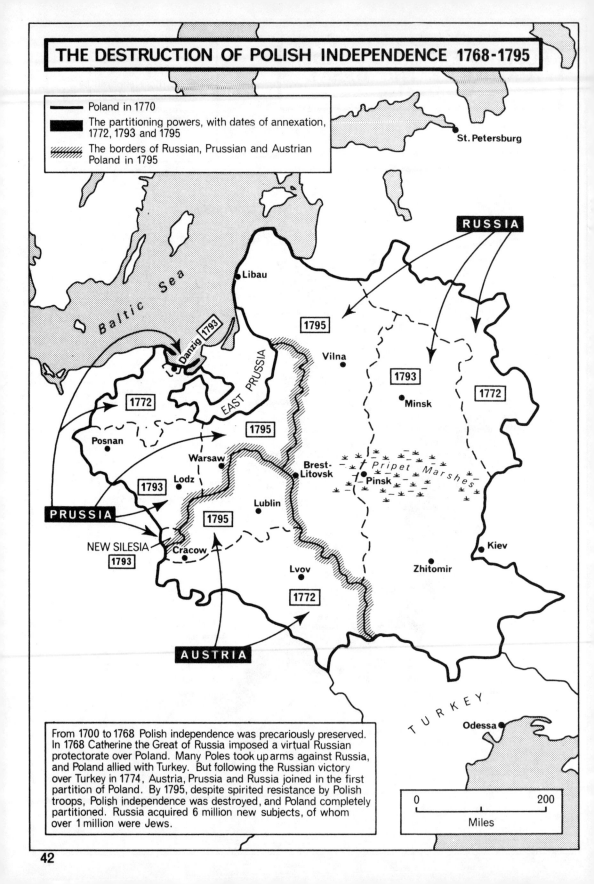

THE DESTRUCTION OF POLISH INDEPENDENCE 1768-1795

Poland in 1770

The partitioning powers, with dates of annexation, 1772, 1793 and 1795

The borders of Russian, Prussian and Austrian Poland in 1795

St. Petersburg

RUSSIA

Baltic Sea

Libau

Danzig 1793

1795

Vilna

1793

EAST PRUSSIA

1772

Minsk

1772

Posnan

1795

Warsaw

Brest-Litovsk

Pripet Marshes

Pinsk

1793

Lodz

Lublin

PRUSSIA

1795

NEW SILESIA

1793

Cracow

Kiev

Lvov

Zhitomir

1772

AUSTRIA

TURKEY

Odessa

From 1700 to 1768 Polish independence was precariously preserved. In 1768 Catherine the Great of Russia imposed a virtual Russian protectorate over Poland. Many Poles took up arms against Russia, and Poland allied with Turkey. But following the Russian victory over Turkey in 1774, Austria, Prussia and Russia joined in the first partition of Poland. By 1795, despite spirited resistance by Polish troops, Polish independence was destroyed, and Poland completely partitioned. Russia acquired 6 million new subjects, of whom over 1 million were Jews.

0   200

Miles

THE RUSSIAN ANNEXATIONS OF POLAND 1772-1795

Baltic Sea

LATVIA

Pskov

0   150
Miles

Windau

Riga

Libau

Mitau

Palanga

Dvinsk

Nevel

Memel

LITHUANIA

Dvina

Polotsk

Königsberg

Kovno

1795

Vitebsk

Smolensk

**EAST
PRUSSIA**

Vilna

Troki

1793

Borisov

1772

Orsha

Suvalki

Mogilev

Mstislav

Dnieper

Lida

Minsk

Grodno

Novogrudok

**WHITE
RUSSIA**

PRUSSIAN-ANNEXED POLAND

Vilkoviski

Mir

Bobruisk

Bialystok

Baranovichi

Slutsk

Gomel

Warsaw

Brest-Litovsk

Pinsk

Pripet   Marshes

Starodub

Pripet

Turov

Mozyr

Lublin

Kovel

Olevsk

Chernigov

VOLHYNIA

Lutsk

**WESTERN
UKRAINE**

UKRAINE

Rovno

Dubno

Zhitomir

Kiev

Lvov

Staro-
Konstantinov

Berdychev

Pereyaslavl

Przemysl

Tarnopol

GALICIA

Vinnitsa

Boguslav

Dnieper

PODOLIA

Stanislavov

Kamenets-
Podolsk

Bug

BESSARABIA

Dniester

Balta

AUSTRIA

**RUSSIAN-
ANNEXED**

TURKEY

Kherson

Dnieper

TURKEY

1791
Odessa

1774

*Black
Sea*

The western part of Russia in 1770

Partition lines

Principal Polish military resistance
to the Russians

The western frontier of Russia 1795

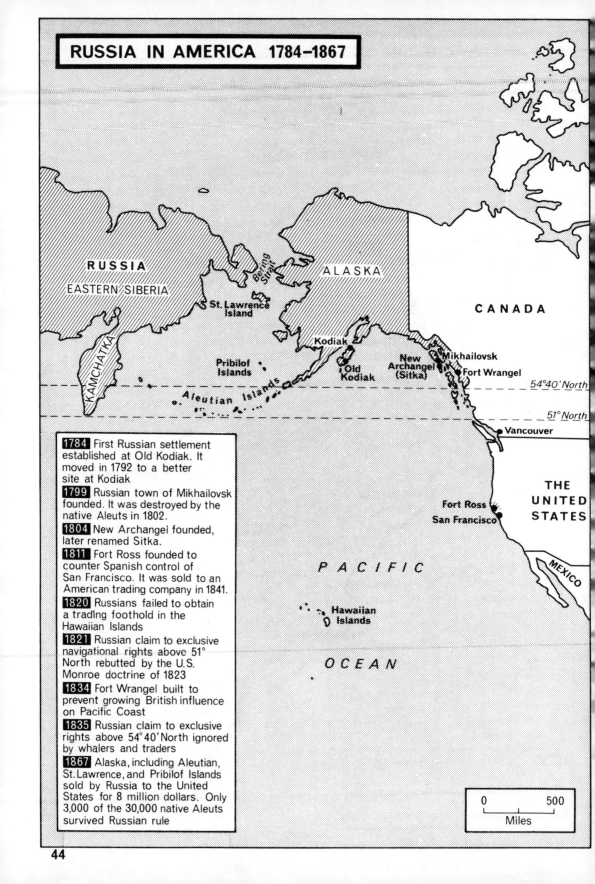

RUSSIA IN AMERICA 1784–1867

RUSSIA

EASTERN SIBERIA

KAMCHATKA

Bering Strait

St. Lawrence Island

ALASKA

CANADA

Pribilof Islands

Kodiak

Old Kodiak

New Archangel (Sitka)

Mikhailovsk

Fort Wrangel

Aleutian Islands

54°40' North

51° North

Vancouver

THE UNITED STATES

Fort Ross

San Francisco

PACIFIC

Hawaiian Islands

OCEAN

MEXICO

1784 First Russian settlement established at Old Kodiak. It moved in 1792 to a better site at Kodiak

1799 Russian town of Mikhailovsk founded. It was destroyed by the native Aleuts in 1802.

1804 New Archangel founded, later renamed Sitka.

1811 Fort Ross founded to counter Spanish control of San Francisco. It was sold to an American trading company in 1841.

1820 Russians failed to obtain a trading foothold in the Hawaiian Islands

1821 Russian claim to exclusive navigational rights above 51° North rebutted by the U.S. Monroe doctrine of 1823

1834 Fort Wrangel built to prevent growing British influence on Pacific Coast

1835 Russian claim to exclusive rights above 54°40' North ignored by whalers and traders

1867 Alaska, including Aleutian, St. Lawrence, and Pribilof Islands sold by Russia to the United States for 8 million dollars. Only 3,000 of the 30,000 native Aleuts survived Russian rule

0   500

Miles

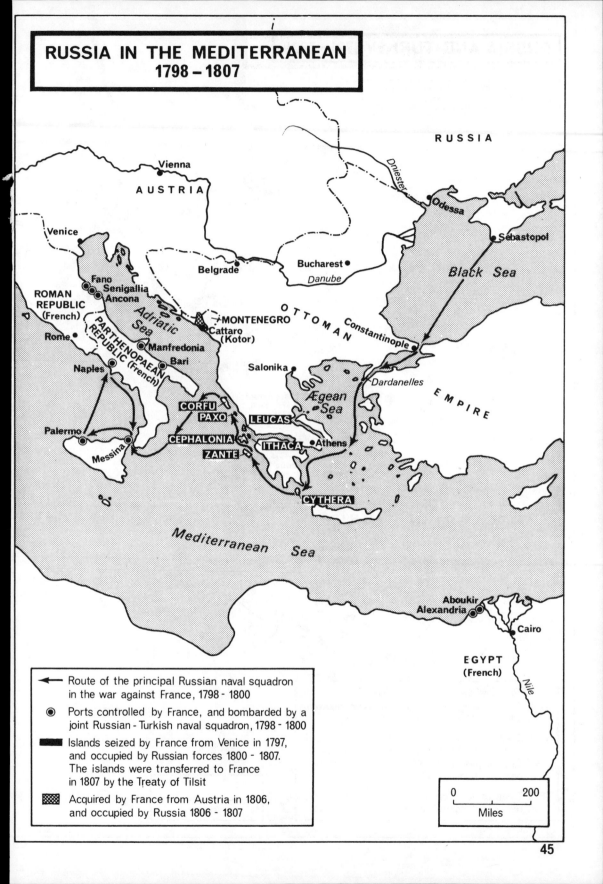

RUSSIA IN THE MEDITERRANEAN
1798 – 1807

i

RUSSIA

Vienna

AUSTRIA

Venice

Dniester

Odessa

Sébastopol

Black Sea

Belgrade

Bucharest

Danube

ROMAN REPUBLIC (French)

Fano
Senigallia
Ancona

Adriatic Sea

MONTENEGRO
Cattaro (Kotor)

O T T O M A N

Constantinople

Rome

PARTHENOPAEAN REPUBLIC (French)

Manfredonia
Bari

Salonika

Dardanelles

E M P I R E

Naples

CORFU
PAXO
LEUCAS

Ægean Sea

CEPHALONIA
ITHACA
Athens

Palermo

ZANTE

Messina

CYTHERA

Mediterranean Sea

Aboukir
Alexandria

Cairo

EGYPT (French)

Nile

— Route of the principal Russian naval squadron in the war against France, 1798 - 1800

⊚ Ports controlled by France, and bombarded by a joint Russian - Turkish naval squadron, 1798 - 1800

■ Islands seized by France from Venice in 1797, and occupied by Russian forces 1800 - 1807. The islands were transferred to France in 1807 by the Treaty of Tilsit

▨ Acquired by France from Austria in 1806, and occupied by Russia 1806 - 1807

0   200
Miles

45

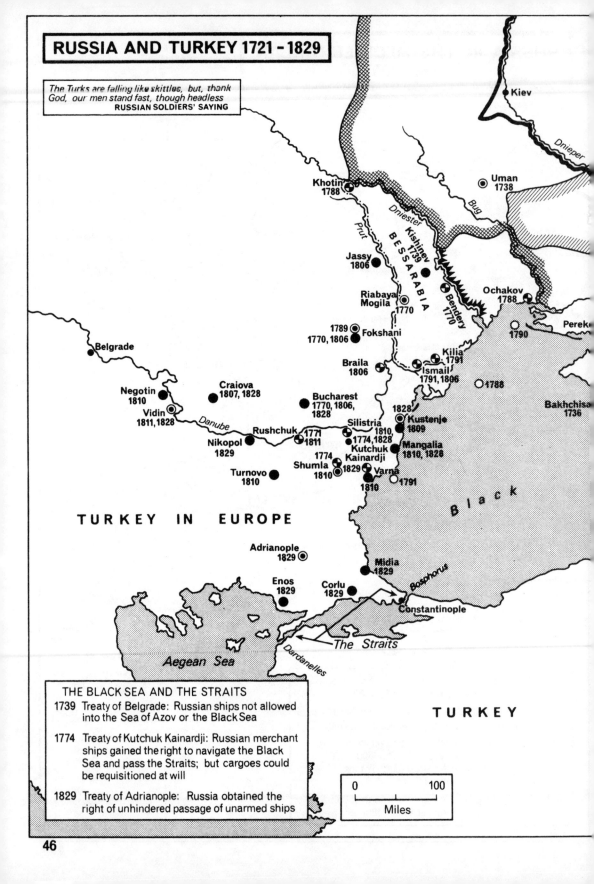

RUSSIA AND TURKEY 1721 - 1829

The Turks are falling like skittles, but, thank
God, our men stand fast, though headless
RUSSIAN SOLDIERS' SAYING

Kiev

Dnieper

Khotin
1788

Uman
1738

Dniester

Bug

Prut

Kishinev
1739
B E S S A R A B I A

Jassy
1806

Riabaya
Mogila
1770

Bendery
1770

Ochakov
1788

Perek

1790

1789
1770, 1806

Fokshani

Kilia
1791

Belgrade

Braila
1806

Ismail
1791, 1806

1788

Bakhchisa
1736

Negotin
1810

Craiova
1807, 1828

Bucharest
1770, 1806,
1828

1828

Kustenje
1809

Vidin
1811, 1828

Danube

Rushchuk
1771
1811

Silistria
1810

1774, 1828

Mangalia
1810, 1828

Nikopol
1829

Kutchuk
Kainardji

1774
Shumla
1810

1829

Varna
1810

1791

Turnovo
1810

T U R K E Y   I N   E U R O P E

B l a c k

Adrianople
1829

Midia
1829

Bosphorus

Enos
1829

Corlu
1829

Constantinople

The Straits

Dardanelles

Aegean Sea

T U R K E Y

THE BLACK SEA AND THE STRAITS

1739 Treaty of Belgrade: Russian ships not allowed
into the Sea of Azov or the Black Sea

1774 Treaty of Kutchuk Kainardji: Russian merchant
ships gained the right to navigate the Black
Sea and pass the Straits; but cargoes could
be requisitioned at will

1829 Treaty of Adrianople: Russia obtained the
right of unhindered passage of unarmed ships

0   100

Miles

46

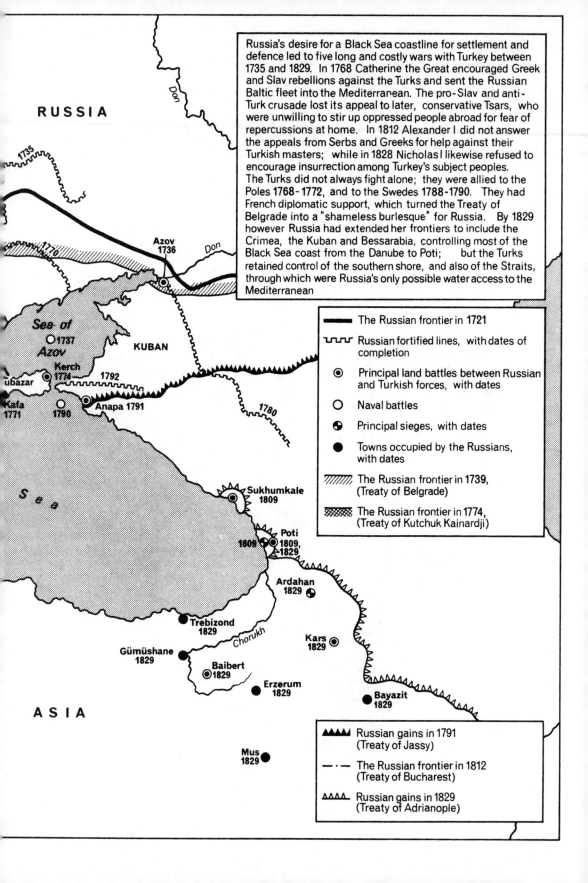

RUSSIA

Don

Russia's desire for a Black Sea coastline for settlement and defence led to five long and costly wars with Turkey between 1735 and 1829. In 1768 Catherine the Great encouraged Greek and Slav rebellions against the Turks and sent the Russian Baltic fleet into the Mediterranean. The pro-Slav and anti-Turk crusade lost its appeal to later, conservative Tsars, who were unwilling to stir up oppressed people abroad for fear of repercussions at home. In 1812 Alexander I did not answer the appeals from Serbs and Greeks for help against their Turkish masters; while in 1828 Nicholas I likewise refused to encourage insurrection among Turkey's subject peoples. The Turks did not always fight alone; they were allied to the Poles 1768-1772, and to the Swedes 1788-1790. They had French diplomatic support, which turned the Treaty of Belgrade into a "shameless burlesque" for Russia. By 1829 however Russia had extended her frontiers to include the Crimea, the Kuban and Bessarabia, controlling most of the Black Sea coast from the Danube to Poti; but the Turks retained control of the southern shore, and also of the Straits, through which were Russia's only possible water access to the Mediterranean

1735

1770

Azov
1736

Don

Sea of
Azov
○1737

KUBAN

Kerch
1774

1792

ubazar

Kafa
1771

1790

Anapa 1791

1780

	The Russian frontier in 1721
ᴸᴸᴸᴸ	Russian fortified lines, with dates of completion
◉	Principal land battles between Russian and Turkish forces, with dates
○	Naval battles
✛	Principal sieges, with dates
●	Towns occupied by the Russians, with dates
▨	The Russian frontier in 1739, (Treaty of Belgrade)
▨	The Russian frontier in 1774, (Treaty of Kutchuk Kainardji)

S e a

Sukhumkale
1809 ◉

Poti
1809 ✛ ◉ 1809,
1829

Ardahan
1829 ✛

Trebizond
1829 ●

Chorukh

Kars
1829 ◉

Gümüshane
1829 ●

Baibert
◉1829

Erzerum
1829 ●

Bayazit
1829 ●

A S I A

Mus
1829 ●

▲▲▲▲	Russian gains in 1791 (Treaty of Jassy)
— · —	The Russian frontier in 1812 (Treaty of Bucharest)
▵▵▵▵	Russian gains in 1829 (Treaty of Adrianople)

RUSSIA AND SWEDEN 1700-1809

0   300
Miles

From 1621 Sweden controlled the
Baltic Sea and the Gulfs of Finland
and Bothnia. In 1700 Peter the
Great allied Russia with Poland
and Denmark, in 1714 with Prussia
and Hanover. His first conquest
was Ingria, giving Russia a small
but valued outlet on the Baltic.
After several defeats, the Russians
finally broke Sweden's dominance
in 1721. Russia's annexation of
Finland in 1809 further extended
her control of the Baltic.

LAPLAND

SWEDEN

Gulf of Bothnia

Tornea

Uleaborg

Vasa

FINLAND

KARELIA

Kexholm

Helsingfors

Nystad
Abo

Vyborg

Nöteborg
St Petersburg

ALAND IS.

Gulf of Finland

Narva

INGRIA

DAGÖ

Reval

ESTLAND

Ivangorod

Novgorod

Stockholm

ÖSEL

Dorpat

Pskov

GOTLAND

LIVLAND

Baltic Sea

Riga

DENMARK

Copenhagen

Stralsund

BORNHOLM

POLAND

SWEDISH POMERANIA

Stettin

HANOVER

PRUSSIA

▬▬▬ Sweden in 1700

■ Swedish territory conquered by
Peter the Great during the Great
Northern War 1700-1721, and annexed
to Russia at the Treaty of Nystad 1721

▨ Conquered by Russia, 1743

▨ Swedish territory conquered by
Alexander I and annexed to Russia
in 1809

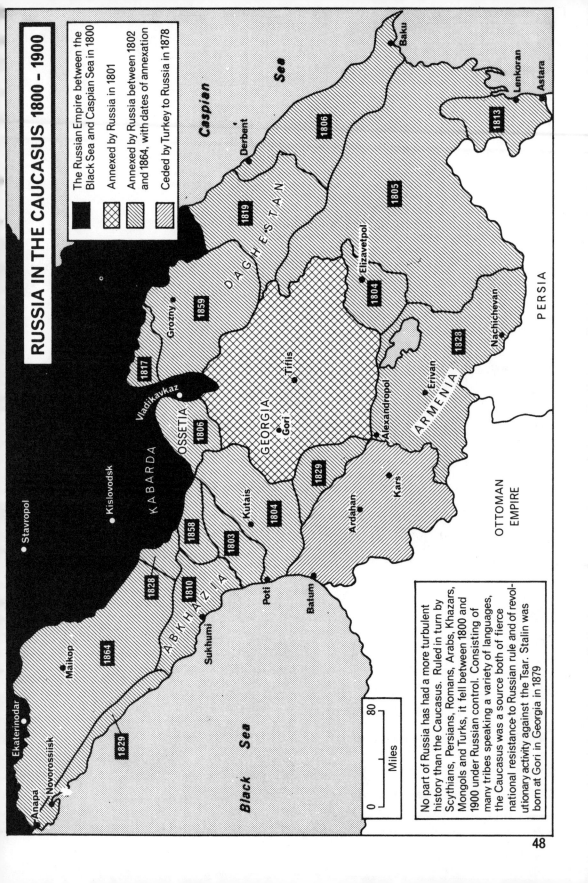

RUSSIA IN THE CAUCASUS 1800 – 1900

The Russian Empire between the Black Sea and Caspian Sea in 1800

Annexed by Russia in 1801

Annexed by Russia between 1802 and 1864, with dates of annexation

Ceded by Turkey to Russia in 1878

No part of Russia has had a more turbulent history than the Caucasus. Ruled in turn by Scythians, Persians, Romans, Arabs, Khazars, Mongols and Turks, it fell between 1800 and 1900 under Russian control. Consisting of many tribes speaking a variety of languages, the Caucasus was a source both of fierce national resistance to Russian rule and of revolutionary activity against the Tsar. Stalin was born at Gori in Georgia in 1879

Miles

0   80

Caspian Sea

Black Sea

PERSIA

OTTOMAN EMPIRE

Baku
Lenkoran
Astara
1813
1806
1805
Derbent
1819
DAGHESTAN
Elizavetpol
1804
1859
Grozny
1817
Nachichevan
1828
Erivan
ARMENIA
Vladikavkaz
OSSETIA
1806
Tiflis
Gori
GEORGIA
Alexandropol
Kislovodsk
KABARDA
1829
Kars
Kutais
1804
Ardahan
Stavropol
1858
1803
ABKHAZIA
1810
1828
Poti
Battum
Maikop
Sukhumi
1864
Ekaterinodar
Novorossiisk
1829
Anapa

48

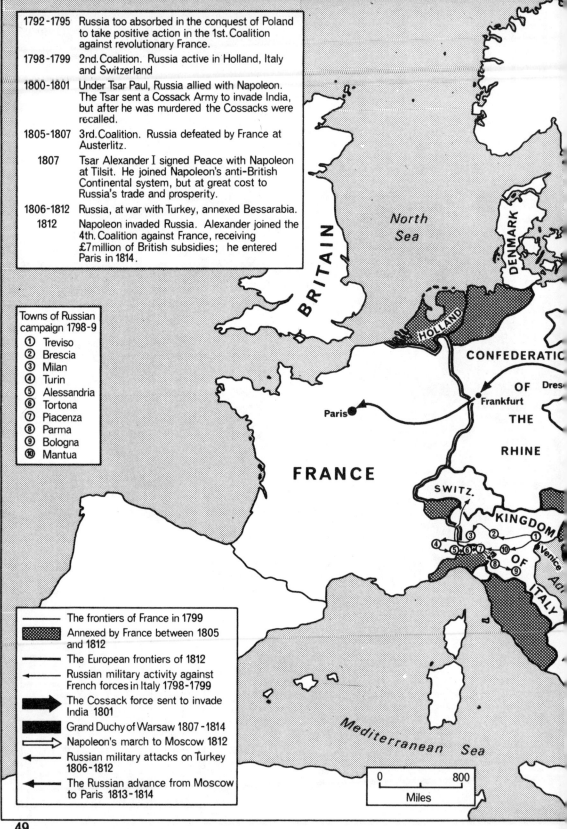

1792-1795   Russia too absorbed in the conquest of Poland to take positive action in the 1st. Coalition against revolutionary France.

1798-1799   2nd. Coalition. Russia active in Holland, Italy and Switzerland

1800-1801   Under Tsar Paul, Russia allied with Napoleon. The Tsar sent a Cossack Army to invade India, but after he was murdered the Cossacks were recalled.

1805-1807   3rd. Coalition. Russia defeated by France at Austerlitz.

1807   Tsar Alexander I signed Peace with Napoleon at Tilsit. He joined Napoleon's anti-British Continental system, but at great cost to Russia's trade and prosperity.

1806-1812   Russia, at war with Turkey, annexed Bessarabia.

1812   Napoleon invaded Russia. Alexander joined the 4th. Coalition against France, receiving £7 million of British subsidies; he entered Paris in 1814.

Towns of Russian campaign 1798-9
① Treviso
② Brescia
③ Milan
④ Turin
⑤ Alessandria
⑥ Tortona
⑦ Piacenza
⑧ Parma
⑨ Bologna
⑩ Mantua

North Sea

BRITAIN

DENMARK

HOLLAND

CONFEDERATIO

OF   Dres

Frankfurt

THE

Paris

RHINE

FRANCE

SWITZ.

KINGDOM

Venice

OF

ITALY

The frontiers of France in 1799

Annexed by France between 1805 and 1812

The European frontiers of 1812

Russian military activity against French forces in Italy 1798-1799

The Cossack force sent to invade India 1801

Grand Duchy of Warsaw 1807-1814

Napoleon's march to Moscow 1812

Russian military attacks on Turkey 1806-1812

The Russian advance from Moscow to Paris 1813-1814

Mediterranean Sea

0   800

Miles

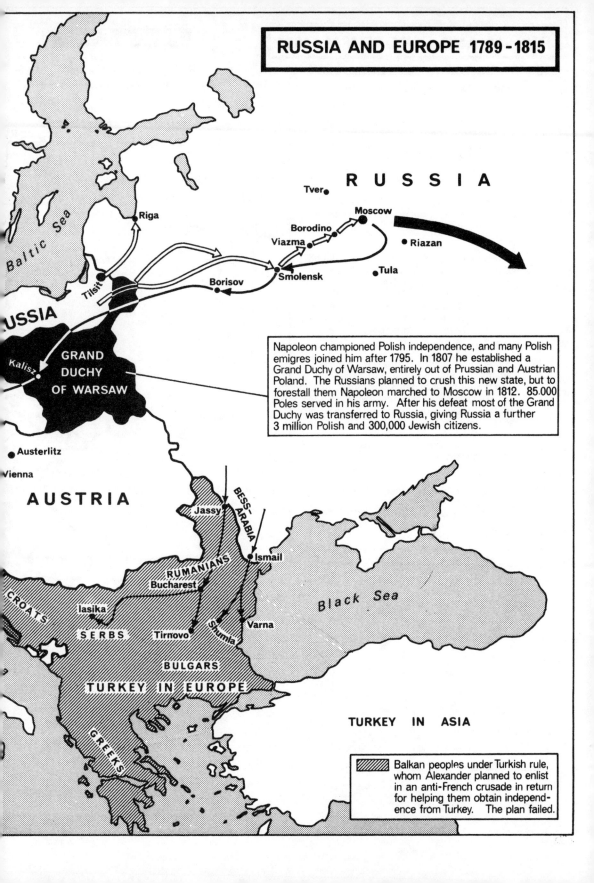

RUSSIA AND EUROPE 1789-1815

RUSSIA

Tver

Moscow

Borodino

Viazma

Riazan

Smolensk

Tula

Riga

Baltic Sea

Tilsit

Borisov

USSIA

Kalisz

GRAND DUCHY OF WARSAW

Napoleon championed Polish independence, and many Polish emigres joined him after 1795. In 1807 he established a Grand Duchy of Warsaw, entirely out of Prussian and Austrian Poland. The Russians planned to crush this new state, but to forestall them Napoleon marched to Moscow in 1812. 85.000 Poles served in his army. After his defeat most of the Grand Duchy was transferred to Russia, giving Russia a further 3 million Polish and 300,000 Jewish citizens.

Austerlitz

Vienna

AUSTRIA

Jassy

BESS-ARABIA

Ismail

RUMANIANS

Bucharest

Black Sea

Iasika

CROATS

SERBS

Tirnovo

Shumla

Varna

BULGARS

TURKEY IN EUROPE

GREEKS

TURKEY IN ASIA

Balkan peoples under Turkish rule, whom Alexander planned to enlist in an anti-French crusade in return for helping them obtain independence from Turkey. The plan failed.

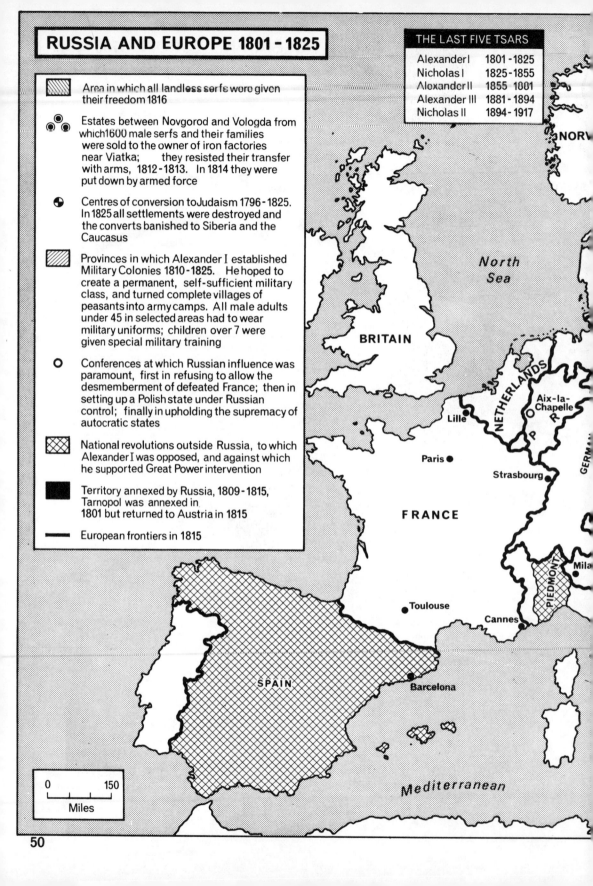

RUSSIA AND EUROPE 1801 - 1825

THE LAST FIVE TSARS

Alexander I	1801 - 1825
Nicholas I	1825 - 1855
Alexander II	1855 - 1881
Alexander III	1881 - 1894
Nicholas II	1894 - 1917

Area in which all landless serfs were given their freedom 1816

Estates between Novgorod and Vologda from which 1600 male serfs and their families were sold to the owner of iron factories near Viatka; they resisted their transfer with arms, 1812 - 1813. In 1814 they were put down by armed force

Centres of conversion to Judaism 1796 - 1825. In 1825 all settlements were destroyed and the converts banished to Siberia and the Caucasus

Provinces in which Alexander I established Military Colonies 1810 - 1825. He hoped to create a permanent, self-sufficient military class, and turned complete villages of peasants into army camps. All male adults under 45 in selected areas had to wear military uniforms; children over 7 were given special military training

Conferences at which Russian influence was paramount, first in refusing to allow the desmemberment of defeated France; then in setting up a Polish state under Russian control; finally in upholding the supremacy of autocratic states

National revolutions outside Russia, to which Alexander I was opposed, and against which he supported Great Power intervention

Territory annexed by Russia, 1809 - 1815, Tarnopol was annexed in 1801 but returned to Austria in 1815

European frontiers in 1815

NORWAY

North Sea

BRITAIN

NETHERLANDS

Aix-la-Chapelle

Lille

EUROPE

GERMANY

Paris

Strasbourg

FRANCE

Milan

PIEDMONT

Toulouse

Cannes

SPAIN

Barcelona

Mediterranean

0   150
Miles

FINLAND

ALAND
ISLANDS

SWEDEN

Baltic Sea

Viatka •

Vologda

St.
Petersburg

Novgorod

Moscow •

Tula ⊕

R U S S I A

Saratov ⊕

Mogilev

Bobrov ⊕

Pavlovsk ⊕

S S I A

POLAND

Carlsbad ○

Prague •

Troppau ○

Lemberg •

Tarnopol

Vienna ○

Ekaterinoslav •

BESSARABIA

AUSTRIA-
HUNGARY

Nikolaev •

Laibach ○

Bucharest •

Belgrade •

T

U

Black Sea

Cattaro •

Constantinople •

R

K E Y

NAPLES

Naples •

GREECE

Athens

Sea

Like Catherine the Great on her accession,
Alexander I was looked to on his accession
(in 1801) as a potential source of liberal-
ization. In the war against Napoleon he acted
as the enemy of tyrants and friend of the
oppressed. But by 1820 he had become a
pillar of autocracy both in Russia and
abroad. Under Alexander, Russia's western
frontier reached its furthest western extent,
and from 1820 to 1917 it was unchanged

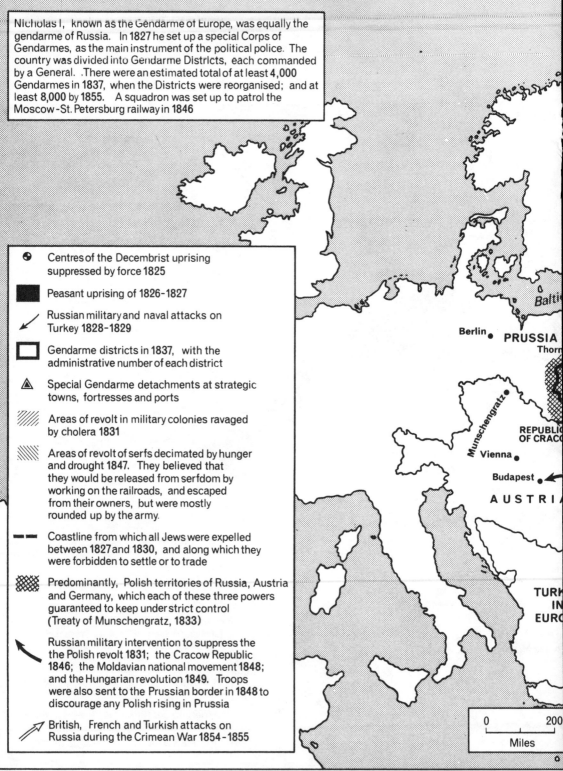

RUSSIA UNDER NICHOLAS I 1825-1855

Nicholas I, known as the Gendarme of Europe, was equally the gendarme of Russia. In 1827 he set up a special Corps of Gendarmes, as the main instrument of the political police. The country was divided into Gendarme Districts, each commanded by a General. .There were an estimated total of at least 4,000 Gendarmes in 1837, when the Districts were reorganised; and at least 8,000 by 1855. A squadron was set up to patrol the Moscow-St. Petersburg railway in 1846

- ⊕ Centres of the Decembrist uprising suppressed by force 1825

- ■ Peasant uprising of 1826-1827

- ✓ Russian military and naval attacks on Turkey 1828-1829

- ☐ Gendarme districts in 1837, with the administrative number of each district

- ▲ Special Gendarme detachments at strategic towns, fortresses and ports

- ▨ Areas of revolt in military colonies ravaged by cholera 1831

- ▨ Areas of revolt of serfs decimated by hunger and drought 1847. They believed that they would be released from serfdom by working on the railroads, and escaped from their owners, but were mostly rounded up by the army.

- ▬ ▬ Coastline from which all Jews were expelled between 1827 and 1830, and along which they were forbidden to settle or to trade

- ▦ Predominantly, Polish territories of Russia, Austria and Germany, which each of these three powers guaranteed to keep under strict control (Treaty of Munschengratz, 1833)

- ↖ Russian military intervention to suppress the the Polish revolt 1831; the Cracow Republic 1846; the Moldavian national movement 1848; and the Hungarian revolution 1849. Troops were also sent to the Prussian border in 1848 to discourage any Polish rising in Prussia

- ↗ British, French and Turkish attacks on Russia during the Crimean War 1854-1855

Berlin • PRUSSIA
Thorn

Baltic

Munschengratz •

REPUBLIC
OF CRACO

Vienna •

Budapest •

AUSTRIA

TURK
IN
EURO

0   200
Miles

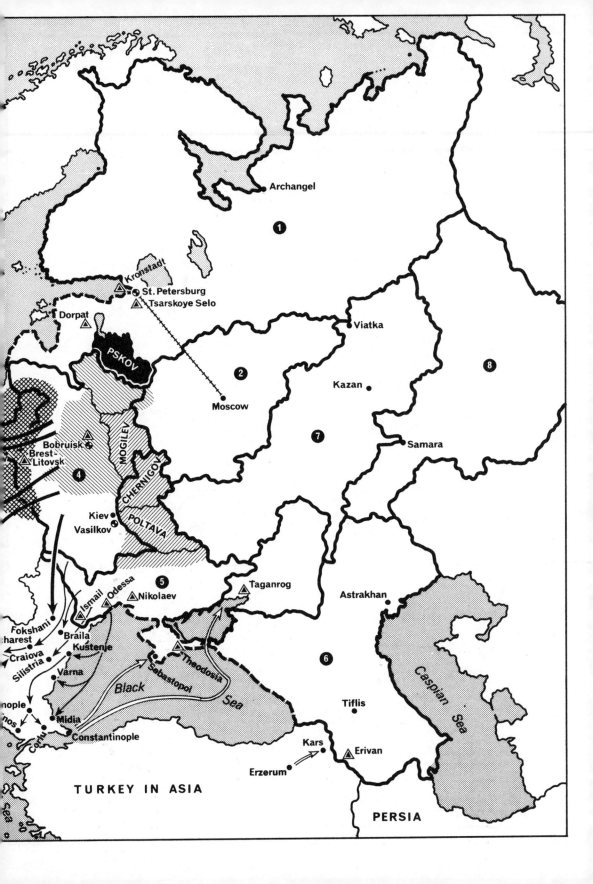

THE POLISH REVOLT IN 1831

After Napoleon's defeat in 1814, Russia set up its new Polish territory as a separate kingdom, CONGRESS POLAND, ruled directly by the Tsar. After 1814, Alexander I adopted a liberal, pro-Polish policy. But in 1825 his successor, Nicholas I, began to restrict Polish liberties. In 1830 the Poles rose in open war against Russian rule. They hoped for help from France, but it never came. The revolt was crushed by superior Russian force.

Palanga

Memel

Königsberg

Danzig

P R U S S I A

Masurian Lakes

Vilna

Suvalki

Grodno

0   50

Miles

Posen

Bialystok

R U S S I A

Kalisz

Lodz

Warsaw

Piotrkow

Pripet Marshes

Brest-Litovsk

Pinsk

Breslau

Czenstochowa

SILESIA

Kovel

Krasnik

REPUBLIC OF CRACOW

Cracow

Tarnow

GALICIA

Przemysl

Lvov

AUSTRIA

Tarnopol

Congress Poland, ruled by the Russian Tsar 1815-1914

Principal areas of Polish partisan activity in 1831 against the local Russian authorities

Battles between Russian and Polish troops in 1831

Polish troop movements. All these ended in exile across the Prussian, Austrian and Cracovian borders

THE POLISH REVOLT IN 1861

The Polish rising of 1831 was largely the work of the Polish aristocracy and land-owners. But by 1860 discontent against Russian rule had spread to the middle classes and intelligentsia. The revolt of 1861 took place throughout Congress Poland. It was crushed after three years of bitter fighting, during which time the Russians had to call in Austrian and Prussian military help

0   50

Miles

Memel

Königsberg

Danzig

PRUSSIA

Masurian Lakes

Kovno

Vilna

Troki

RUSSIA

Mlava

Bialystok

Kalisz

Warsaw

Pripet

Marshes

Radomsk

Lublin

Kovel

Czenstochowa

Krasnik

Zamosc

Cracow

Tarnow

Brody

Lvov

Przemysl

AUSTRIA

Congress Poland, ruled by the Russian Tsar 1815 - 1914

○   Centres of the Polish revolt 1861-1863

Prussian and Austrian troops helping Russia to suppress the uprising

⊙   Principal battles

THE SIBERIAN EXILES 1648-1917

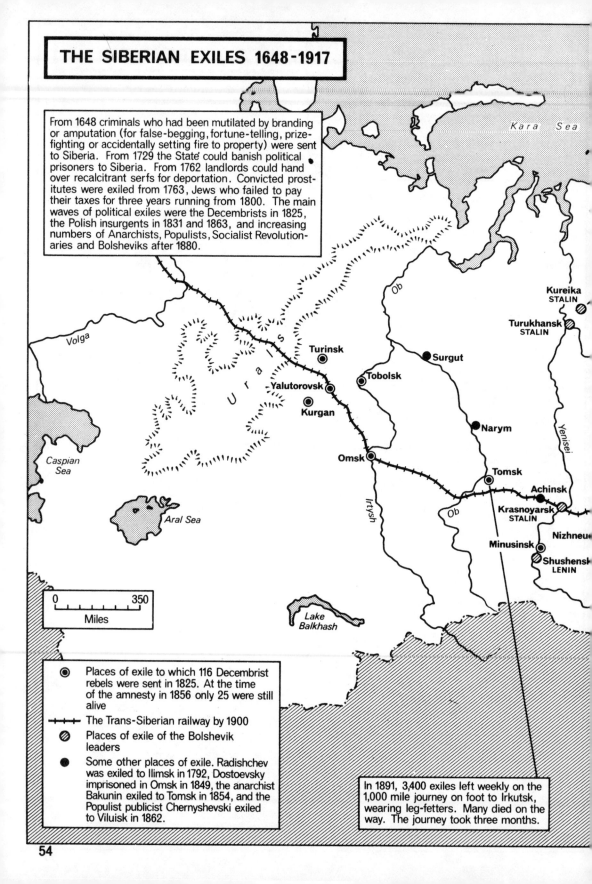

From 1648 criminals who had been mutilated by branding or amputation (for false-begging, fortune-telling, prize-fighting or accidentally setting fire to property) were sent to Siberia. From 1729 the State could banish political prisoners to Siberia. From 1762 landlords could hand over recalcitrant serfs for deportation. Convicted prostitutes were exiled from 1763, Jews who failed to pay their taxes for three years running from 1800. The main waves of political exiles were the Decembrists in 1825, the Polish insurgents in 1831 and 1863, and increasing numbers of Anarchists, Populists, Socialist Revolutionaries and Bolsheviks after 1880.

Kara Sea

Volga

Urals

Kureika
STALIN

Turukhansk
STALIN

Ob

Turinsk

Surgut

Yalutorovsk

Tobolsk

Kurgan

Narym

Caspian Sea

Omsk

Yenisei

Tomsk

Achinsk

Aral Sea

Irtysh

Ob

Krasnoyarsk
STALIN

Nizhneu

Minusinsk

Shushensk
LENIN

0 ——————— 350
Miles

Lake Balkhash

⦿ Places of exile to which 116 Decembrist rebels were sent in 1825. At the time of the amnesty in 1856 only 25 were still alive

+++ The Trans-Siberian railway by 1900

⊘ Places of exile of the Bolshevik leaders

● Some other places of exile. Radishchev was exiled to Ilimsk in 1792, Dostoevsky imprisoned in Omsk in 1849, the anarchist Bakunin exiled to Tomsk in 1854, and the Populist publicist Chernyshevski exiled to Viluisk in 1862.

In 1891, 3,400 exiles left weekly on the 1,000 mile journey on foot to Irkutsk, wearing leg-fetters. Many died on the way. The journey took three months.

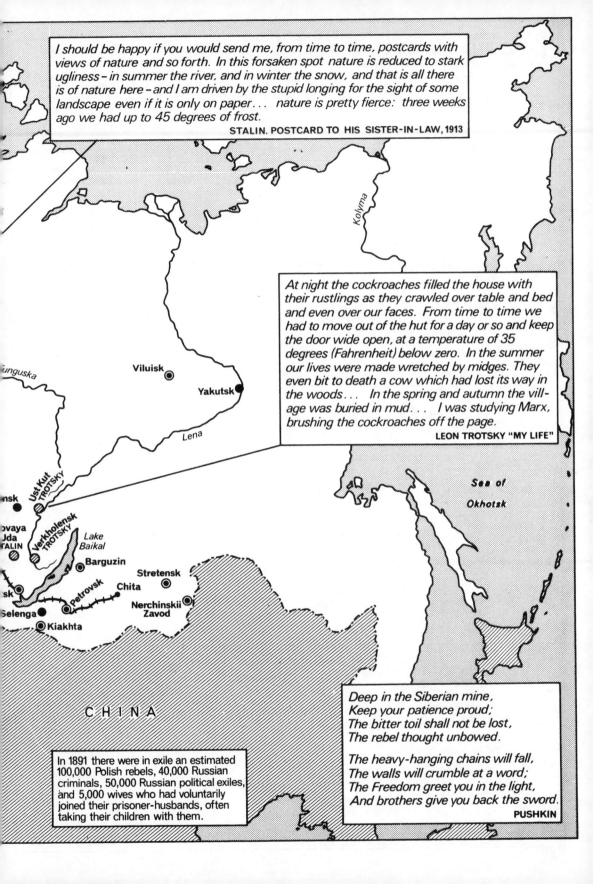

I should be happy if you would send me, from time to time, postcards with views of nature and so forth. In this forsaken spot nature is reduced to stark ugliness – in summer the river, and in winter the snow, and that is all there is of nature here – and I am driven by the stupid longing for the sight of some landscape even if it is only on paper... nature is pretty fierce: three weeks ago we had up to 45 degrees of frost.

STALIN. POSTCARD TO HIS SISTER-IN-LAW, 1913

At night the cockroaches filled the house with their rustlings as they crawled over table and bed and even over our faces. From time to time we had to move out of the hut for a day or so and keep the door wide open, at a temperature of 35 degrees (Fahrenheit) below zero. In the summer our lives were made wretched by midges. They even bit to death a cow which had lost its way in the woods... In the spring and autumn the village was buried in mud... I was studying Marx, brushing the cockroaches off the page.

LEON TROTSKY "MY LIFE"

Kolyma

Tunguska

Viluisk

Yakutsk

Lena

nsk

Ust Kut TROTSKY

ovaya Jda STALIN

Verkholensk TROTSKY

Lake Baikal

Barguzin

Stretensk

Petrovsk

Chita

sk

Selenga

Kiakhta

Nerchinskii Zavod

Sea of Okhotsk

C H I N A

In 1891 there were in exile an estimated 100,000 Polish rebels, 40,000 Russian criminals, 50,000 Russian political exiles, and 5,000 wives who had voluntarily joined their prisoner-husbands, often taking their children with them.

Deep in the Siberian mine,
Keep your patience proud;
The bitter toil shall not be lost,
The rebel thought unbowed.

The heavy-hanging chains will fall,
The walls will crumble at a word;
The Freedom greet you in the light,
And brothers give you back the sword.

PUSHKIN

THE ANARCHISTS 1840-1906

"What is property? Property is theft" wrote the French philosopher Proudhon, the father of anarchism, in 1840. He urged the destruction of officialdom, bureaucracy money and state organisation in order to make all men equal and free. But he shunned violent revolt, fearing that revolution might bring new tyranny. The Russian, Bakunin, bent anarchism to violence. "The passion to destroy is at the same time a passion to create," he wrote in 1842. Bakunin believed that the Russian peasant would be the instrument of anarchic revolt, and encouraged terrorist acts. The murder of Tsar Alexander II at St. Petersburg in 1881 encouraged further assassinations, aimed at provoking revolution. The Russian anarchist, Prince Kropotkin, said after the execution of one of the 5 assassins: "By her death she was dealing an even more terrible blow, from which the autocracy will never recover."

St.Petersburg

Viatka

Baltic Sea

Riga

LITHUANIA

Kovno

Vilna

Minsk

Grodno

Bialystok

Warsaw

POLAND

Moscow

Nizhni Novgorod

Volga

Tula

Orel

Samara

Nezhin

Kiev

Kharkov

UKRAINE

Ekaterinoslav

Kishinev

Odessa

Sebastopol

Yalta

Black Sea

Volga

Caspian Sea

Batum

Tiflis

CAUCASIA

Baku

Legend

⊙ Anarchist groups meeting from the 1840's to 1880's

● Revolutionary anarchist groups in existence from 1903 and "revolting" in 1905 - 1906

▨ The "Forest Brethren" carrying out terrorist activity in 1905 - 1906

0   300

Miles

RUSSIAN INDUSTRY BY 1860

0 ——— 200
Miles

Archangel

Urals

Vyborg
Schlüsselburg
Reval
St. Petersburg 540,000
LEATHER
Narva
WOOL
Dorpat
Pskov
Riga 77,000
Libau
Mitau
Dvinsk
WOOL
Kovno
Vilna 69,000
Grodno
Bialystok
Warsaw
LINEN
Lodz
LINEN

Viatka

Kama
Perm
COAL GOLD
COAL COPPER
LEATHER
Ufa
COPPER

Yaroslavl
LINEN
Volga
Kazan 63,000
Tver
Vladimir
Yegorevsk
LEATHER
Moscow 460,000
Nizhni Novgorod
LEATHER
Riazan
Kaluga Tula
LINEN
LEATHER
Orel
WOOL
Voronezh
Saratov 84,000

Ural

LINEN
Chernigov

Kiev 68,000
LINEN
Kharkov
Poltava
Donets
COAL
Don
Volga

Kishinev 94,000
64,000
Nikolaev
Odessa
120,000

TOBACCO
Caucasus

Caspian Sea

Baku
OIL

Black Sea

Dnieper

POPULATION
1811: 41,000,000
1863: 74,000,000

—— The Russian frontier 1815 - 1914

● Principal cities, with their estimated population in 1860

╫╫ Railways built by 1860

+++ Railways under construction in 1860

◉ Factory development before 1860

◒ Towns with large factory growth from 1860

▮ Industries expanding rapidly from 1860

▦ Centres of the iron and steel production

▨ Sugar factories

PRINCIPAL IMPORTS: Cotton, machine tools, alcohol, dyes, fruit and nuts, wool, tea, olive and vegetable oil, silk, sugar, zinc, steel, iron, copper, horses. cattle. poultry, salt. Over 80% of all imports and exports went through the ports of St. Petersburg and Odessa

PRINCIPAL EXPORTS: Wheat, rye, cereals, flour, flax, hemp, wool, animal fat, lard, seeds, wood, wood products, paper

56

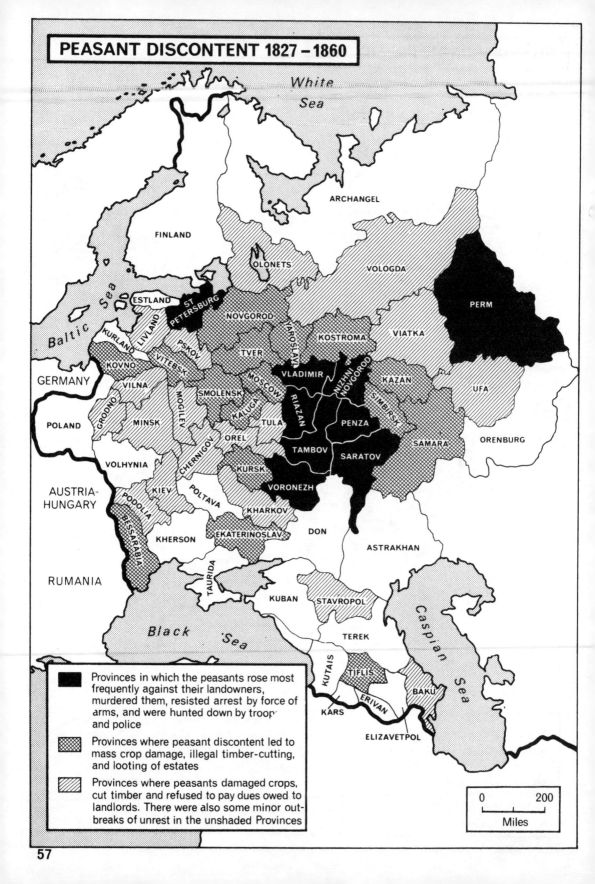

PEASANT DISCONTENT 1827-1860

White Sea

ARCHANGEL

FINLAND

OLONETS

VOLOGDA

Baltic Sea

ESTLAND

ST PETERSBURG

NOVGOROD

PERM

KURLAND

LIVLAND

PSKOV

YAROSLAVL

KOSTROMA

VIATKA

VITEBSK

TVER

KOVNO

MOSCOW

VLADIMIR

NIZHNI NOVGOROD

KAZAN

GERMANY

VILNA

SMOLENSK

KALUGA

RIAZAN

SIMBIRSK

UFA

GRODNO

MOGILEV

TULA

PENZA

ORENBURG

POLAND

MINSK

OREL

SAMARA

VOLHYNIA

CHERNIGOV

KURSK

TAMBOV

SARATOV

AUSTRIA-HUNGARY

PODOLIA

KIEV

POLTAVA

VORONEZH

BESSARABIA

KHARKOV

DON

ASTRAKHAN

KHERSON

EKATERINOSLAV

RUMANIA

TAURIDA

KUBAN

STAVROPOL

Black Sea

TEREK

Caspian Sea

KUTAIS

TIFLIS

BAKU

KARS

ERIVAN

ELIZAVETPOL

Provinces in which the peasants rose most frequently against their landowners, murdered them, resisted arrest by force of arms, and were hunted down by troops and police

Provinces where peasant discontent led to mass crop damage, illegal timber-cutting, and looting of estates

Provinces where peasants damaged crops, cut timber and refused to pay dues owed to landlords. There were also some minor outbreaks of unrest in the unshaded Provinces

0   200
Miles

57

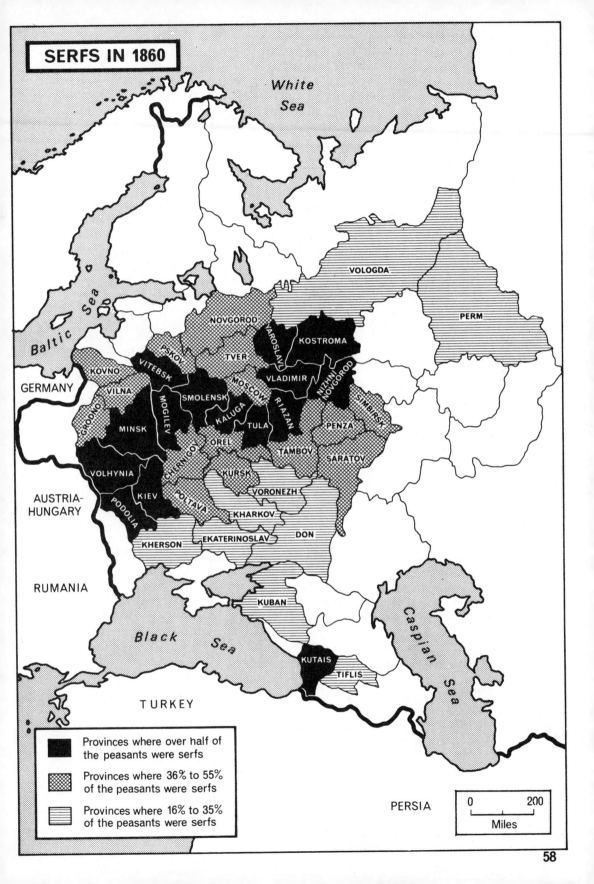

SERFS IN 1860

White Sea

Baltic Sea

GERMANY

AUSTRIA-HUNGARY

RUMANIA

VOLOGDA

PERM

NOVGOROD

PSKOV

VITEBSK

KOVNO

VILNA

GRODNO

MOGILEV

MINSK

TVER

MOSCOW

SMOLENSK

KALUGA

VOLHYNIA

KIEV

PODOLIA

CHERNIGOV

POLTAVA

OREL

KURSK

TULA

YAROSLAVL

KOSTROMA

VLADIMIR

RIAZAN

NIZHNI NOVGOROD

SIMBIRSK

PENZA

TAMBOV

SARATOV

VORONEZH

KHARKOV

EKATERINOSLAV

DON

KHERSON

KUBAN

Black Sea

Caspian Sea

KUTAIS

TIFLIS

PERSIA

TURKEY

Provinces where over half of
the peasants were serfs

Provinces where 36% to 55%
of the peasants were serfs

Provinces where 16% to 35%
of the peasants were serfs

0   200
Miles

58

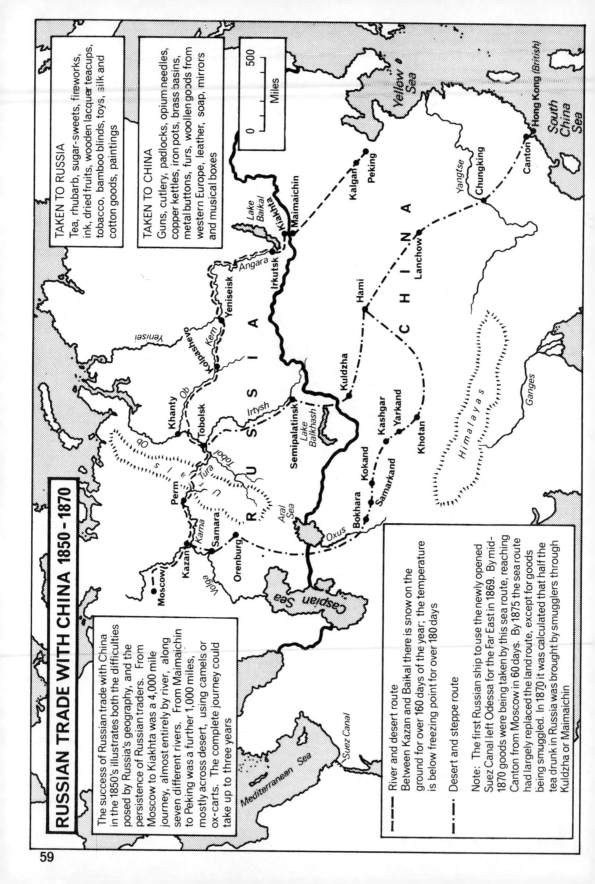

RUSSIAN TRADE WITH CHINA 1850 – 1870

The success of Russian trade with China in the 1850's illustrates both the difficulties posed by Russia's geography, and the persistence of Russian traders. From Moscow to Kiakhta was a 4,000 mile journey, almost entirely by river, along seven different rivers. From Maimaichin to Peking was a further 1,000 miles, mostly across desert, using camels or ox-carts. The complete journey could take up to three years

TAKEN TO RUSSIA
Tea, rhubarb, sugar-sweets, fireworks, ink, dried fruits, wooden lacquer teacups, tobacco, bamboo blinds, toys, silk and cotton goods, paintings

TAKEN TO CHINA
Guns, cutlery, padlocks, opium needles, copper kettles, iron pots, brass basins, metal buttons, furs, woollen goods from western Europe, leather, soap, mirrors and musical boxes

- - - River and desert route
Between Kazan and Baikal there is snow on the ground for over 160 days of the year; the temperature is below freezing point for over 180 days

-·-·- Desert and steppe route

Note: The first Russian ship to use the newly opened Suez Canal left Odessa for the Far East in 1869. By mid-1870 goods were being taken by this sea route, reaching Canton from Moscow in 60 days. By 1875 the sea route had largely replaced the land route, except for goods being smuggled. In 1870 it was calculated that half the tea drunk in Russia was brought by smugglers through Kuldzha or Maimaichin

59

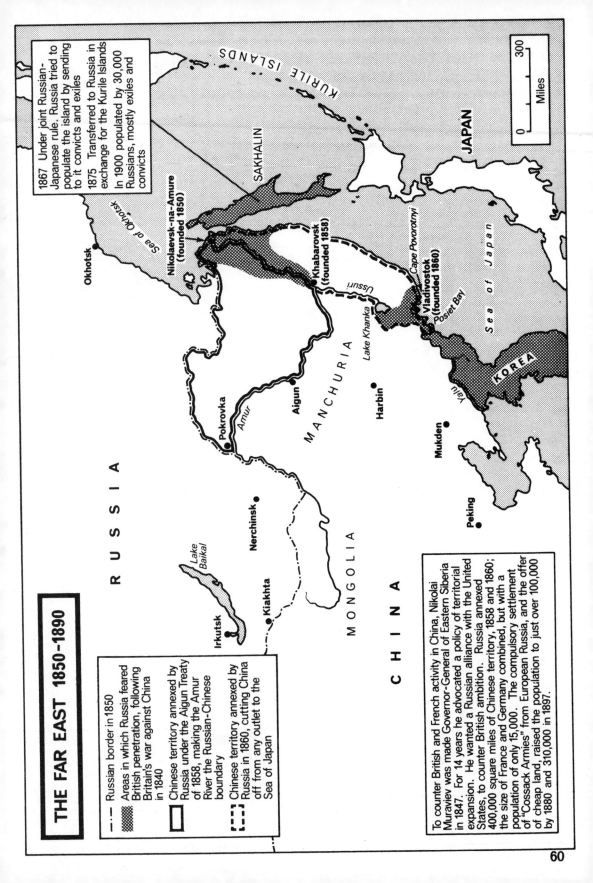

THE FAR EAST 1850-1890

Legend:

- –·– Russian border in 1850
- Areas in which Russia feared British penetration, following Britain's war against China in 1840
- ☐ Chinese territory annexed by Russia under the Aigun Treaty of 1858, making the Amur River the Russian-Chinese boundary
- ⌐ ⌐ ⌐ Chinese territory annexed by Russia in 1860, cutting China off from any outlet to the Sea of Japan

1867 Under joint Russian-Japanese rule. Russia tried to populate the island by sending to it convicts and exiles

1875 Transferred to Russia in exchange for the Kurile Islands In 1900 populated by 30,000 Russians, mostly exiles and convicts

To counter British and French activity in China, Nikolai Muraviev was made Governor-General of Eastern Siberia in 1847. For 14 years he advocated a policy of territorial expansion. He wanted a Russian alliance with the United States, to counter British ambition. Russia annexed 400,000 square miles of Chinese territory, 1858 and 1860; the size of France and Germany combined, but with a population of only 15,000. The compulsory settlement of "Cossack Armies" from European Russia, and the offer of cheap land, raised the population to just over 100,000 by 1880 and 310,000 in 1897.

KURILE ISLANDS

JAPAN

300
0
Miles

Sea of Okhotsk

Okhotsk

SAKHALIN

Nikolaevsk-na-Amure (founded 1850)

Khabarovsk (founded 1858)

Cape Povorotnyi

Vladivostok (founded 1860)

Posiet Bay

Sea of Japan

Ussuri

Lake Khanka

KOREA

Yalu

MANCHURIA

Pokrovka

Aigun

Harbin

Amur

Mukden

RUSSIA

Lake Baikal

Nerchinsk

Irkutsk

Kiakhta

MONGOLIA

Peking

CHINA

60

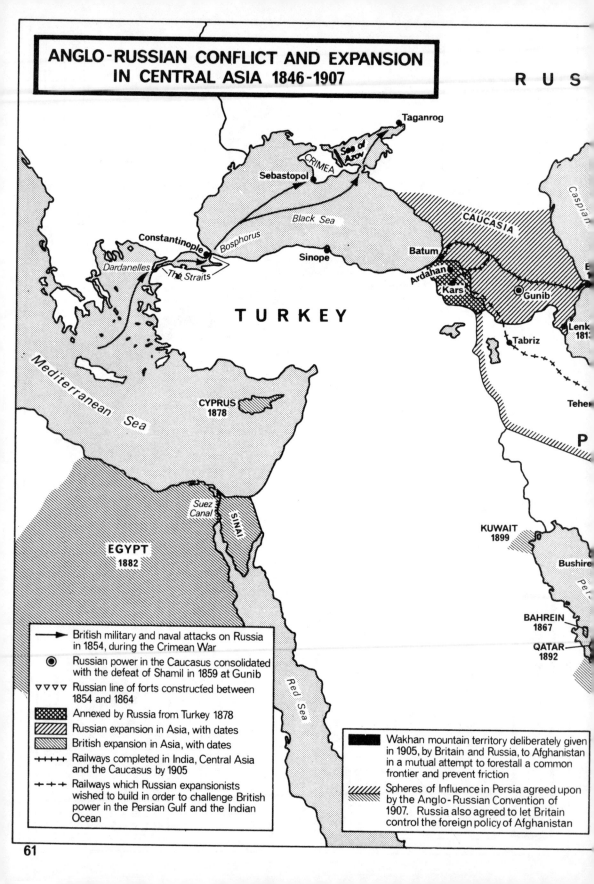

ANGLO-RUSSIAN CONFLICT AND EXPANSION IN CENTRAL ASIA 1846-1907

R U S

Taganrog

Sea of Azov

CRIMEA

Sebastopol

Black Sea

CAUCASIA

Caspian

Constantinople

Bosphorus

Batum

Dardanelles

The Straits

Sinope

Ardahan

Kars

Gunib

T U R K E Y

Lenk
181

Tabriz

Tehe

CYPRUS
1878

Mediterranean Sea

P

Suez
Canal

SINAI

KUWAIT
1899

EGYPT
1882

Bushire

Red Sea

BAHREIN
1867

QATAR
1892

→ British military and naval attacks on Russia in 1854, during the Crimean War

◉ Russian power in the Caucasus consolidated with the defeat of Shamil in 1859 at Gunib

▽▽▽▽ Russian line of forts constructed between 1854 and 1864

▨ Annexed by Russia from Turkey 1878

▧ Russian expansion in Asia, with dates

▩ British expansion in Asia, with dates

+++++ Railways completed in India, Central Asia and the Caucasus by 1905

+-+-+ Railways which Russian expansionists wished to build in order to challenge British power in the Persian Gulf and the Indian Ocean

■ Wakhan mountain territory deliberately given in 1905, by Britain and Russia, to Afghanistan in a mutual attempt to forestall a common frontier and prevent friction

▨ Spheres of Influence in Persia agreed upon by the Anglo-Russian Convention of 1907. Russia also agreed to let Britain control the foreign policy of Afghanistan

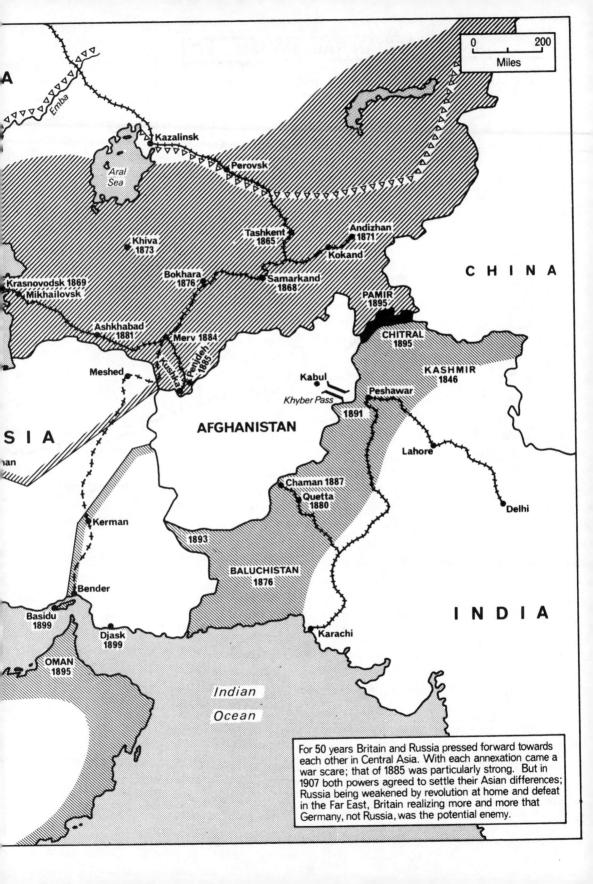

Miles
0   200

Emba

Kazalinsk

Perovsk

Aral
Sea

Tashkent
1865

Andizhan
1871

Kokand

C H I N A

Khiva
1873

Krasnovodsk 1869
Mikhailovsk

Bokhara
1876

Samarkand
1868

PAMIR
1895

Ashkhabad
1881

Merv 1884

Penjdeh
1885

CHITRAL
1895

KASHMIR
1846

Meshed

Kabul

Peshawar

A

Khyber Pass

1891

S I A

AFGHANISTAN

Lahore

Kerman

Chaman 1887

Quetta
1880

Delhi

Bender

1893

Basidu
1899

Djask
1899

BALUCHISTAN
1876

I N D I A

OMAN
1895

Karachi

Indian

Ocean

For 50 years Britain and Russia pressed forward towards
each other in Central Asia. With each annexation came a
war scare; that of 1885 was particularly strong. But in
1907 both powers agreed to settle their Asian differences;
Russia being weakened by revolution at home and defeat
in the Far East, Britain realizing more and more that
Germany, not Russia, was the potential enemy.

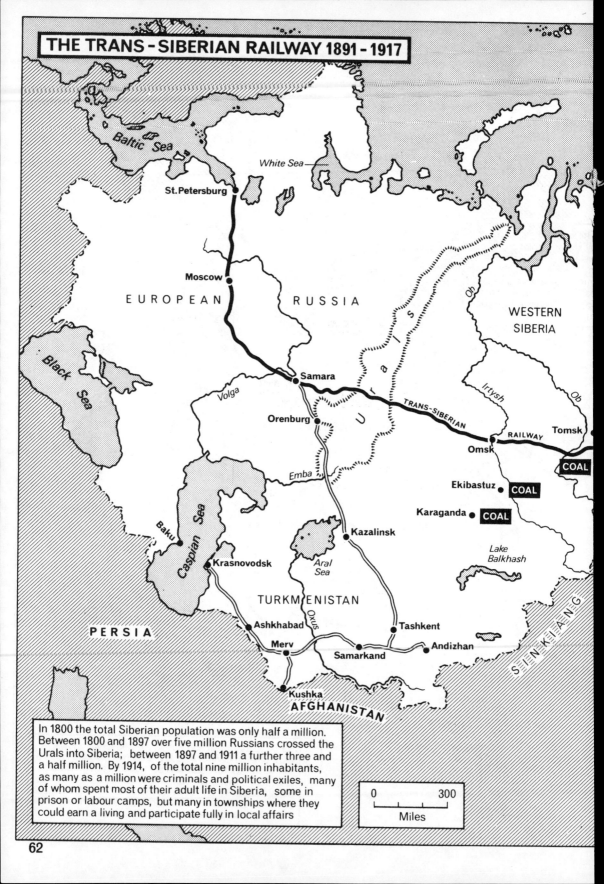

THE TRANS-SIBERIAN RAILWAY 1891-1917

Baltic Sea

White Sea

St. Petersburg

Moscow

E U R O P E A N   R U S S I A

WESTERN
SIBERIA

Black Sea

Samara

Volga

Ob

Urals

Orenburg

Irtysh

TRANS-SIBERIAN

Ob

Tomsk

RAILWAY

Emba

Omsk

COAL

Ekibastuz   **COAL**

Karaganda   **COAL**

Baku

Caspian Sea

Kazalinsk

Aral Sea

Lake Balkhash

Krasnovodsk

TURKMENISTAN

Oxus

S I N K I A N G

P E R S I A

Ashkhabad

Tashkent

Merv

Andizhan

Samarkand

Kushka

AFGHANISTAN

In 1800 the total Siberian population was only half a million.
Between 1800 and 1897 over five million Russians crossed the
Urals into Siberia; between 1897 and 1911 a further three and
a half million. By 1914, of the total nine million inhabitants,
as many as a million were criminals and political exiles, many
of whom spent most of their adult life in Siberia, some in
prison or labour camps, but many in townships where they
could earn a living and participate fully in local affairs

```
0            300
|__|__|__|__|__|
      Miles
```

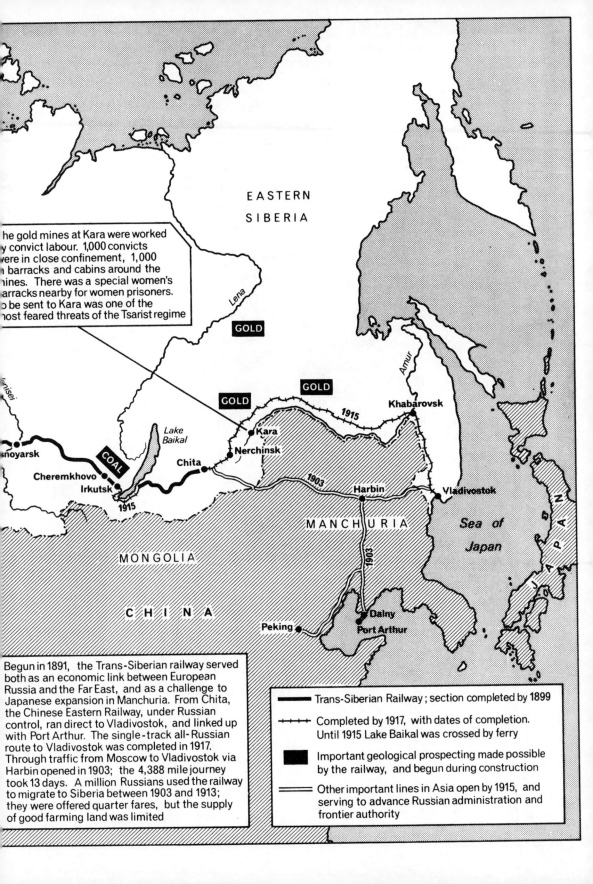

EASTERN
SIBERIA

Lena

GOLD

he gold mines at Kara were worked
y convict labour. 1,000 convicts
vere in close confinement, 1,000
n barracks and cabins around the
nines. There was a special women's
arracks nearby for women prisoners.
o be sent to Kara was one of the
nost feared threats of the Tsarist regime

GOLD

Amur

GOLD

Khabarovsk

1915

noyarsk

enisei

COAL

Lake
Baikal

Kara

Nerchinsk

Cheremkhovo

Chita

1903

Irkutsk

1915

Harbin

Vladivostok

MANCHURIA

Sea of
Japan

MONGOLIA

1903

CHINA

Dalny

J A P A N

Peking

Port Arthur

Begun in 1891, the Trans-Siberian railway served
both as an economic link between European
Russia and the Far East, and as a challenge to
Japanese expansion in Manchuria. From Chita,
the Chinese Eastern Railway, under Russian
control, ran direct to Vladivostok, and linked up
with Port Arthur. The single-track all-Russian
route to Vladivostok was completed in 1917.
Through traffic from Moscow to Vladivostok via
Harbin opened in 1903; the 4,388 mile journey
took 13 days. A million Russians used the railway
to migrate to Siberia between 1903 and 1913;
they were offered quarter fares, but the supply
of good farming land was limited

Trans-Siberian Railway; section completed by 1899

+++++ Completed by 1917, with dates of completion.
Until 1915 Lake Baikal was crossed by ferry

Important geological prospecting made possible
by the railway, and begun during construction

Other important lines in Asia open by 1915, and
serving to advance Russian administration and
frontier authority

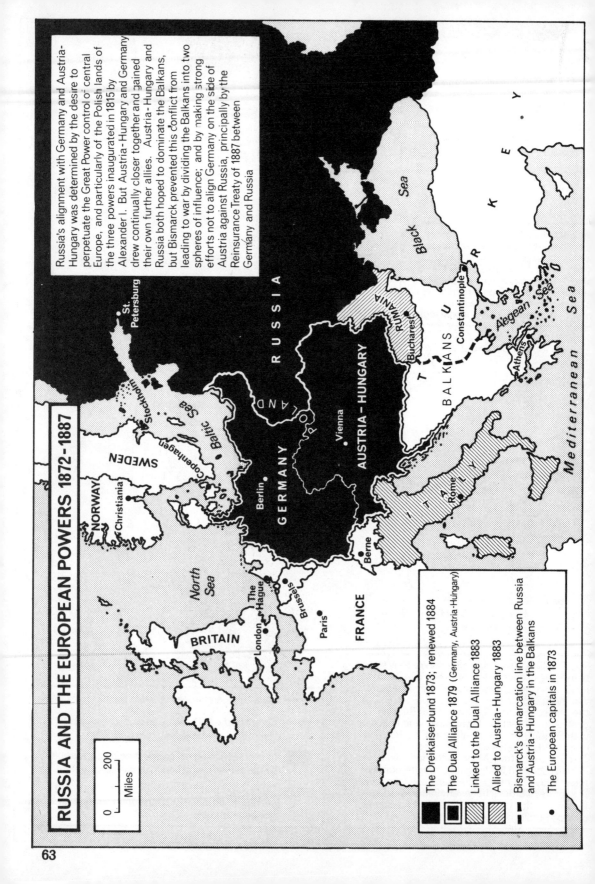

RUSSIA AND THE EUROPEAN POWERS 1872-1887

Russia's alignment with Germany and Austria-Hungary was determined by the desire to perpetuate the Great Power control of central Europe, and particularly of the Polish lands of the three powers inaugurated in 1815 by Alexander I. But Austria-Hungary and Germany drew continually closer together and gained their own further allies. Austria-Hungary and Russia both hoped to dominate the Balkans, but Bismarck prevented this conflict from leading to war by dividing the Balkans into two spheres of influence; and by making strong efforts not to align Germany on the side of Austria against Russia, principally by the Reinsurance Treaty of 1887 between Germany and Russia

0   200
Miles

The Dreikaiserbund 1873; renewed 1884

The Dual Alliance 1879 (Germany, Austria-Hungary)

Linked to the Dual Alliance 1883

Allied to Austria-Hungary 1883

Bismarck's demarcation line between Russia and Austria-Hungary in the Balkans

The European capitals in 1873

NORWAY
Christiania

SWEDEN
Stockholm

St. Petersburg

RUSSIA

Baltic Sea

Copenhagen

BRITAIN

North Sea

London
The Hague
Brussels

Berlin
GERMANY

POLAND

Vienna
AUSTRIA-HUNGARY

RUMANIA
Bucharest

Black Sea

TURKEY

BALKANS

Constantinople

Aegean Sea

Athens

Paris
FRANCE

Berne

ITALY
Rome

Mediterranean Sea

63

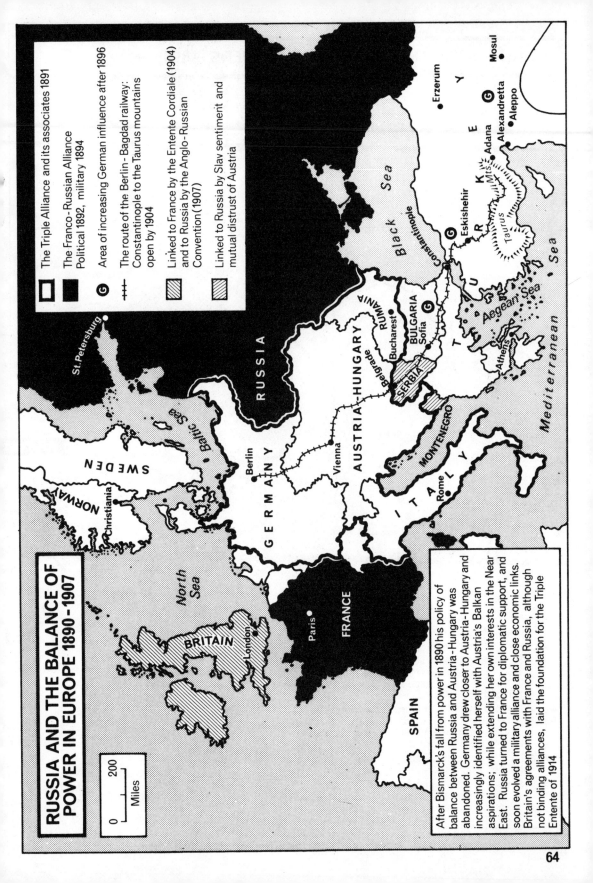

RUSSIA AND THE BALANCE OF POWER IN EUROPE 1890–1907

	The Triple Alliance and its associates 1891
	The Franco-Russian Alliance Political 1892, military 1894
Ⓖ	Area of increasing German influence after 1896
┼┼┼	The route of the Berlin-Bagdad railway: Constantinople to the Taurus mountains open by 1904
▨	Linked to France by the Entente Cordiale (1904) and to Russia by the Anglo-Russian Convention (1907)
▨	Linked to Russia by Slav sentiment and mutual distrust of Austria

0   200
Miles

After Bismarck's fall from power in 1890 his policy of balance between Russia and Austria-Hungary was abandoned. Germany drew closer to Austria-Hungary and increasingly identified herself with Austria's Balkan aspirations; while extending her own interests in the Near East. Russia turned to France for diplomatic support, and soon evolved a military alliance and close economic links. Britain's agreements with France and Russia, although not binding alliances, laid the foundation for the Triple Entente of 1914

SWEDEN

NORWAY

Christiania

RUSSIA

St. Petersburg

Baltic Sea

North Sea

BRITAIN

London

FRANCE

Paris

SPAIN

GERMANY

Berlin

Vienna

AUSTRIA-HUNGARY

ITALY

Rome

Black Sea

RUMANIA

Bucharest

Belgrade

SERBIA

MONTENEGRO

BULGARIA

Sofia Ⓖ

Constantinople Ⓖ

Athens

Aegean Sea

Mediterranean Sea

T U R K E Y

Eskishehir

Taurus Mts.

Adana

Alexandretta Ⓖ

Aleppo

Mosul

Erzerum Ⓖ

CHINA AND THE EUROPEAN POWERS 1898-1904

RUSSIA

Lake Balkhash

Tashkent

Issyk Kul

Kuldzha

Hami

AFGHANISTAN

Kashgar

S I N K I A N G

Lop Nor

Yarkand

Khotan

Peshawar

Koko Nor

K A S H M I R

Indus

T I B E T

Delhi

BRITAI

Lhasa

Guru

Ganges

BRITISH

INDIA

B E N G A L

Yun

Calcutta

BURMA

Bay of Bengal

Indian Ocean

SIA

Legend:

— The Chinese frontier in 1897

● Ports annexed by the European Powers in 1898

◉ Port which the United States wished to annex in 1900, but was stopped from doing so by Japan. In 1898 the United States had defeated Spain and annexed the Philippines

—·—) Proposed partition of China between Russia, Britain, France and Germany. The idea was abandoned, as too many interests clashed. The British in India, for example, wanted to control the area ⊠⊠⊠

→ Russian exploration, trade and diplomatic influence in Tibet, 1900-1904, resented by Britain

⟫⟫⟫ British military Mission under Younghusband, which defeated the Tibetans at Guru in 1904 and entered Lhasa. In 1907 Russia agreed to allow Britain to be the dominant foreign power in Tibet

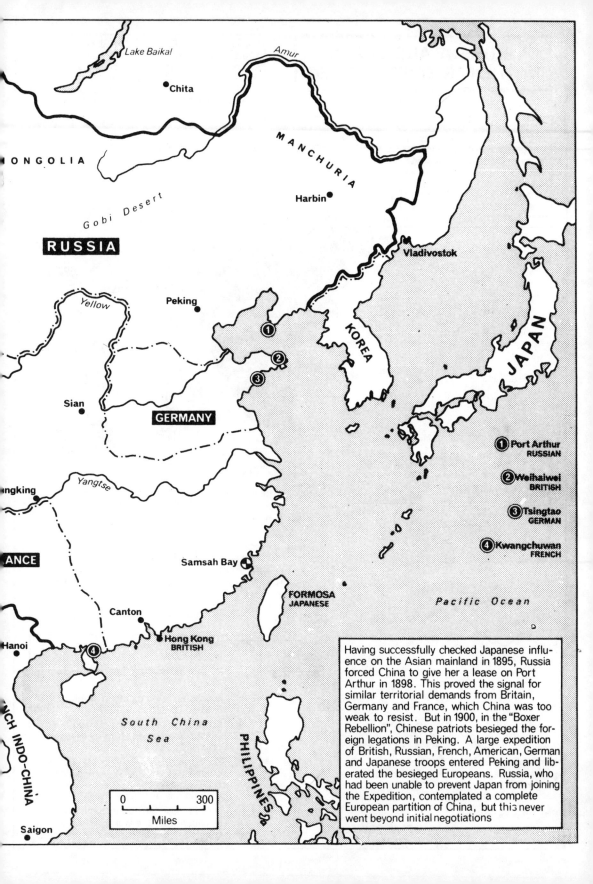

Lake Baikal

•Chita

Amur

M A N C H U R I A

MONGOLIA

Gobi Desert

Harbin•

RUSSIA

Vladivostok

Yellow

Peking •

KOREA

JAPAN

Sian •

GERMANY

ngking

Yangtse

① **Port Arthur**
RUSSIAN

② **Weihaiwei**
BRITISH

③ **Tsingtao**
GERMAN

④ **Kwangchuwan**
FRENCH

ANCE

Samsah Bay ⊕

FORMOSA
JAPANESE

Pacific Ocean

Canton •

• Hong Kong
BRITISH

Hanoi •

④

South China
Sea

P H I L I P P I N E S

Having successfully checked Japanese influence on the Asian mainland in 1895, Russia
forced China to give her a lease on Port
Arthur in 1898. This proved the signal for
similar territorial demands from Britain,
Germany and France, which China was too
weak to resist. But in 1900, in the "Boxer
Rebellion", Chinese patriots besieged the foreign legations in Peking. A large expedition
of British, Russian, French, American, German
and Japanese troops entered Peking and liberated the besieged Europeans. Russia, who
had been unable to prevent Japan from joining
the Expedition, contemplated a complete
European partition of China, but this never
went beyond initial negotiations

NCH INDO-CHINA

Saigon •

0 — 300
Miles

Kamchatka: part of Russia in 1650. Since 1750 used largely as a place of exile for criminals and political prisoners. Russian schoolboys were often threatened that slackers would be "sent to Kamchatka"—the furthest corner of the classroom. The peninsula has over 20 active volcanoes.

The struggle between Russia and Japan in the Far East was long and bitter. In 1860 Russia acquired an outlet on the Sea of Japan. The Japanese at once adopted a forward policy in China and Korea. When Japan defeated China in 1895 she expected to make wide territorial gains. But Russia, France, Britain and Germany combined to deprive Japan of the fruits of victory. This led to deep anti-Russian resentment throughout Japan. Throughout this period, European penetration in south China continued unabated.

RUSSIA

Amur

SIBERIA

KAMCHATKA

Sea of Okhotsk

Petropavlovsk

MANCHURIA

EASTERN

Nikolaevsk

Khabarosvk

SAKHALIN

Harbin

Sungari

Ussuri

KURILE ISLANDS

Uruppu

Changchun   Kirin

Etorofu

Mukden

Vladivostok

Peking

Yalu

Sea of Japan

Pacific

Tientsin

Port Arthur   Wonsan

Weihaiwei

Seoul   **KOREA**

Ocean

Yellow

Inchon

Yellow Sea

Pusan

JAPAN

Tsingtao

0   500

Miles

Nanking

Hankow   Shanghai

Yangtse

Oshima

Okinawa

Macao (Portuguese 1557)

Kowloon (British 1861)

RYUKYU ISLANDS

Hongkong
(British 1841)

FORMOSA

South China Sea

PHILIPPINES
(Spanish 1521)

Territory annexed by Russia from China in 1858-1860

Islands annexed by Japan from China in 1874

Islands annexed by Japan in return for Russian control of Sakhalin

Korean ports open, as the result of Japanese pressure, to Japanese trade 1876-1878

Occupied by Japan during the war with China, 1894-95. Russia, France, Britain and Germany combined to prevent Japan keeping any of this territory

Only Chinese territory actually annexed by Japan after the war of 1894-1895

**THE RUSSIAN RESPONSE
IN THE FAR EAST 1895-1905**

WAR DEAD 1904-05	
Russian	120,000
Japanese	75,000

R U S S I A

Chita

Nerchinsk

Amur

Nikolaevsk

Argun

Hailar

M A N C H U R I A

Tsitsihar

Khabarovsk

Amur

S A K H A L I N

Harbin

Sungari

CHINA

Mukden

Peking

Yalu

Vladivostok

Sea of Japan

Port
Arthur

Seoul

KOREA

J A P A N

Yellow
Sea

Tsushima Strait

Tokyo

The Trans-Siberian Railway by 1895

Under increasing Russian control after 1895

Leased by Russia from China in 1898, together with the right to build a railway to Harbin; (completed by 1904)

The Chinese Eastern Railway, controlled by Russia after its completion in 1903

Russian economic penetration. Russia refused to allow Japan a sphere of influence in Korea

Japanese naval and military attacks 1904-1905

Annexed by Japan in 1905

After successfully halting Japanese expansion in 1895, the Russians adopted an active expansionist policy. For 10 years they pressed forward in Manchuria, and discussed the partition of China with the British Government in 1900. But Japan sought revenge for the humiliation of 1895, and in 1902 neutralized Britain by the Anglo-Japanese Alliance. In February 1904, under Russian provocation, Japan attacked Port Arthur. Russia was defeated on land and sea, and a peace treaty was signed in the United States in Sept. 1905. The grave demoralization created by Russia's defeat led to a mass of revolutionary outbreaks in Russia, and to a serious weakening of the Tsarist mystique.

PRELUDE TO REVOLUTION 1894 - 1904

Despite the abolition of Serfdom in 1860, peasant poverty remained widespread. Despite Russia's economic expansion in the 1890's, urban hardship was widespread. Revolutionary groups competed for allegiance, offering various panaceas: anarchy, the total destruction of the autocracy, and a new world based upon the dignity of labour. There were frequent strikes and riots after 1890. The Tsarist police struggled to prevent the mounting violence. An increasing number of political activists were exiled to Siberia. Discontent continued unabated: the General Jewish Labour League (the 'Bund') was founded in 1897, the Social Democrat Labour Party in 1898, the Socialist Revolutionary Party in 1901. By 1904 every town in Russia, and almost every factory, however small, was caught in the upsurge of popular revolt, strikes and riots

The emperor of all the Russias is an autocratic and unlimited monarch. God himself commands that his supreme power be obeyed, out of conscience as well as fear

ARTICLE ONE, FUNDAMENTAL LAWS OF THE EMPIRE 1892

Ufa 1903

Volga

Ivanovo

Moscow

RIAZAN

TULA

OREL

St. Petersburg 1902, 1904

FINNS

BALTS

Riga

Minsk

Baltic Sea

POLES

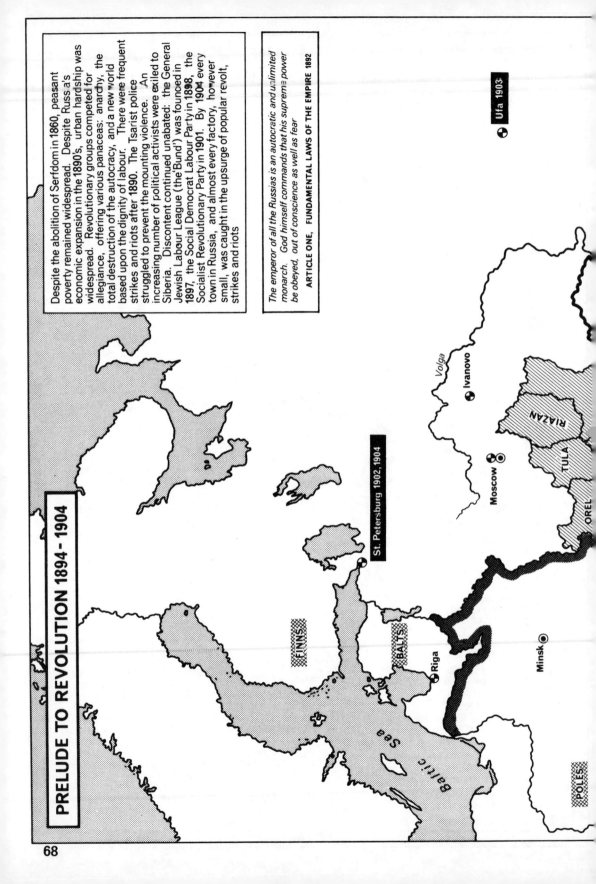

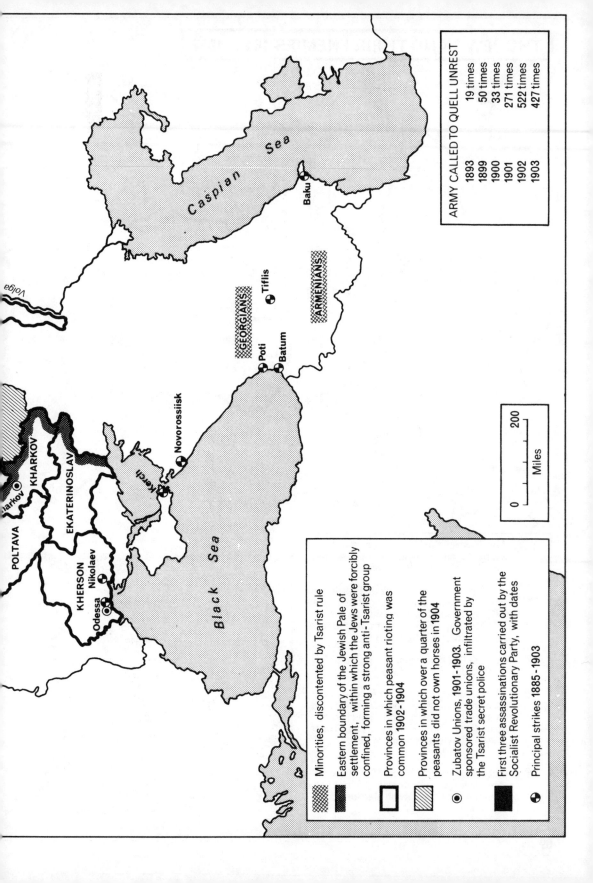

ARMY CALLED TO QUELL UNREST

1893	19 times
1899	50 times
1900	33 times
1901	271 times
1902	522 times
1903	427 times

Volga

Caspian Sea

Baku

GEORGIANS

Tiflis

ARMENIANS

Poti
Batum

Novorossiisk

Kerch

POLTAVA

KHARKOV
Kharkov

EKATERINOSLAV

KHERSON
Nikolaev
Odessa

Black Sea

0   200

Miles

Minorities, discontented by Tsarist rule

Eastern boundary of the Jewish Pale of
settlement, within which the Jews were forcibly
confined, forming a strong anti-Tsarist group

Provinces in which peasant rioting was
common 1902-1904

Provinces in which over a quarter of the
peasants did not own horses in 1904

Zubatov Unions, 1901-1903. Government
sponsored trade unions, infiltrated by
the Tsarist secret police

First three assassinations carried out by the
Socialist Revolutionary Party, with dates

Principal strikes 1885-1903

THE JEWS AND THEIR ENEMIES 1648-1917

1903
1906 St. Petersburg
Tsarskoye Selo 1905

1891. 2,000 Jews depor
many of them in chains

Baltic Sea

Dusiata

Mogilev

Minsk

Starodub

Bialystok

Gomel

Berlin
1911

Sedlits

Brest Litovsk

Konotop
Nezhin

Xanten

GERMANY

Lodz

Czestochowa

Kiev

Zhitomir

Sm

Pereyaslavl

Tisza-Eszlar

AUSTRIA - HUNGARY

Elizavetgra
Balta

Anana
Nikolaevk

Kishinev

Odessa

RUMANIA

BULGARIA

///// Area in which the Ukrainian peasantry,
led by Bogdan Khmelnitski, massacred
over 100,000 Jews 1648-1656

☐ The Pale of Settlement inside Russia, to
which Russian Jews were confined by law
1815-1917. Of Russia's 5 million Jews
in 1880, only 300,000 had managed to
live outside, mostly illegally

◉ Principal mob attacks, or "pogroms",
against Jews, 1871-1906

✪ Ritual murder charges, in Russia and
elsewhere, in which Jews were accused
of using the blood of Christian children
to mix with their Passover bread. These
charges led to harsh mob violence
against the Jews

⚠ Publishing centres before 1917 of the anti-
semitic forgery, "Protocols of Zion", which
claimed to be the Jewish plan for world
domination

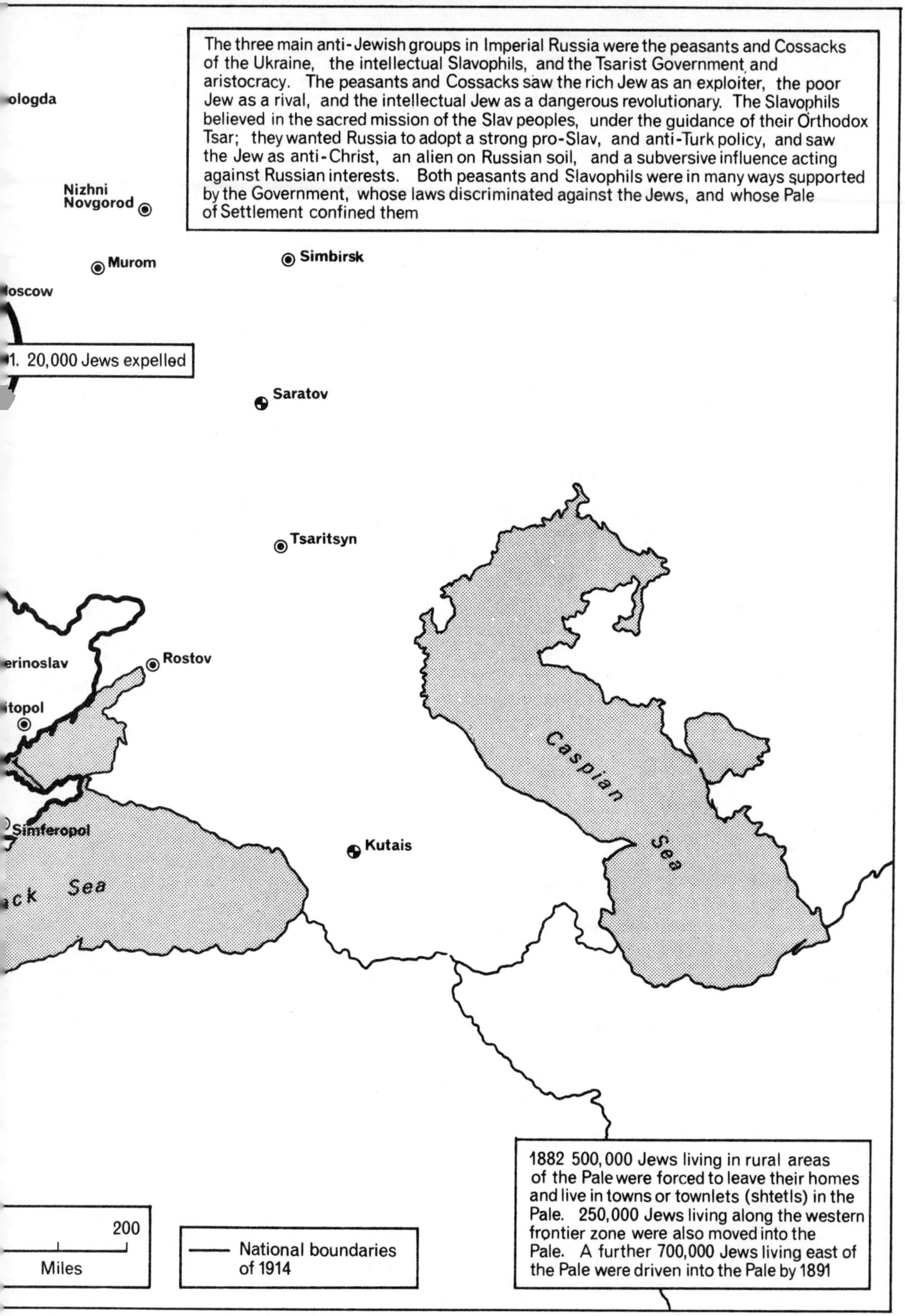
The three main anti-Jewish groups in Imperial Russia were the peasants and Cossacks of the Ukraine, the intellectual Slavophils, and the Tsarist Government and aristocracy. The peasants and Cossacks saw the rich Jew as an exploiter, the poor Jew as a rival, and the intellectual Jew as a dangerous revolutionary. The Slavophils believed in the sacred mission of the Slav peoples, under the guidance of their Orthodox Tsar; they wanted Russia to adopt a strong pro-Slav, and anti-Turk policy, and saw the Jew as anti-Christ, an alien on Russian soil, and a subversive influence acting against Russian interests. Both peasants and Slavophils were in many ways supported by the Government, whose laws discriminated against the Jews, and whose Pale of Settlement confined them
ologda
Nizhni Novgorod
Murom
Simbirsk
loscow
1. 20,000 Jews expelled
Saratov
Tsaritsyn
erinoslav
Rostov
itopol
Simferopol
Kutais
Caspian Sea
ck Sea
200
Miles
National boundaries of 1914
1882 500,000 Jews living in rural areas of the Pale were forced to leave their homes and live in towns or townlets (shtetls) in the Pale. 250,000 Jews living along the western frontier zone were also moved into the Pale. A further 700,000 Jews living east of the Pale were driven into the Pale by 1891

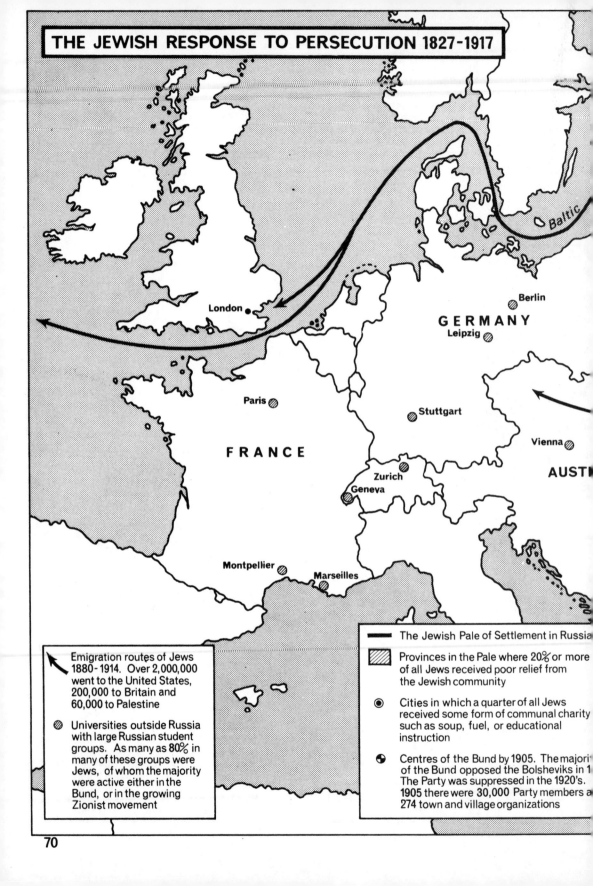

THE JEWISH RESPONSE TO PERSECUTION 1827-1917

Berlin

GERMANY
Leipzig

Paris

Stuttgart

Vienna

FRANCE

AUST

Zurich
Geneva

London

Baltic

Montpellier
Marseilles

Emigration routes of Jews
1880-1914. Over 2,000,000
went to the United States,
200,000 to Britain and
60,000 to Palestine

Universities outside Russia
with large Russian student
groups. As many as 80% in
many of these groups were
Jews, of whom the majority
were active either in the
Bund, or in the growing
Zionist movement

The Jewish Pale of Settlement in Russia

Provinces in the Pale where 20% or more
of all Jews received poor relief from
the Jewish community

Cities in which a quarter of all Jews
received some form of communal charity
such as soup, fuel, or educational
instruction

Centres of the Bund by 1905. The majori
of the Bund opposed the Bolsheviks in 1
The Party was suppressed in the 1920's.
1905 there were 30,000 Party members a
274 town and village organizations

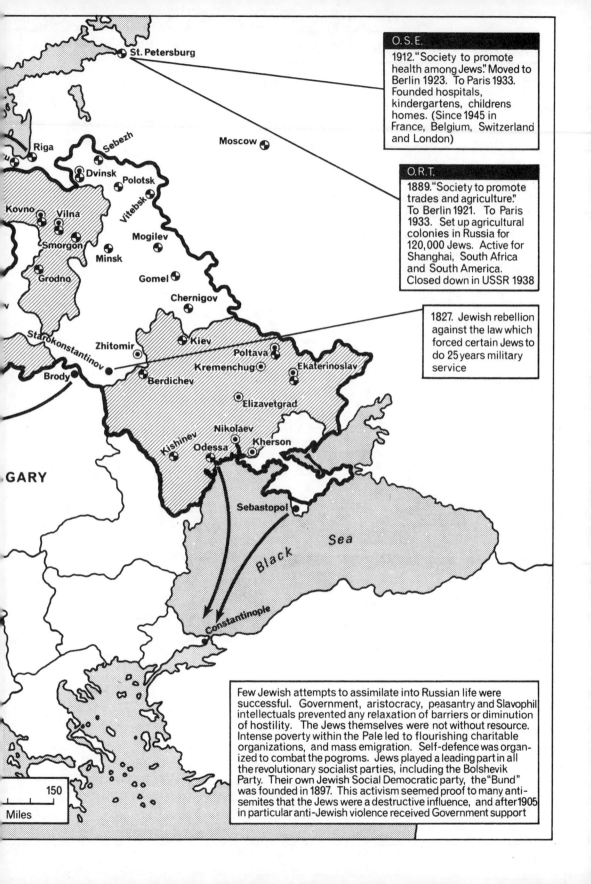

St. Petersburg

Moscow ⊕

Riga
Sebezh
Dvinsk ⊕
Polotsk
Kovno
Vilna ⊕
Vitebsk ⊕
Smorgon
Mogilev ⊕
Grodno
Minsk ⊕
Gomel ⊕
Chernigov ⊕
Starokonstantinov
Zhitomir ⊙
Kiev ⊕
Poltava ⊕
Kremenchug ⊙
Ekaterinoslav ⊕
Brody
Berdichev
Elizavetgrad ⊙
Nikolaev
Kishinev ⊕
Odessa ⊙
Kherson ⊙

GARY

Sebastopol

Black Sea

Constantinople

O.S.E.
1912. "Society to promote health among Jews." Moved to Berlin 1923. To Paris 1933. Founded hospitals, kindergartens, childrens homes. (Since 1945 in France, Belgium, Switzerland and London)

O.R.T.
1889. "Society to promote trades and agriculture." To Berlin 1921. To Paris 1933. Set up agricultural colonies in Russia for 120,000 Jews. Active for Shanghai, South Africa and South America. Closed down in USSR 1938

1827. Jewish rebellion against the law which forced certain Jews to do 25 years military service

Few Jewish attempts to assimilate into Russian life were successful. Government, aristocracy, peasantry and Slavophil intellectuals prevented any relaxation of barriers or diminution of hostility. The Jews themselves were not without resource. Intense poverty within the Pale led to flourishing charitable organizations, and mass emigration. Self-defence was organized to combat the pogroms. Jews played a leading part in all the revolutionary socialist parties, including the Bolshevik Party. Their own Jewish Social Democratic party, the "Bund" was founded in 1897. This activism seemed proof to many anti-semites that the Jews were a destructive influence, and after 1905 in particular anti-Jewish violence received Government support

150
Miles

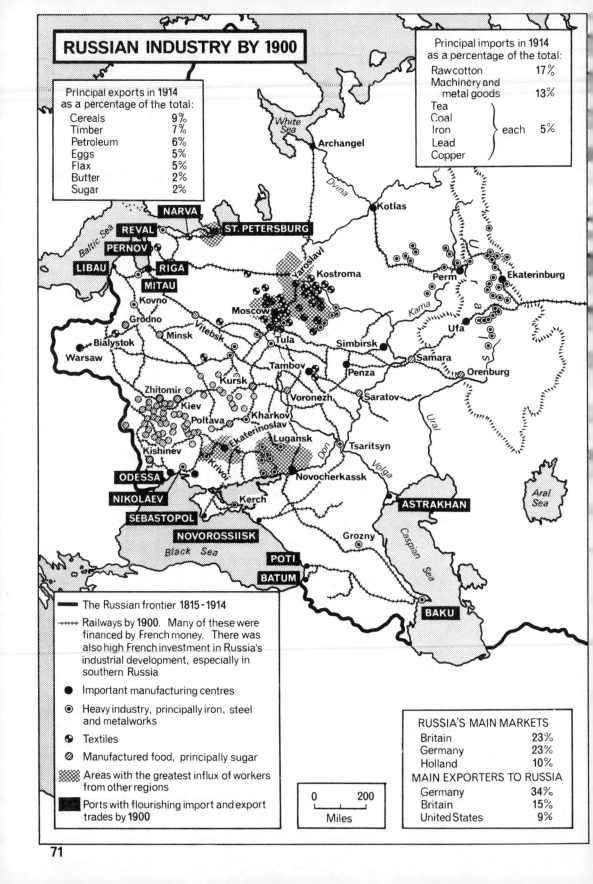

RUSSIAN INDUSTRY BY 1900

Principal exports in 1914
as a percentage of the total:

Cereals	9%
Timber	7%
Petroleum	6%
Eggs	5%
Flax	5%
Butter	2%
Sugar	2%

White Sea

Archangel

Dvina

Kotlas

NARVA

REVAL

PERNOV

ST. PETERSBURG

Baltic Sea

LIBAU

RIGA

MITAU

Kovno

Yaroslavl

Kostroma

Perm

Ekaterinburg

Ural

Grodno

Moscow

Kama

Minsk

Vitebsk

Tula

Ufa

Bialystok

Simbirsk

Warsaw

Samara

Tambov

Penza

Orenburg

Kursk

Zhitomir

Voronezh

Saratov

Kiev

Poltava

Kharkov

Kishinev

Ekaterinoslav

Lugansk

Tsaritsyn

Krivoi

Don

Volga

Ural

ODESSA

Novocherkassk

Aral Sea

NIKOLAEV

Kerch

ASTRAKHAN

SEBASTOPOL

NOVOROSSIISK

Black Sea

Grozny

Caspian Sea

POTI

BATUM

BAKU

71

The Russian frontier 1815-1914

┼┼┼┼┼ Railways by 1900. Many of these were financed by French money. There was also high French investment in Russia's industrial development, especially in southern Russia

● Important manufacturing centres

◉ Heavy industry, principally iron, steel and metalworks

◕ Textiles

◒ Manufactured food, principally sugar

▨ Areas with the greatest influx of workers from other regions

▉ Ports with flourishing import and export trades by 1900

0   200

Miles

RUSSIA'S MAIN MARKETS

Britain	23%
Germany	23%
Holland	10%

MAIN EXPORTERS TO RUSSIA

Germany	34%
Britain	15%
United States	9%

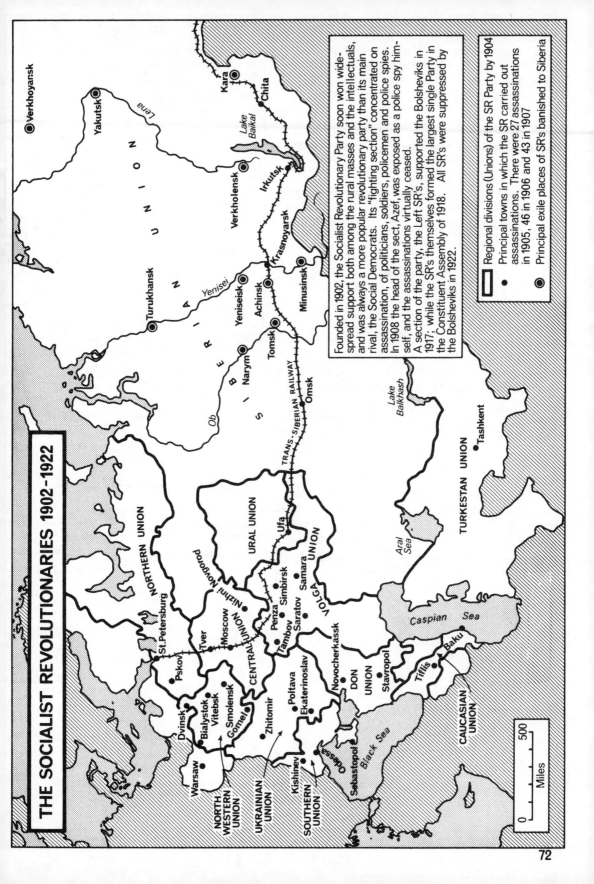

THE SOCIALIST REVOLUTIONARIES 1902–1922

Founded in 1902, the Socialist Revolutionary Party soon won wide-spread support both among the rural masses and the intellectuals, and was always a more popular revolutionary party than its main rival, the Social Democrats. Its "fighting section" concentrated on assassination, of politicians, soldiers, policemen and police spies. In 1908 the head of the sect, Azef, was exposed as a police spy himself, and the assassinations virtually ceased.
A section of the party, the Left SR's, supported the Bolsheviks in 1917; while the SR's themselves formed the largest single Party in the Constituent Assembly of 1918. All SR's were suppressed by the Bolsheviks in 1922.

☐ Regional divisions (Unions) of the SR Party by 1904
• Principal towns in which the SR carried out assassinations. There were 27 assassinations in 1905, 46 in 1906 and 43 in 1907
◉ Principal exile places of SR's banished to Siberia

Verkhoyansk

Yakutsk

Kara

Chita

Lena

Lake Baikal

Irkutsk

Verkholensk

Krasnoyarsk

Turukhansk

Yeniseisk

Achinsk

Minusinsk

U N I O N

Yenisei

Narym

Tomsk

Ob

Omsk

S I B E R I A

TRANS-SIBERIAN RAILWAY

Lake Balkhash

Tashkent

TURKESTAN UNION

Aral Sea

NORTHERN UNION

URAL UNION

Ufa

Samara

VOLGA UNION

Simbirsk

Penza

Saratov

Tambov

Nizhni Novgorod

Moscow

Tver

St. Petersburg

Pskov

Dvinsk

Bialystok

Vitebsk

Smolensk

Gomel

CENTRAL UNION

Zhitomir

Poltava

Ekaterinoslav

Novocherkassk

DON UNION

Stavropol

Caspian Sea

Baku

Tiflis

CAUCASIAN UNION

Black Sea

Odessa

Sebastopol

Kishinev

SOUTHERN UNION

Warsaw

NORTH WESTERN UNION

UKRAINIAN UNION

500

0

Miles

72

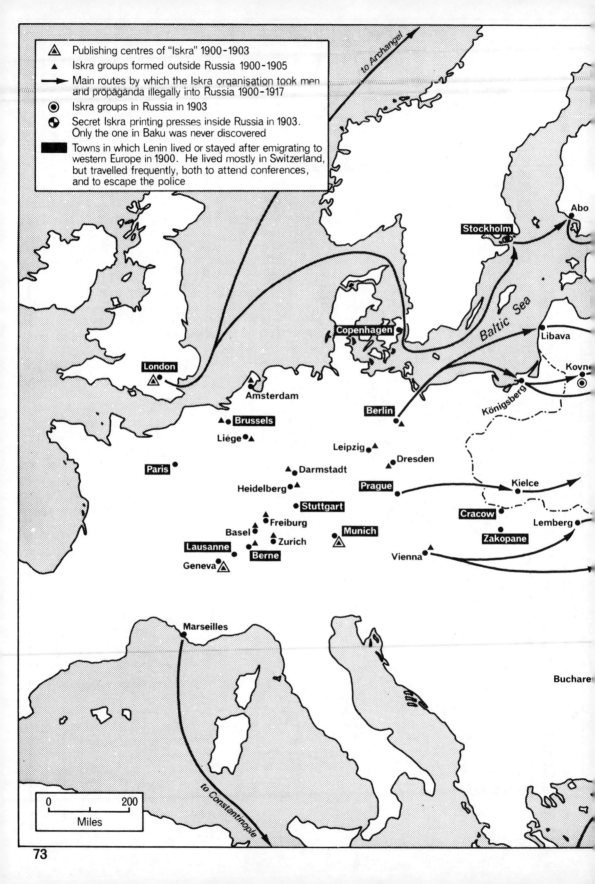

Publishing centres of "Iskra" 1900-1903

Iskra groups formed outside Russia 1900-1905

Main routes by which the Iskra organisation took men and propaganda illegally into Russia 1900-1917

Iskra groups in Russia in 1903

Secret Iskra printing presses inside Russia in 1903. Only the one in Baku was never discovered

Towns in which Lenin lived or stayed after emigrating to western Europe in 1900. He lived mostly in Switzerland, but travelled frequently, both to attend conferences, and to escape the police

to Archangel

Baltic Sea

Abo

Stockholm

Copenhagen

Libava

Kovn

London

Amsterdam

Berlin

Königsberg

Brussels

Liége

Leipzig

Dresden

Paris

Darmstadt

Heidelberg

Prague

Kielce

Stuttgart

Cracow

Lemberg

Freiburg

Munich

Basel

Zurich

Zakopane

Lausanne

Berne

Vienna

Geneva

Marseilles

Buchare

0   200

Miles

to Constantinople

73

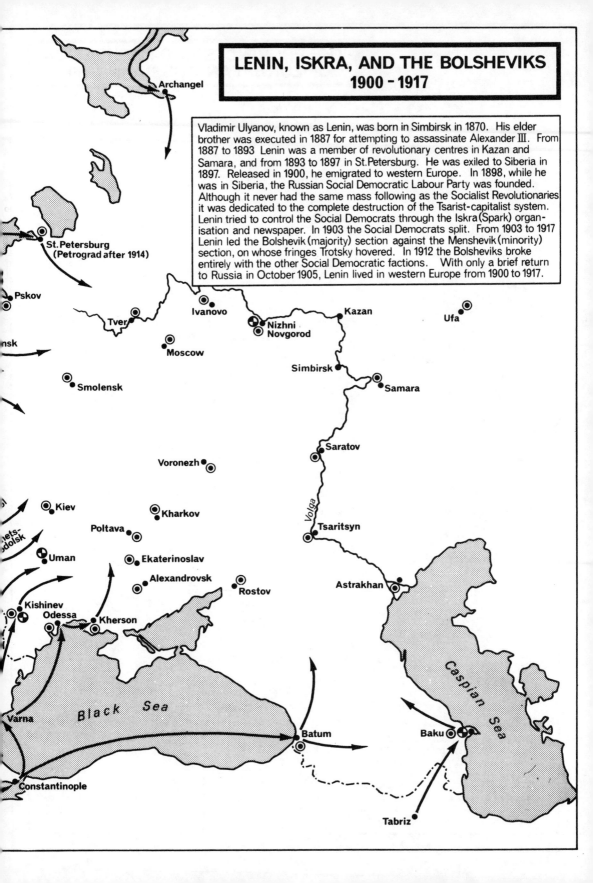

LENIN, ISKRA, AND THE BOLSHEVIKS
1900 - 1917

Vladimir Ulyanov, known as Lenin, was born in Simbirsk in 1870. His elder
brother was executed in 1887 for attempting to assassinate Alexander III. From
1887 to 1893 Lenin was a member of revolutionary centres in Kazan and
Samara, and from 1893 to 1897 in St.Petersburg. He was exiled to Siberia in
1897. Released in 1900, he emigrated to western Europe. In 1898, while he
was in Siberia, the Russian Social Democratic Labour Party was founded.
Although it never had the same mass following as the Socialist Revolutionaries
it was dedicated to the complete destruction of the Tsarist-capitalist system.
Lenin tried to control the Social Democrats through the Iskra (Spark) organisation and newspaper. In 1903 the Social Democrats split. From 1903 to 1917
Lenin led the Bolshevik (majority) section against the Menshevik (minority)
section, on whose fringes Trotsky hovered. In 1912 the Bolsheviks broke
entirely with the other Social Democratic factions.   With only a brief return
to Russia in October 1905, Lenin lived in western Europe from 1900 to 1917.

Archangel

St.Petersburg
(Petrograd after 1914)

Pskov

Tver

Ivanovo

Nizhni
Novgorod

Kazan

Ufa

nsk

Moscow

Simbirsk

Samara

Smolensk

Saratov

Voronezh

Volga

Kiev

Kharkov

Poltava

Tsaritsyn

nets-
odolsk

Uman

Ekaterinoslav

Alexandrovsk

Rostov

Astrakhan

Kishinev
Odessa

Kherson

Caspian Sea

Black Sea

Varna

Batum

Baku

Constantinople

Tabriz

THE PROVINCES AND POPULATION OF EUROPEAN RUSSIA IN 1900

NORWAY

White Sea

SWEDEN

Baltic Sea

ARCHANGEL

FINLAND

OLONETS

VOLOGDA

PERM

ESTLAND
ST PETERSBURG

NOVGOROD

KURLAND
LIVLAND

PSKOV

VIATKA

KOSTROMA

KOVNO

VITEBSK

TVER

YAROSLAVL

GERMANY

VILNA

SMOLENSK

MOSCOW

VLADIMIR

NIZHNI NOVGOROD

KAZAN

UFA

GRODNO

MOGILEV

KALUGA

TULA

RIAZAN

SIMBIRSK

POLISH PROVINCES

MINSK

OREL

PENZA

ORENBURG

SAMARA

VOLHYNIA

CHERNIGOV

KURSK

TAMBOV

SARATOV

AUSTRIA-HUNGARY

KIEV

POLTAVA

VORONEZH

PODOLIA

KHARKOV

BESSARABIA

KHERSON

EKATERINOSLAV

DON

ASTRAKHAN

RUMANIA

TAURIDA

Black Sea

KUBAN

STAVROPOL

Caspian Sea

TEREK

TURKEY

TRANS-CAUCASIAN PROVINCES

PERSIA

The first official Russian census was held in 1897. The total population was just over 129 million - nearly as large as the combined populations of Britain, France, and Germany. Over 80% of all Russians were peasants. Finland was an autonomous Duchy, and, like Poland, was subdivided into Provinces

MAIN NATIONAL & ETHNIC GROUPS IN EUROPEAN RUSSIA IN 1900	
Russians	55 million
Ukrainians	22 million
Poles	8 million
White Russians	6 million
Jews	5 million
Balts	4 million
Caucasians	3 million
Germans	2 million

THE 1905 REVOLUTION IN THE COUNTRYSIDE

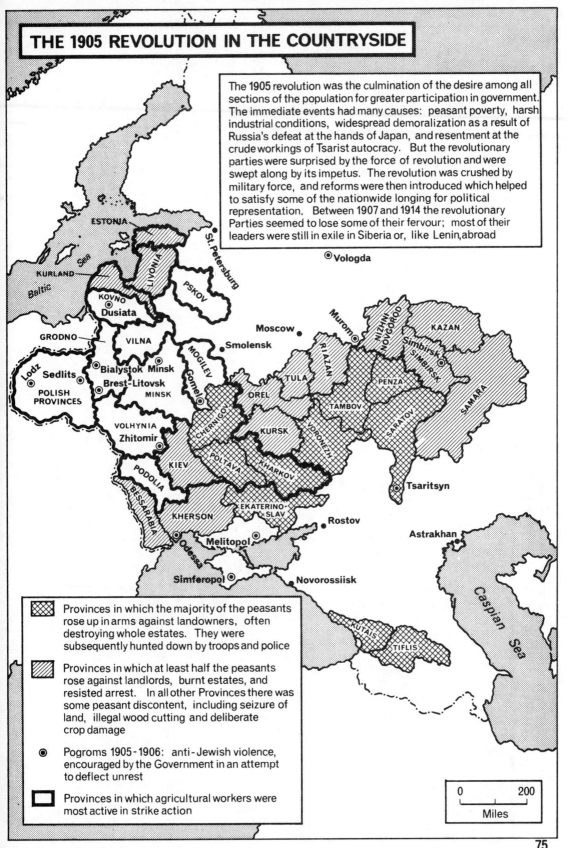

The 1905 revolution was the culmination of the desire among all sections of the population for greater participation in government. The immediate events had many causes: peasant poverty, harsh industrial conditions, widespread demoralization as a result of Russia's defeat at the hands of Japan, and resentment at the crude workings of Tsarist autocracy. But the revolutionary parties were surprised by the force of revolution and were swept along by its impetus. The revolution was crushed by military force, and reforms were then introduced which helped to satisfy some of the nationwide longing for political representation. Between 1907 and 1914 the revolutionary Parties seemed to lose some of their fervour; most of their leaders were still in exile in Siberia or, like Lenin, abroad

Provinces in which the majority of the peasants rose up in arms against landowners, often destroying whole estates. They were subsequently hunted down by troops and police

Provinces in which at least half the peasants rose against landlords, burnt estates, and resisted arrest. In all other Provinces there was some peasant discontent, including seizure of land, illegal wood cutting and deliberate crop damage

Pogroms 1905-1906: anti-Jewish violence, encouraged by the Government in an attempt to deflect unrest

Provinces in which agricultural workers were most active in strike action

0   200

Miles

75

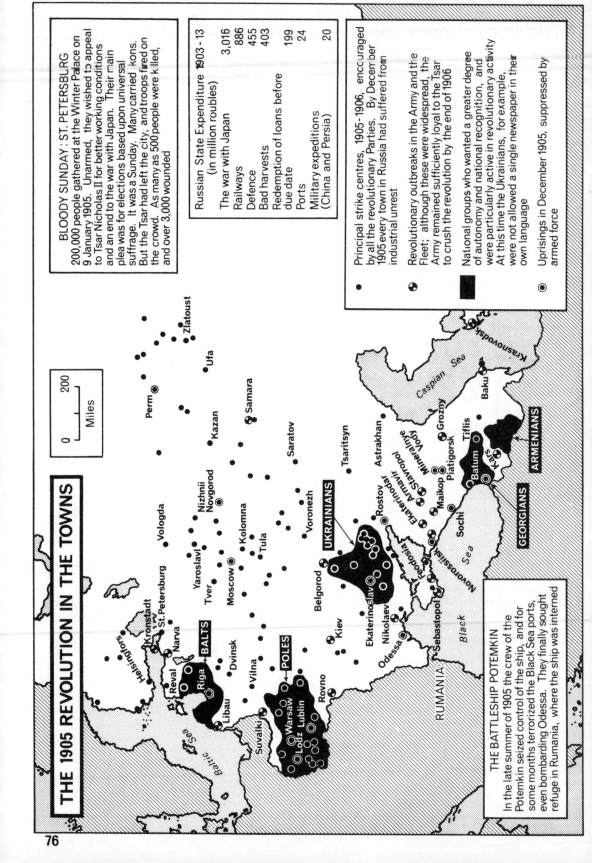

THE 1905 REVOLUTION IN THE TOWNS

BLOODY SUNDAY : ST. PETERSBURG

200,000 people gathered at the Winter Palace on 9 January 1905. Unarmed, they wished to appeal to Tsar Nicholas II for better working conditions and an end to the war with Japan. Their main plea was for elections based upon universal suffrage. It was a Sunday. Many carried ikons. But the Tsar had left the city, and troops fired on the crowd. As many as 500 people were killed, and over 3,000 wounded

Russian State Expenditure 1903 - 13 (in million roubles)	
The war with Japan	3,016
Railways	886
Defence	455
Bad harvests	403
Redemption of loans before due date	199
Ports	24
Military expeditions (China and Persia)	20

- Principal strike centres, 1905-1906, encouraged by all the revolutionary Parties. By December 1905 every town in Russia had suffered from industrial unrest

- Revolutionary outbreaks in the Army and the Fleet; although these were widespread, the Army remained sufficiently loyal to the Tsar to crush the revolution by the end of 1906

- National groups who wanted a greater degree of autonomy and national recognition, and were particularly active in revolutionary activity. At this time the Ukrainians, for example, were not allowed a single newspaper in their own language

- Uprisings in December 1905, suppressed by armed force

THE BATTLESHIP POTEMKIN

In the late summer of 1905 the crew of the Potemkin seized control of the ship, and for some months terrorized the Black Sea ports, even bombarding Odessa. They finally sought refuge in Rumania, where the ship was interned

Zlatoust

Ufa

Perm

Samara

Kazan

Saratov

Vologda

Nizhnii Novgorod

Tsaritsyn

Astrakhan

Yaroslavl

Tver

Moscow

Kolomna

Tula

Voronezh

St. Petersburg

Kronstadt

Narva

Reval

Riga

Dvinsk

Vilna

Suvalki

Rovno

Warsaw

Lodz Lublin

Belgorod

Kiev

Ekaterinoslav

Nikolaev

Odessa

Rostov

Sebastopol

Feodosia

Novorossiisk

Sochi

Batum

Tiflis

Kars

Baku

Grozny

Piatigorsk

Maikop

Mineralnye Vody

Ekaterinodar

Stavropol

Armavir

Krasnovodsk

Helsingfors

Libau

BALTS

POLES

UKRAINIANS

GEORGIANS

ARMENIANS

RUMANIA

Baltic Sea

Black Sea

Caspian Sea

0   200
Miles

THE MOSCOW UPRISING 1905

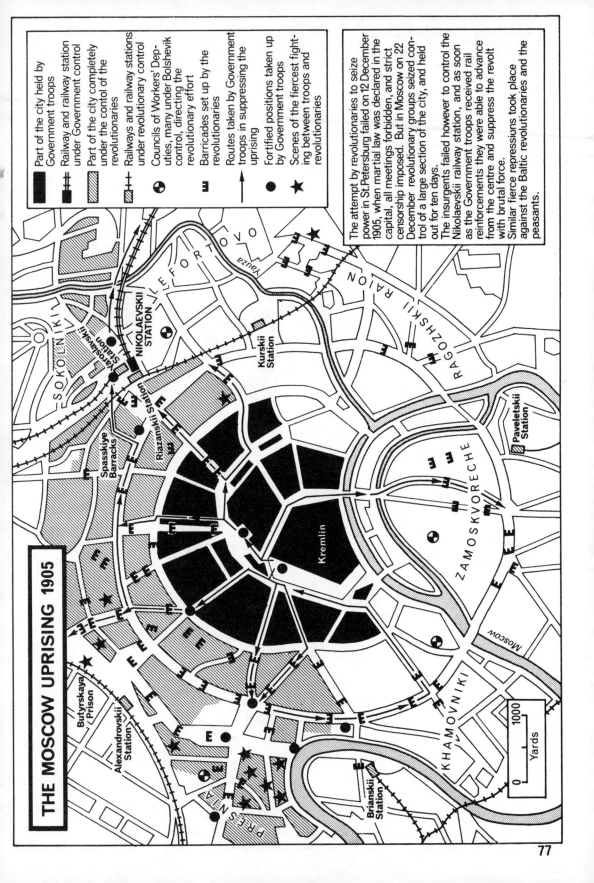

Legend:

- Part of the city held by Government troops
- Railway and railway station under Government control
- Part of the city completely under the control of the revolutionaries
- Railways and railway stations under revolutionary control
- Councils of Workers' Deputies, many under Bolshevik control, directing the revolutionary effort
- Barricades set up by the revolutionaries
- Routes taken by Government troops in suppressing the uprising
- Fortified positions taken up by Government troops
- Scenes of the fiercest fighting between troops and revolutionaries

The attempt by revolutionaries to seize power in St.Petersburg failed on 12 December 1905, when martial law was declared in the capital, all meetings forbidden, and strict censorship imposed. But in Moscow on 22 December revolutionary groups seized control of a large section of the city, and held out for ten days.

The insurgents failed however to control the Nikolaevskii railway station, and as soon as the Government troops received rail reinforcements they were able to advance from the centre and suppress the revolt with brutal force.

Similar fierce repressions took place against the Baltic revolutionaries and the peasants.

Labels on map: SOKOLNIKI, LEFORTOVO, Yauza, NIKOLAEVSKII STATION, Yaroslavskii Station, Kurskii Station, RAGOZHSKII RAION, Spasskiye Barracks, Riazanskii Station, Paveletskii Station, Kremlin, ZAMOSKVORECHE, Butyrskaya Prison, Alexandrovskii Station, KHAMOVNIKI, Moscow, PRESNIA, Brianskii Station

Scale: 0 — 1000 Yards

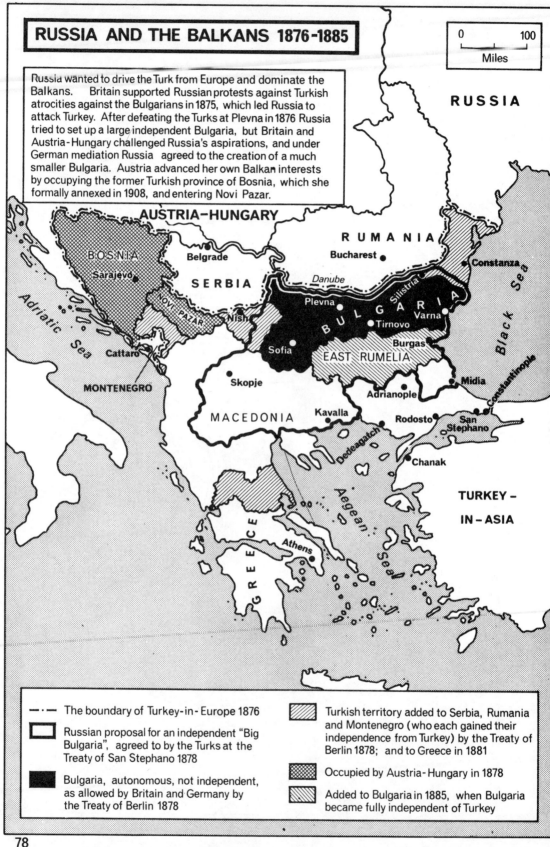

RUSSIA AND THE BALKANS 1876-1885

Russia wanted to drive the Turk from Europe and dominate the Balkans. Britain supported Russian protests against Turkish atrocities against the Bulgarians in 1875, which led Russia to attack Turkey. After defeating the Turks at Plevna in 1876 Russia tried to set up a large independent Bulgaria, but Britain and Austria-Hungary challenged Russia's aspirations, and under German mediation Russia agreed to the creation of a much smaller Bulgaria. Austria advanced her own Balkan interests by occupying the former Turkish province of Bosnia, which she formally annexed in 1908, and entering Novi Pazar.

RUSSIA

AUSTRIA-HUNGARY

BOSNIA
Sarajevo

Belgrade

RUMANIA

Bucharest

Constanza

SERBIA

Danube

NOVI PAZAR

Plevna

Silistria

BULGARIA

Varna

Nish

Tirnovo

Adriatic Sea

Cattaro

Sofia

Burgas

EAST RUMELIA

Black Sea

MONTENEGRO

Skopje

Adrianople

Midia

MACEDONIA

Kavalla

Rodosto

San Stephano

Constantinople

Dedeagatch

Chanak

Aegean Sea

TURKEY – IN – ASIA

GREECE

Athens

—·— The boundary of Turkey-in-Europe 1876

☐ Russian proposal for an independent "Big Bulgaria", agreed to by the Turks at the Treaty of San Stephano 1878

■ Bulgaria, autonomous, not independent, as allowed by Britain and Germany by the Treaty of Berlin 1878

▨ Turkish territory added to Serbia, Rumania and Montenegro (who each gained their independence from Turkey) by the Treaty of Berlin 1878; and to Greece in 1881

▨ Occupied by Austria-Hungary in 1878

▨ Added to Bulgaria in 1885, when Bulgaria became fully independent of Turkey

RUSSIA, THE BALKANS, AND THE COMING OF WAR 1912–1914

0 — 500
Miles

North Sea

Baltic

BRITAIN

FRANCE

Paris

GERMANY

Berlin

Breslau

Danzig

Warsaw

POLISH PROVINCES

Vienna

Budapest

AUSTRIA – HUNGARY

BOSNIA

Sarajevo

Belgrade

SERBIA

MONTENEGRO

Skopje

ALBANIA

GREECE

Adriatic Sea

Reval

Riga

BALTIC PROVINCES

St. Petersburg

Moscow

RUSSIA

Pripet Marshes

Kiev

VOLHYNIA

Lemberg

RUMANIA

BULGARIA

Black Sea

Constantinople

Bosphorus

Dardanelles

TURKEY

Russia's mid-century alignment with Germany was changed during the 1880's to a new alignment with France, while at the same time Austria and Germany drew closer together. In the two Balkan Wars of 1912 and 1913 Turkey was driven almost entirely from Europe, but Russia's position did not improve; for as a result of Turkey's defeat Austrian influence increased even further. In June 1914 a Bosnian Serb murdered the Austrian heir to the throne, Archduke Franz-Ferdinand, at Sarajevo. Austria invaded Serbia on 28 July 1914. Russia then declared war on Austria. Germany supported her ally Austria and declared war on Russia. France and Britain joined Russia against Germany and Austria. Turkey attacked Russia in October 1914

Countries in which Austrian and German influence worked against Russia. Greece had a pro-German King; Turkey a pro-German Minister of War and virtual dictator; Bulgaria and Rumania had both accepted alliance with the Central Powers

Area of Russia in which Germany hoped to expand as a result of war

Russia's only two Balkan Allies, both threatened by Austria. Austria had created the state of Albania in 1912 in order to cut Serbia off from the sea.

Countries in western Europe sympathetic to Russia. France had a military alliance with Russia dating from 1894. Britain a convention dating from 1907

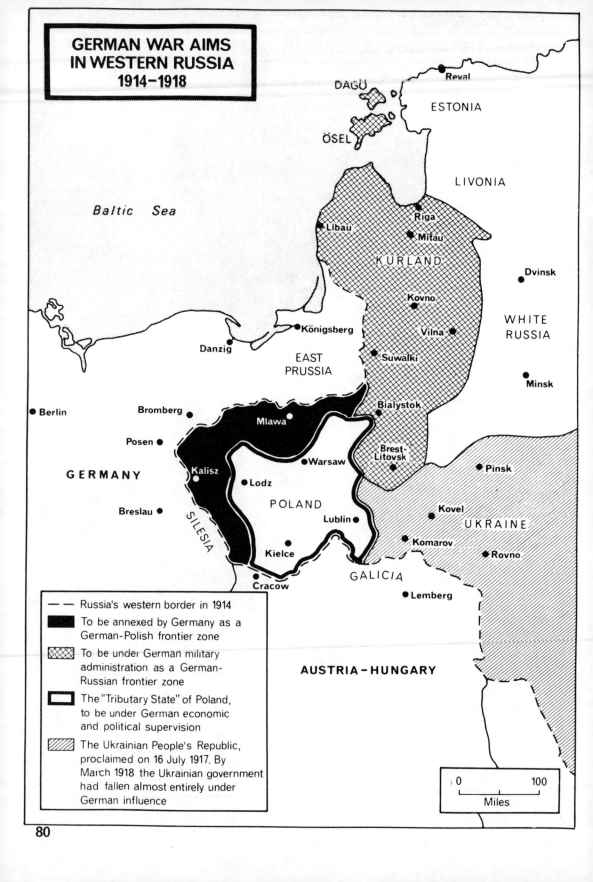

GERMAN WAR AIMS IN WESTERN RUSSIA 1914-1918

DAGÜ

Reval

ESTONIA

ÖSEL

LIVONIA

Baltic Sea

Riga

Libau

Mitau

KURLAND

Dvinsk

Kovno

Königsberg

WHITE RUSSIA

Danzig

Vilna

EAST PRUSSIA

Suwalki

Minsk

Berlin

Bromberg

Mlawa

Bialystok

Posen

Warsaw

Brest-Litovsk

Pinsk

GERMANY

Kalisz

Lodz

POLAND

Kovel

UKRAINE

Breslau

SILESIA

Lublin

Kielce

Komarov

Rovno

Cracow

GALICIA

Lemberg

AUSTRIA-HUNGARY

--- Russia's western border in 1914

To be annexed by Germany as a German-Polish frontier zone

To be under German military administration as a German-Russian frontier zone

The "Tributary State" of Poland, to be under German economic and political supervision

The Ukrainian People's Republic, proclaimed on 16 July 1917. By March 1918 the Ukrainian government had fallen almost entirely under German influence

0   100

Miles

80

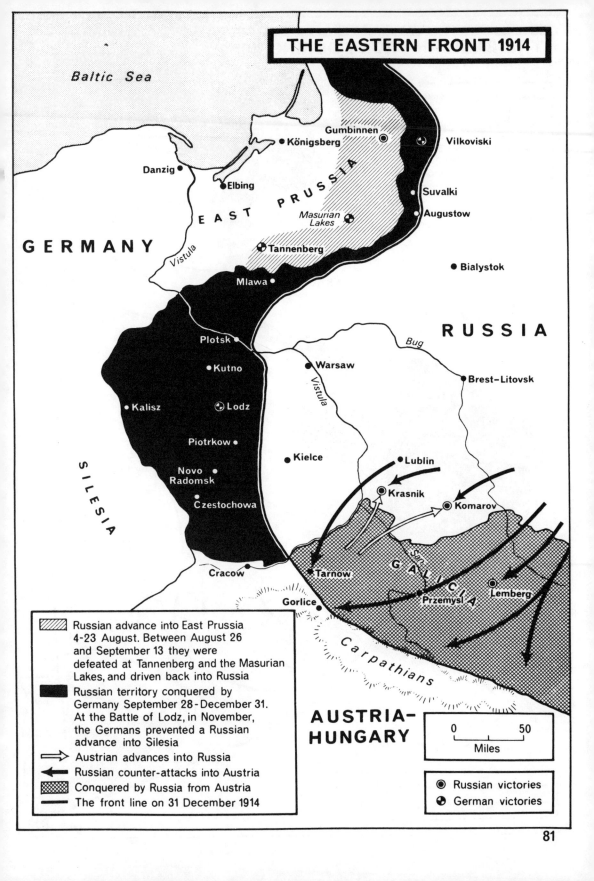

THE EASTERN FRONT 1914

Baltic Sea

GERMANY

EAST PRUSSIA

- Danzig
- Königsberg
- Elbing
- Gumbinnen ⊙
- ⊕ Vilkoviski
- Suvalki
- Augustow
- Masurian Lakes ⊕
- Tannenberg ⊕
- Mlawa
- Bialystok

Vistula

RUSSIA

- Plotsk
- Kutno
- Warsaw
- Brest–Litovsk

Bug

Vistula

- Kalisz
- ⊕ Lodz
- Piotrkow
- Kielce
- Lublin
- Krasnik ⊙
- Komarov ⊙

SILESIA

- Novo Radomsk
- Czestochowa
- Cracow
- Tarnow
- Gorlice

GALICIA

San

- Przemysl
- Lemberg

Carpathians

AUSTRIA-
HUNGARY

Russian advance into East Prussia
4-23 August. Between August 26
and September 13 they were
defeated at Tannenberg and the Masurian
Lakes, and driven back into Russia

Russian territory conquered by
Germany September 28 - December 31.
At the Battle of Lodz, in November,
the Germans prevented a Russian
advance into Silesia

⇨ Austrian advances into Russia

⬅ Russian counter-attacks into Austria

▨ Conquered by Russia from Austria

— The front line on 31 December 1914

```
0          50
     Miles
```

⊙ Russian victories
⊕ German victories

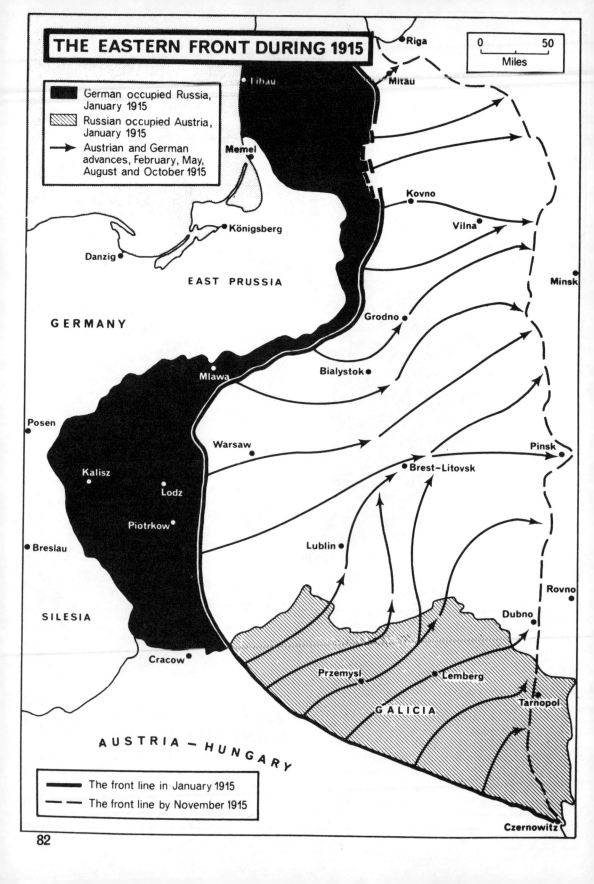

THE EASTERN FRONT DURING 1915

0   50
Miles

Legend:
- German occupied Russia, January 1915
- Russian occupied Austria, January 1915
- Austrian and German advances, February, May, August and October 1915

Riga

Mitau

Libau

Memel

Kovno

Vilna

Minsk

Königsberg

Danzig

EAST PRUSSIA

GERMANY

Grodno

Mlawa

Bialystok

Posen

Warsaw

Pinsk

Kalisz

Lodz

Brest–Litovsk

Piotrkow

Breslau

Lublin

Rovno

Dubno

SILESIA

Cracow

Przemysl

Lemberg

Tarnopol

GALICIA

AUSTRIA – HUNGARY

The front line in January 1915
The front line by November 1915

Czernowitz

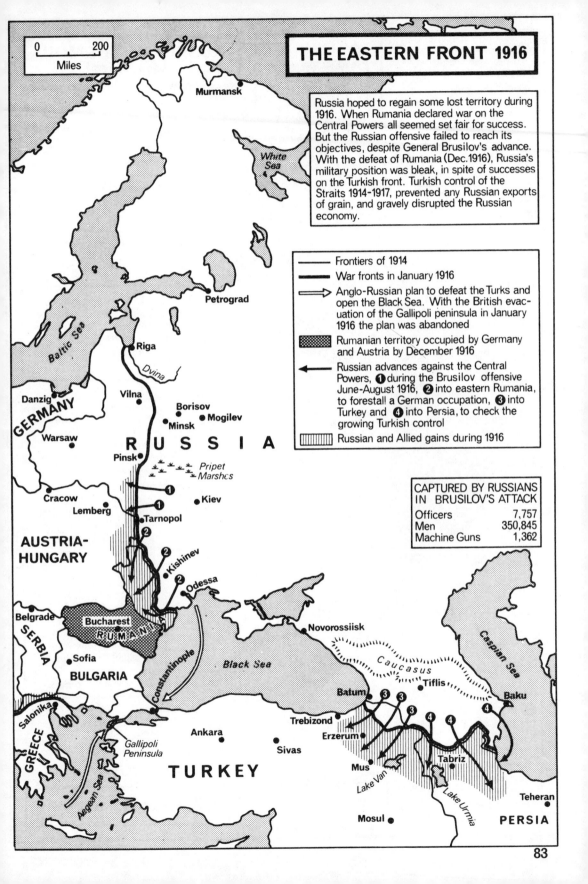

THE EASTERN FRONT 1916

Russia hoped to regain some lost territory during 1916. When Rumania declared war on the Central Powers all seemed set fair for success. But the Russian offensive failed to reach its objectives, despite General Brusilov's advance. With the defeat of Rumania (Dec.1916), Russia's military position was bleak, in spite of successes on the Turkish front. Turkish control of the Straits 1914-1917, prevented any Russian exports of grain, and gravely disrupted the Russian economy.

Frontiers of 1914

War fronts in January 1916

Anglo-Russian plan to defeat the Turks and open the Black Sea. With the British evacuation of the Gallipoli peninsula in January 1916 the plan was abandoned

Rumanian territory occupied by Germany and Austria by December 1916

Russian advances against the Central Powers, ❶ during the Brusilov offensive June-August 1916, ❷ into eastern Rumania, to forestall a German occupation, ❸ into Turkey and ❹ into Persia, to check the growing Turkish control

Russian and Allied gains during 1916

CAPTURED BY RUSSIANS IN BRUSILOV'S ATTACK	
Officers	7,757
Men	350,845
Machine Guns	1,362

0 — 200 Miles

Murmansk

White Sea

Petrograd

Baltic Sea

Riga

Dvina

GERMANY

Danzig

Vilna

Borisov

Mogilev

Minsk

Warsaw

R U S S I A

Pinsk

Pripet Marshes

Cracow

Lemberg

Tarnopol

Kiev

AUSTRIA-HUNGARY

Kishinev

Odessa

Belgrade

Bucharest

RUMANIA

SERBIA

Sofia

BULGARIA

Constantinople

Black Sea

Novorossiisk

Caucasus

Caspian Sea

Tiflis

Baku

Salonika

GREECE

Gallipoli Peninsula

Aegean Sea

Ankara

Sivas

Batum

Trebizond

Erzerum

Mus

Lake Van

TURKEY

Tabriz

Lake Urmia

Teheran

Mosul

PERSIA

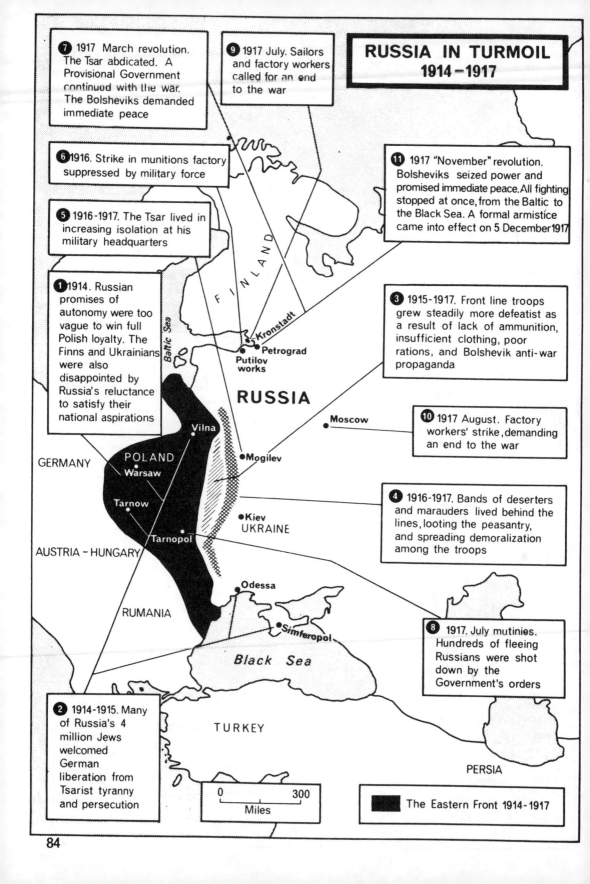

RUSSIA IN TURMOIL 1914–1917

7 1917 March revolution. The Tsar abdicated. A Provisional Government continued with the war. The Bolsheviks demanded immediate peace

9 1917 July. Sailors and factory workers called for an end to the war

6 1916. Strike in munitions factory suppressed by military force

11 1917 "November" revolution. Bolsheviks seized power and promised immediate peace. All fighting stopped at once, from the Baltic to the Black Sea. A formal armistice came into effect on 5 December 1917

5 1916-1917. The Tsar lived in increasing isolation at his military headquarters

1 1914. Russian promises of autonomy were too vague to win full Polish loyalty. The Finns and Ukrainians were also disappointed by Russia's reluctance to satisfy their national aspirations

3 1915-1917. Front line troops grew steadily more defeatist as a result of lack of ammunition, insufficient clothing, poor rations, and Bolshevik anti-war propaganda

10 1917 August. Factory workers' strike, demanding an end to the war

FINLAND

Baltic Sea

Kronstadt
Petrograd
Putilov works

RUSSIA

Vilna

POLAND
Warsaw

Tarnow

Moscow

Mogilev

Kiev
UKRAINE

4 1916-1917. Bands of deserters and marauders lived behind the lines, looting the peasantry, and spreading demoralization among the troops

GERMANY

AUSTRIA – HUNGARY

Tarnopol

RUMANIA

Odessa

Simferopol

Black Sea

8 1917. July mutinies. Hundreds of fleeing Russians were shot down by the Government's orders

2 1914-1915. Many of Russia's 4 million Jews welcomed German liberation from Tsarist tyranny and persecution

TURKEY

PERSIA

0   300
Miles

■ The Eastern Front 1914-1917

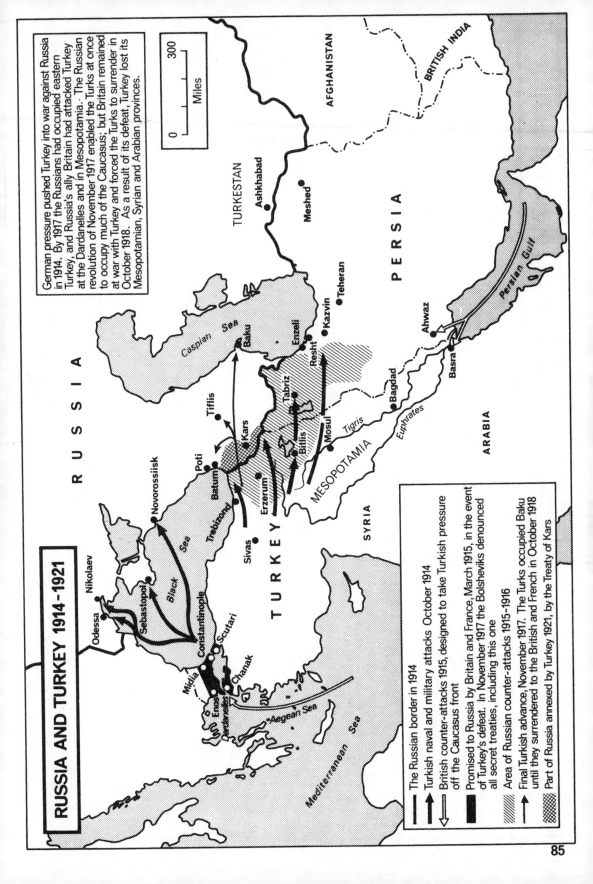

RUSSIA AND TURKEY 1914–1921

German pressure pushed Turkey into war against Russia in 1914. By 1917 the Russians had occupied eastern Turkey, and Russia's ally Britain had attacked Turkey at the Dardanelles and in Mesopotamia.. The Russian revolution of November 1917 enabled the Turks at once to occupy much of the Caucasus; but Britain remained at war with Turkey and forced the Turks to surrender in October 1918. As a result of its defeat, Turkey lost its Mesopotamian, Syrian and Arabian provinces.

0 — 300
Miles

AFGHANISTAN

BRITISH INDIA

TURKESTAN

Ashkhabad

Meshed

PERSIA

Teheran

Kazvin

Ahwaz

Persian Gulf

Basra

Bagdad

Euphrates

ARABIA

MESOPOTAMIA

Tigris

Mosul

Resht

Enzeli

Baku

Caspian Sea

Tabriz

Bitlis

Kars

Tiflis

Erzerum

Poti

Batum

Trebizond

RUSSIA

Novorossiisk

Sivas

TURKEY

SYRIA

Black Sea

Sebastopol

Nikolaev

Odessa

Constantinople

Scutari

Chanak

Midia

Enos

Dardanelles

Aegean Sea

Mediterranean Sea

—— The Russian border in 1914

▲ Turkish naval and military attacks October 1914

▷ British counter-attacks 1915, designed to take Turkish pressure off the Caucasus front

■ Promised to Russia by Britain and France, March 1915, in the event of Turkey's defeat. In November 1917 the Bolsheviks denounced all secret treaties, including this one

▨ Area of Russian counter-attacks 1915-1916

↑ Final Turkish advance, November 1917. The Turks occupied Baku until they surrendered to the British and French in October 1918

▨ Part of Russia annexed by Turkey 1921, by the Treaty of Kars

85

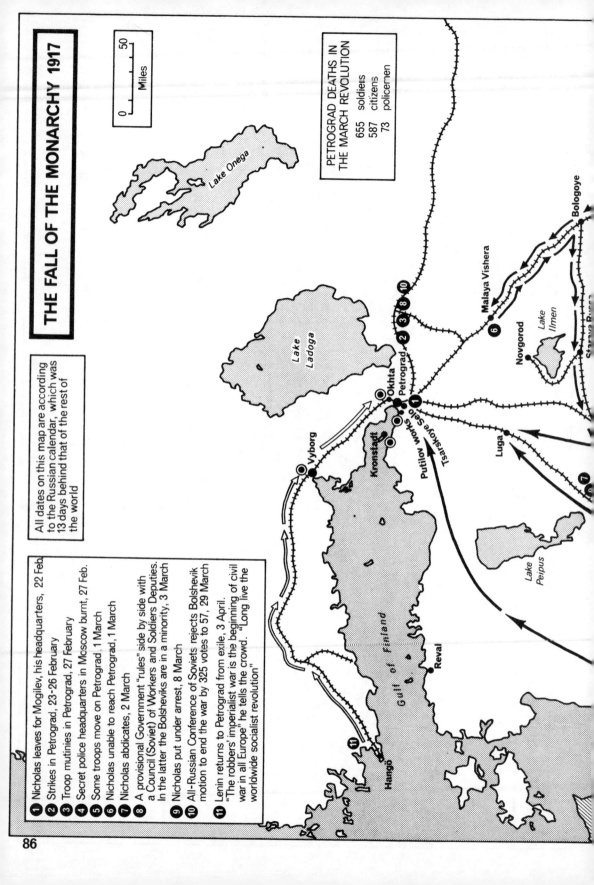

THE FALL OF THE MONARCHY 1917

Miles
0 · · · 50

All dates on this map are according to the Russian calendar, which was 13 days behind that of the rest of the world

PETROGRAD DEATHS IN THE MARCH REVOLUTION

655	soldiers
587	citizens
73	policemen

1. Nicholas leaves for Mogilev, his headquarters, 22 Feb.
2. Strikes in Petrograd, 23-26 February
3. Troop mutinies in Petrograd, 27 February
4. Secret police headquarters in Moscow burnt, 27 Feb.
5. Some troops move on Petrograd, 1 March
6. Nicholas unable to reach Petrograd, 1 March
7. Nicholas abdicates, 2 March
8. A provisional Government "rules" side by side with a Council (Soviet) of Workers and Soldiers Deputies. In the latter the Bolsheviks are in a minority, 3 March
9. Nicholas put under arrest, 8 March
10. All-Russian Conference of Soviets rejects Bolshevik motion to end the war by 325 votes to 57, 29 March
11. Lenin returns to Petrograd from exile, 3 April. "The robbers' imperialist war is the beginning of civil war in all Europe" he tells the crowd. "Long live the worldwide socialist revolution"

Lake Onega

Lake Ladoga

Lake Ilmen

Lake Peipus

Gulf of Finland

Bologoye

Malaya Vishera

Novgorod

Staraya Russa

Okhta
Petrograd
Kronstadt
Putilov works
Tsarskoye Selo
Luga

Vyborg

Hangö

Reval

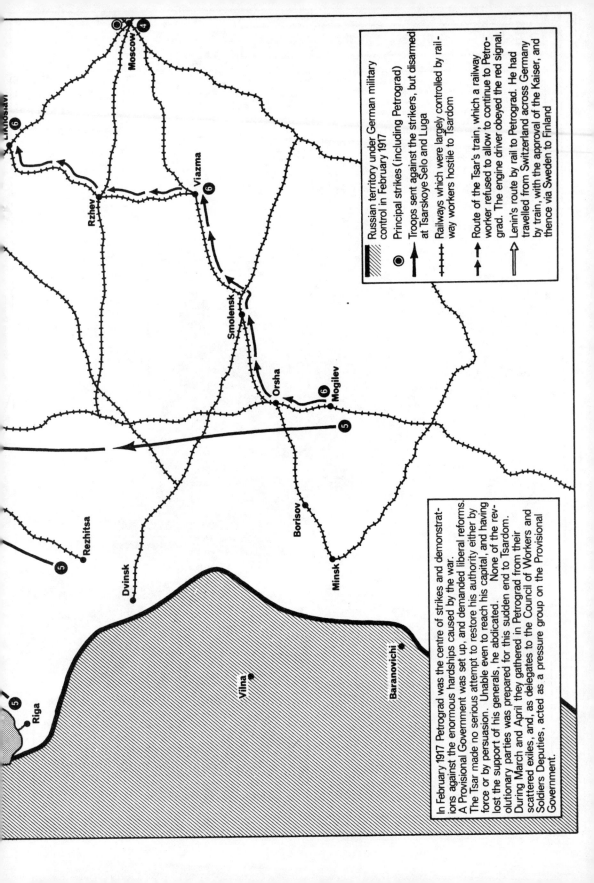

Russian territory under German military control in February 1917

● Principal strikes (including Petrograd)

Troops sent against the strikers, but disarmed at Tsarskoye Selo and Luga

Railways which were largely controlled by railway workers hostile to Tsardom

Route of the Tsar's train, which a railway worker refused to allow to continue to Petrograd. The engine driver obeyed the red signal.

Lenin's route by rail to Petrograd. He had travelled from Switzerland across Germany by train, with the approval of the Kaiser, and thence via Sweden to Finland

In February 1917 Petrograd was the centre of strikes and demonstrations against the enormous hardships caused by the war. A Provisional Government was set up, and demanded liberal reforms. The Tsar made no serious attempt to restore his authority either by force or by persuasion. Unable even to reach his capital, and having lost the support of his generals, he abdicated. None of the revolutionary parties was prepared for this sudden end to Tsardom. During March and April they gathered in Petrograd from their scattered exiles, and, as delegates to the Council of Workers and Soldiers Deputies, acted as a pressure group on the Provisional Government.

Moscow

Viazma

Rzhev

Smolensk

Orsha

Mogilev

Borisov

Minsk

Rezhitsa

Dvinsk

Vilna

Baranovichi

Riga

LENIN'S RETURN TO RUSSIA 1917

Our tactics: absolute distrust; no support of new Government; Kerensky particularly suspect; to arm proletariat only guarantee; no rapprochement with other parties. This last is conditio sine qua non

**LENIN TO BOLSHEVIKS IN SWEDEN
TELEGRAM FROM BERN 26 MARCH 1917**

0   250
Miles

North Cape

Murmansk

SWEDEN

Scapa Flow

North Sea

BRITAIN

Liverpool

London

English Channel

Paris

FRANCE

Berne
SWITZ

Innsbruck

Vienna

Cracow

ITALY

Stockholm

Trelleborg

Berlin

GERMANY

Baltic Sea

Hangö

Vyborg

Petrograd

AUSTRIA-HUNGARY

BULGARIA

RUSSIA

Odessa

Black Sea

TURKEY

Aegean Sea

On 7 August 1914 Lenin was arrested in Cracow by the Austrians as an enemy alien and spy. He was released on 23 Aug., the Austrian Government having been persuaded that he was even more an enemy of Tsardom, and could "render great services" to Austria by fomenting anti-Tsarist troubles

The Central Powers and their conquests in February 1917

Lenin's route from Austria to Switzerland, 1914

Lenin's first proposed route back to Russia, which proved impossible for fear of arrest by the British

Lenin's actual route 9-16 April 1917

Sea routes to Russia closed by Central Power minefields

When revolution broke out in Petrograd in February 1917, Lenin, the Bolshevik leader, was in Switzerland. Wartime was not conducive to travel, nor did his plan to go through Britain prove possible. Instead, the German Government, eager to see dissension and chaos in Russia, agreed with alacrity to his request to travel across "enemy" territory, and provided him with facilities. Thus Imperial Germany served as a hand-maiden to the Russian revolution of October 1917

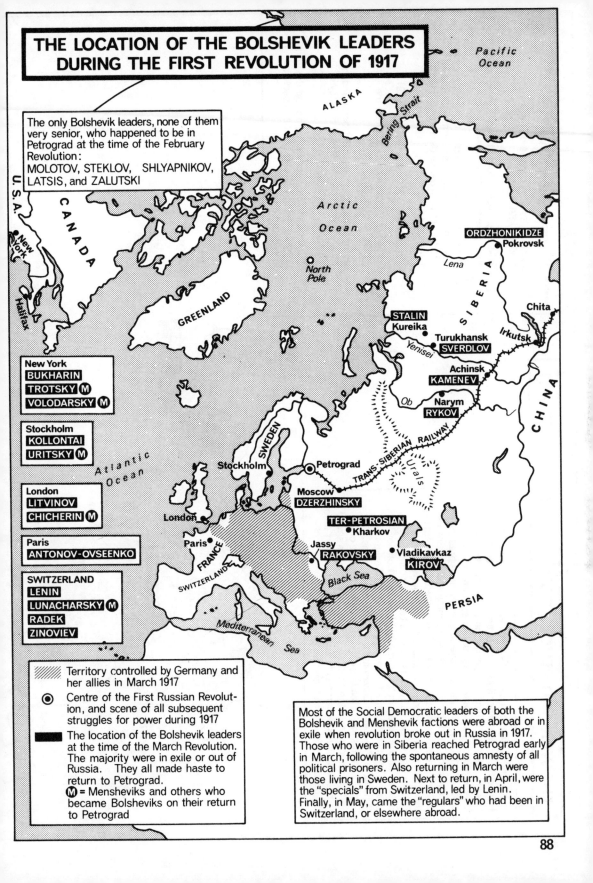

THE LOCATION OF THE BOLSHEVIK LEADERS DURING THE FIRST REVOLUTION OF 1917

The only Bolshevik leaders, none of them very senior, who happened to be in Petrograd at the time of the February Revolution:
MOLOTOV, STEKLOV, SHLYAPNIKOV, LATSIS, and ZALUTSKI

Pacific Ocean

ALASKA

Bering Strait

Arctic Ocean

○ *North Pole*

GREENLAND

New York
BUKHARIN
TROTSKY Ⓜ
VOLODARSKY Ⓜ

Stockholm
KOLLONTAI
URITSKY Ⓜ

London
LITVINOV
CHICHERIN Ⓜ

Paris
ANTONOV-OVSEENKO

SWITZERLAND
LENIN
LUNACHARSKY Ⓜ
RADEK
ZINOVIEV

U.S.A.

CANADA

New York
Halifax

Atlantic Ocean

SWEDEN

Stockholm

London

Paris
FRANCE
SWITZERLAND

Mediterranean Sea

ORDZHONIKIDZE
● Pokrovsk

Lena

SIBERIA

Chita

STALIN
Kureika
Turukhansk
SVERDLOV
Irkutsk

Achinsk
KAMENEV

Yenisei

Ob
Narym
RYKOV

CHINA

Petrograd

Moscow
DZERZHINSKY

TRANS-SIBERIAN RAILWAY

Urals

TER-PETROSIAN
● Kharkov

Jassy
RAKOVSKY

● Vladikavkaz
KIROV

Black Sea

PERSIA

▨ Territory controlled by Germany and her allies in March 1917

◉ Centre of the First Russian Revolution, and scene of all subsequent struggles for power during 1917

▬ The location of the Bolshevik leaders at the time of the March Revolution. The majority were in exile or out of Russia. They all made haste to return to Petrograd.

Ⓜ = Mensheviks and others who became Bolsheviks on their return to Petrograd

Most of the Social Democratic leaders of both the Bolshevik and Menshevik factions were abroad or in exile when revolution broke out in Russia in 1917. Those who were in Siberia reached Petrograd early in March, following the spontaneous amnesty of all political prisoners. Also returning in March were those living in Sweden. Next to return, in April, were the "specials" from Switzerland, led by Lenin. Finally, in May, came the "regulars" who had been in Switzerland, or elsewhere abroad.

THE WAR AND REVOLUTION JULY AND AUGUST 1917

In March 1917 the Provisional Government assured Britain and France that it would continue the war against the Central Powers. But the offensive launched on 1 July ended two weeks later in mutiny and failure. Mass demonstrations in Petrograd on 16 and 17 July, though leaderless, showed how hated the war had become, and the Bolsheviks soon dominated the Soviets by their cry of "Bread and Peace". The Provisional Government then published evidence of financial dealings between the Bolsheviks and German agents, forced Lenin to go into hiding in Finland, and arrested Trotsky. In August General Kornilov led an army against Petrograd, intending to crush the Soviets and stiffen the Provisional Government against concessions.

The Bolsheviks took a leading part in the defence of the city, and greatly increased their military power, having been armed by the Provisional Government. They also gained support among the masses, who feared the return of autocracy

▮	The eastern front on 1 July 1917
⬚	Austrian territory conquered by Russia 1 - 16 July 1917
⬃	Russian proposals for further offensive action during the second two weeks of July
▨	Subject peoples insisting on independence from Russian rule, and gravely hampering the war effort when their demands were rejected or disregarded
☼	Principal areas of mutiny 17 - 30 July 1917
↻	Kornilov's unsuccessful attack on the capital August 1917
◉	Factory groups between Petrograd and the front with increasingly strong Bolshevik influence July - September 1917
●	Military units between Petrograd and the front with increasingly strong Bolshevik sections July - September 1917

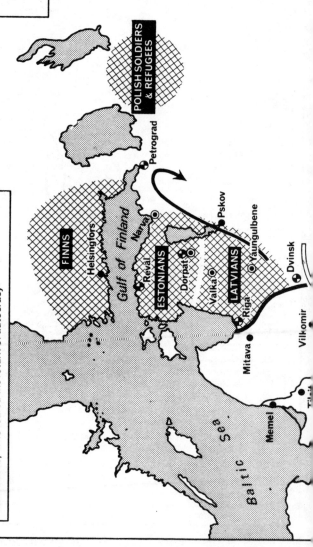

POLISH SOLDIERS & REFUGEES

Petrograd

FINNS

Helsingfors

Gulf of Finland

Narva

Pskov

Reval

ESTONIANS

Dorpat

Valka

Yaungulbene

Dvinsk

LATVIANS

Riga

Baltic Sea

Mitava

Memel

Vilkomir

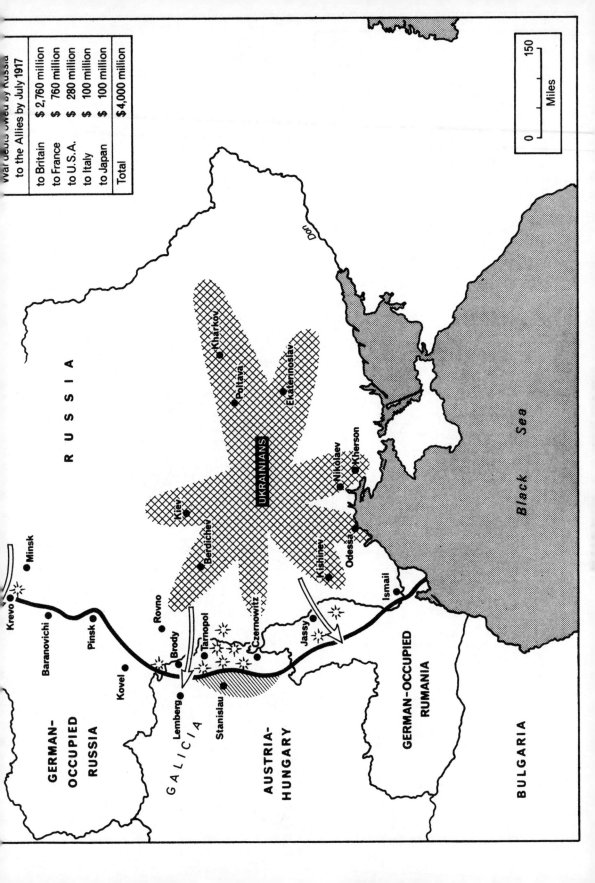

War debts owed by Russia to the Allies by July 1917

to Britain	$	2,760 million
to France	$	760 million
to U.S.A.	$	280 million
to Italy	$	100 million
to Japan	$	100 million
Total	$	4,000 million

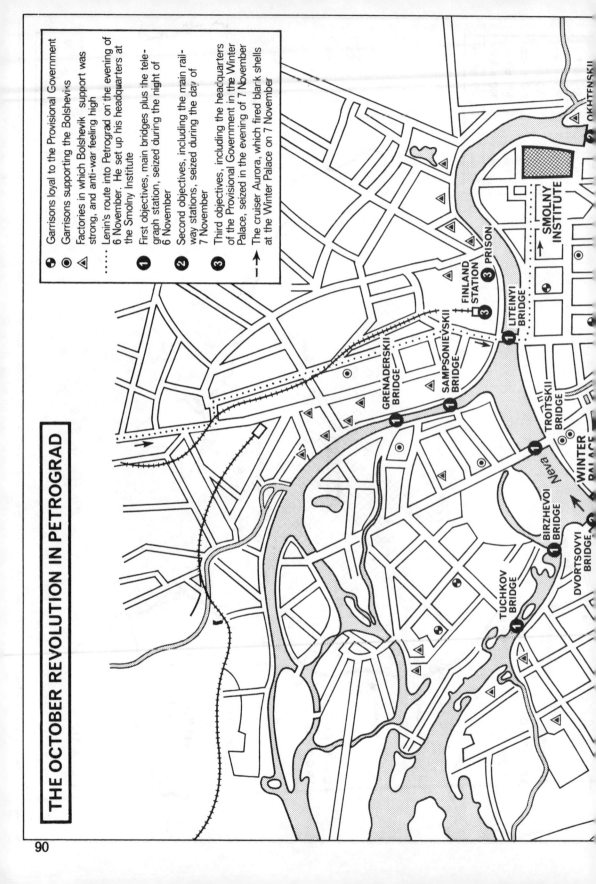

THE OCTOBER REVOLUTION IN PETROGRAD

Garrisons loyal to the Provisional Government

Garrisons supporting the Bolsheviks

Factories in which Bolshevik support was strong, and anti-war feeling high

Lenin's route into Petrograd on the evening of 6 November. He set up his headquarters at the Smolny Institute

1 First objectives, main bridges plus the telegraph station, seized during the night of 6 November

2 Second objectives, including the main railway stations, seized during the day of 7 November

3 Third objectives, including the headquarters of the Provisional Government in the Winter Palace, seized in the evening of 7 November

The cruiser Aurora, which fired blank shells at the Winter Palace on 7 November

SMOLNY INSTITUTE

OKHTENSKII

PRISON

FINLAND STATION

LITEINYI BRIDGE

GRENADERSKII BRIDGE

SAMPSONIEVSKII BRIDGE

TROITSKII BRIDGE

WINTER PALACE

Neva

BIRZHEVOI BRIDGE

DVORTSOVYI BRIDGE

TUCHKOV BRIDGE

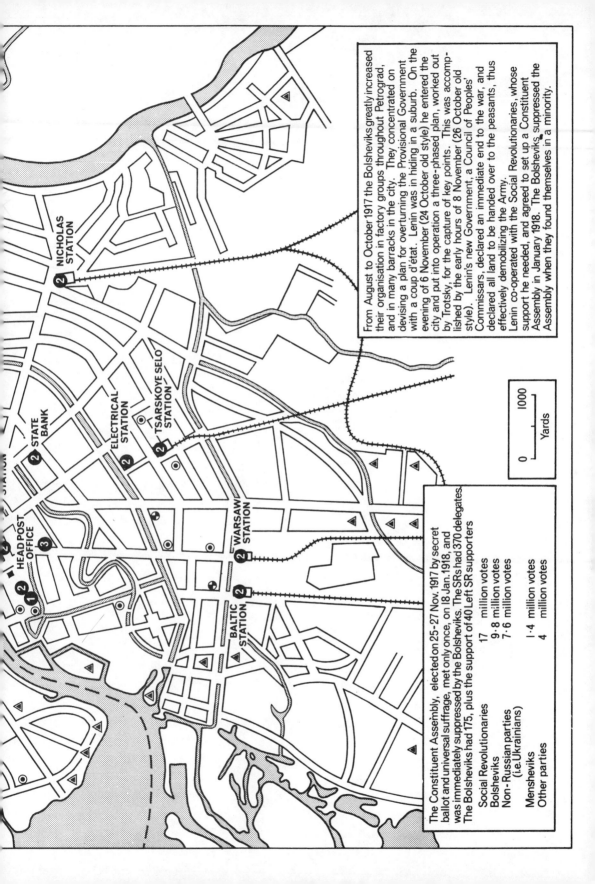

NICHOLAS STATION

STATE BANK

ELECTRICAL STATION

TSARSKOYE SELO STATION

HEAD POST OFFICE

WARSAW STATION

BALTIC STATION

From August to October 1917 the Bolsheviks greatly increased their organisation in factory groups throughout Petrograd, and in many barracks in the city. They concentrated on devising a plan for overturning the Provisional Government with a coup d'état. Lenin was in hiding in a suburb. On the evening of 6 November (24 October old style) he entered the city and put into operation a three-phased plan, worked out by Trotsky, for the capture of key points. This was accomplished by the early hours of 8 November (26 October old style). Lenin's new Government, a Council of Peoples' Commissars, declared an immediate end to the war, and declared all land to be handed over to the peasants, thus effectively demobilizing the Army.
Lenin co-operated with the Social Revolutionaries, whose support he needed, and agreed to set up a Constituent Assembly in January 1918. The Bolsheviks suppressed the Assembly when they found themselves in a minority.

0   1000
Yards

The Constituent Assembly, elected on 25-27 Nov. 1917 by secret ballot and universal suffrage, met only once, on 18 Jan. 1918, and was immediately suppressed by the Bolsheviks. The SRs had 370 delegates. The Bolsheviks had 175, plus the support of 40 Left SR supporters

Social Revolutionaries	17	million votes
Bolsheviks	9·8	million votes
Non-Russian parties (i.e. Ukrainians)	7·6	million votes
Mensheviks	1·4	million votes
Other parties	4	million votes

Section Three

THE SOVIET UNION

Independence from Russia
achieved on 31 December 1917

THE RUSSIAN REVOLUTION
NOVEMBER 1917 – MARCH 1918

Russian territory
occupied by Germany
from November 1917

FINLAND

Murmansk

White Sea

Archangel

Helsinki

Petrograd

Baltic Sea

Riga

Pskov

Moscow

Kazan

Vilna

Kaluga

Smolensk

Penza

Orenburg

GERMANY

POLAND

Warsaw

Brest-
Litovsk

Zhitomir

Voronezh

Saratov

Kiev

Poltava

Kharkov

AUSTRIA-
HUNGARY

Ekaterinoslav

Mariupol

Novocherkassk

Astrakhan

Odessa

Nikolaev

Rostov

RUMANIA

Caspian Sea

Simferopol

Black Sea

Batum

Tiflis

Baku

Kars

The eastern front on
7 November 1917

Principal towns in which the
Bolsheviks seized power
in November and December

Further Bolshevik
activity, January and
February 1918

Occupied by British
troops in March 1918

Occupied by German
troops in March 1918, as a
result of the Bolshevik-German
treaty of Brest-Litovsk

Tabriz

TURKEY

PERSIA

Occupied by Turkish
troops in March 1918

0   300
Miles

91

THE WAR AGAINST BOLSHEVISM 1918-1919

In SIBERIA:
AMERICANS
BRITISH
JAPANESE

Murmansk
BRITISH
SERBS

ITALIANS
AMERICANS
BRITISH

White Sea

Kem
Archangel
FINNS
Onega

Perm
CZECHS

FINNS

Vologda

Petrograd

Nizhni-Novgorod
Kazan

Ufa

Tver

Moscow

Samara

RUSSIANS

Baltic Sea

RUSSIANS

LETTS
BALTIC GERMANS
LITHUANIANS

Vitebsk

Tula

Tambov

Minsk

Orel

Gurev

POLES

RUSSIANS
Kiev
Kharkov
UKRAINIANS

Astrakhan

The anti-Bolshevik armies, even at the height of their success in 1919, were too disunited in aims and methods to prevail over the Bolshevik "Red Army" with its combination of communist ideology and the national defence of mother Russia against the foreign foe

COSSACKS
RUSSIANS
Rostov

RUMANIANS
FRENCH
Odessa

Novo - Rossiisk

Caspian Sea

Tiflis

Baku
BRITISH

Black Sea

Batum
BRITISH

Erivan

0   200
Miles

☐ Under Bolshevik rule November 1918
■ Principal armies attempting to destroy Bolshevism
◣ Maximum advance of the anti-Bolshevik forces 1918-1919
▨ Remnant of anti-Bolshevik forces, defeated 1920-1921
•••• Established Russian frontiers, March 1921- October 1939

92

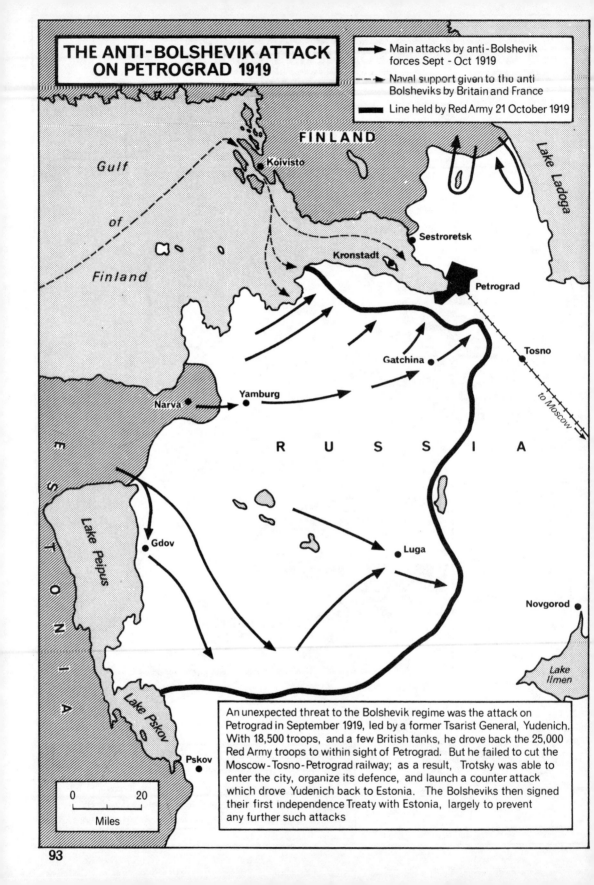

THE ANTI-BOLSHEVIK ATTACK ON PETROGRAD 1919

→ Main attacks by anti-Bolshevik forces Sept - Oct 1919

┅➤ Naval support given to the anti Bolsheviks by Britain and France

━ Line held by Red Army 21 October 1919

FINLAND

Gulf
of
Finland

Koivisto

Lake Ladoga

Sestroretsk

Kronstadt

Petrograd

Tosno

Gatchina

to Moscow

Yamburg

Narva

R U S S I A

E
S
T
O
N
I
A

Lake Peipus

Gdov

Luga

Novgorod

Lake
Ilmen

Lake Pskov

Pskov

0   20

Miles

An unexpected threat to the Bolshevik regime was the attack on
Petrograd in September 1919, led by a former Tsarist General, Yudenich.
With 18,500 troops, and a few British tanks, he drove back the 25,000
Red Army troops to within sight of Petrograd. But he failed to cut the
Moscow-Tosno-Petrograd railway; as a result, Trotsky was able to
enter the city, organize its defence, and launch a counter attack
which drove Yudenich back to Estonia. The Bolsheviks then signed
their first independence Treaty with Estonia, largely to prevent
any further such attacks

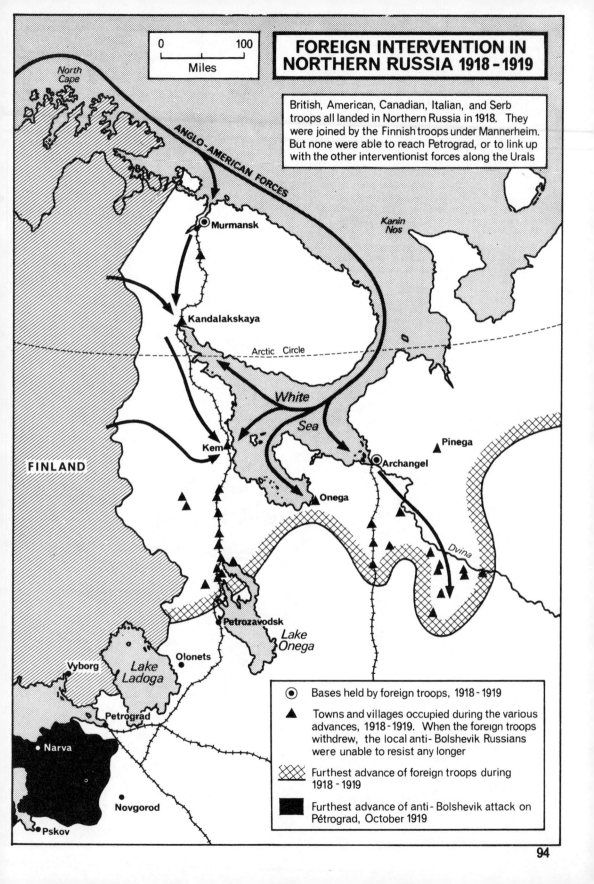

FOREIGN INTERVENTION IN NORTHERN RUSSIA 1918-1919

British, American, Canadian, Italian, and Serb troops all landed in Northern Russia in 1918. They were joined by the Finnish troops under Mannerheim. But none were able to reach Petrograd, or to link up with the other interventionist forces along the Urals

0   100
Miles

North Cape

ANGLO-AMERICAN FORCES

Kanin Nos

⊙ Murmansk

Kandalakskaya

Arctic Circle

White

Sea

▲ Pinega

Kem

FINLAND

⊙ Archangel

▲ Onega

Dvina

Petrozavodsk

Lake Onega

Olonets

Vyborg

Lake Ladoga

Petrograd

• Narva

Novgorod

• Pskov

⊙   Bases held by foreign troops, 1918-1919

▲   Towns and villages occupied during the various advances, 1918-1919. When the foreign troops withdrew, the local anti-Bolshevik Russians were unable to resist any longer

▨   Furthest advance of foreign troops during 1918-1919

■   Furthest advance of anti-Bolshevik attack on Pétrograd, October 1919

94

MAKHNO AND THE ANARCHISTS 1917-1920

Nestor Makhno, the Ukrainian anarchist, was imprisoned for terrorism in 1907, at the age of eighteen. Released in February 1917, he organized a peasant army, and established control over a large area of southern Russia. He defeated the Austrians at Dibrivki (Sept 1918) and the Ukrainian nationalists at Ekaterinoslav (Nov 1918). In 1919 he allied with the Bolsheviks, defeating two anti-Bolshevik armies, Denikin's at Peregonovka (Sept 1919) and Wrangel's in the Crimea (June 1920). Makhno himself was then attacked continuously by the Bolsheviks and fled (November 1920) via Rumania to France, where he died in 1935

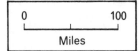

- ⊙ Centres of the Confederation of Anarchist Organizations (Nabat), 1918
- ▨ Anarchist conferences, with dates
- ◕ Makhno's Headquarters 1918-1920
- → Makhno's principal military activities

```
0                    100
|____|____|____|____|
        Miles
```

Kursk
NOV. 1918

Kiev

Kharkov

Poltava

Peregonovka

UKRAINE

Lozovaya

Dnieper

Elizavetgrad
APRIL 1919

Dibrivki

Ekaterinoslav

Alexandrovsk

Nikopol

Guliai Pole

Pologi

Mariupol

Dniester

Berdiansk

Odessa

RUMANIA

Sea of
Azov

CRIMEA

Black   Sea

THE RUSSO-POLISH WAR 1920

Poland's established frontiers, June 1920

The eastern extent of Polish conquests, April, May and June 1920

Russian attacks following the Polish occupation of Kiev in June 1920

Polish lines of defence, August 1920

The 'Miracle of the Vistula'. Russian armies were defeated; they retreated to Russia

Seized by Poland from Lithuania, October 1920

Annexed by Poland from Russia, Treaty of Riga, March 1921

Poland's eastern frontier from 1921 to 1939

ESTONIA

LATVIA

LITHUANIA

Baltic Sea.

DANZIG

EAST PRUSSIA

GERMANY

RUSSIA

Vilna

Minsk

Grodno

Bialystok

Plotsk

Poznan

Warsaw

Pinsk

POLAND

Radom

Lublin

Kholm

Kiev

GERMANY

Vistula

Cracow

Lvov

Kamenets Podolsk

CZECHOSLOVAKIA

0   100
Miles

HUNGARY

RUMANIA

96

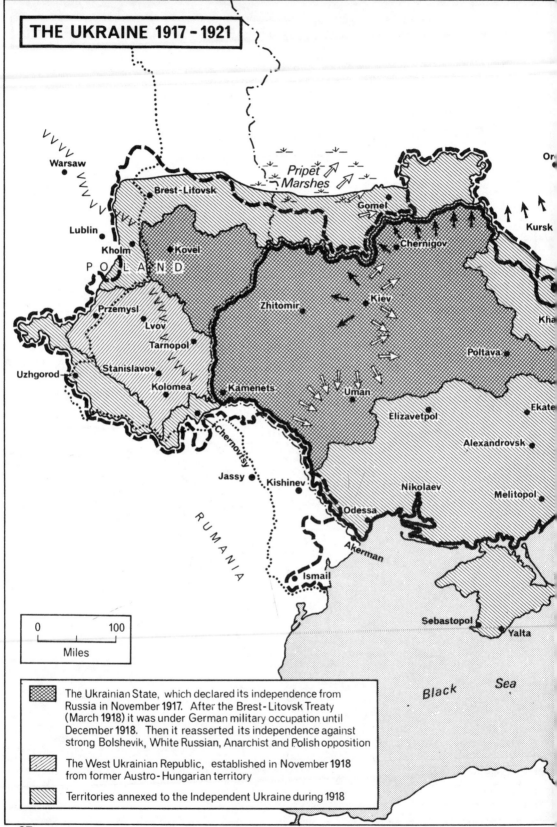

THE UKRAINE 1917 - 1921

Warsaw

Pripet Marshes

Brest-Litovsk

Gomel

Or

Lublin

Kursk

Kholm •Kovel

Chernigov

P O L A N D

Zhitomir

Kiev

Kha

Przemysl

•Lvov

Poltava

Tarnopol

Uzhgorod

Stanislavov

Kolomea

Kamenets

Uman

Ekate

Elizavetpol

Chernovitsy

Alexandrovsk

Jassy •Kishinev

Nikolaev

Melitopol

R U M A N I A

Odessa

Akerman

Ismail

Sebastopol

Yalta

0   100

Miles

Black   Sea

The Ukrainian State, which declared its independence from
Russia in November 1917. After the Brest-Litovsk Treaty
(March 1918) it was under German military occupation until
December 1918. Then it reasserted its independence against
strong Bolshevik, White Russian, Anarchist and Polish opposition

The West Ukrainian Republic, established in November 1918
from former Austro-Hungarian territory

Territories annexed to the Independent Ukraine during 1918

97

Legend

- ▬ ▬ ▬ Territory claimed by the Ukrainian nationalists as part of the "ethnographic" Ukraine
- ▬▬▬ Boundary of the Ukrainian Soviet Socialist Republic **1921**
- — · — · Western boundary of the Soviet Union **1921-1939**
- ············ Western boundary of the Soviet Union since **1945**

Furthest northern advance of Denikin's anti-Bolshevik armies, November **1919**. Denikin's Great Russian policies failed to gain him much Ukrainian support

Furthest eastern advance of the Polish Army in June **1920**

Furthest western advance of the Red Army by August **1920**

Voronezh

Buturlinovka

Lugansk

Taganrog

Rostov

ariupol

Astrakhan

Ekaterinodar

Stavropol

Armavir

Novorossiisk

Mineralnye Vody

Mozdok

Tuapse

Sochi

Batum

Caucasus

Caspian Sea

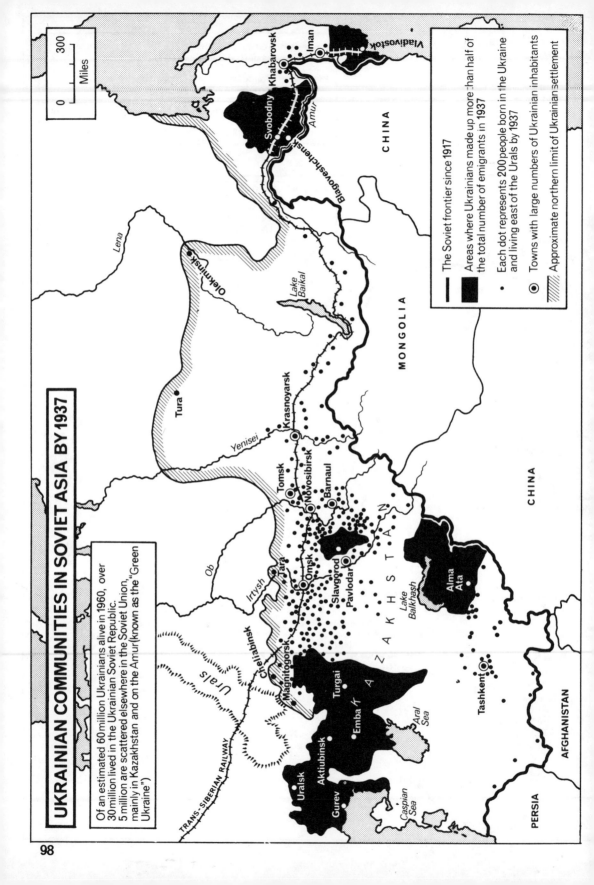

UKRAINIAN COMMUNITIES IN SOVIET ASIA BY 1937

Of an estimated 60 million Ukrainians alive in 1960, over 30 million lived in the Ukrainian Soviet Republic. 5 million are scattered elsewhere in the Soviet Union, mainly in Kazakhstan and on the Amur (known as the "Green Ukraine")

The Soviet frontier since 1917

Areas where Ukrainians made up more than half of the total number of emigrants in 1937

Each dot represents 200 people born in the Ukraine and living east of the Urals by 1937

Towns with large numbers of Ukrainian inhabitants

Approximate northern limit of Ukrainian settlement

300

0

Miles

CHINA

MONGOLIA

KAZAKHSTAN

CHINA

PERSIA

AFGHANISTAN

Vladivostok

Iman

Khabarovsk

Svobodny

Amur

Blagoveshchensk

Olekminsk

Lena

Lake Baikal

Tura

Krasnoyarsk

Yenisei

Tomsk

Novosibirsk

Barnaul

Omsk

Slavgorod

Pavlodar

Tara

Irtysh

Ob

Alma Ata

Lake Balkhash

Tashkent

Cheliabinsk

Magnitogorsk

Turgai

Urals

Emba

Aral Sea

Aktiubinsk

Uralsk

Gurev

Caspian Sea

TRANS-SIBERIAN RAILWAY

98

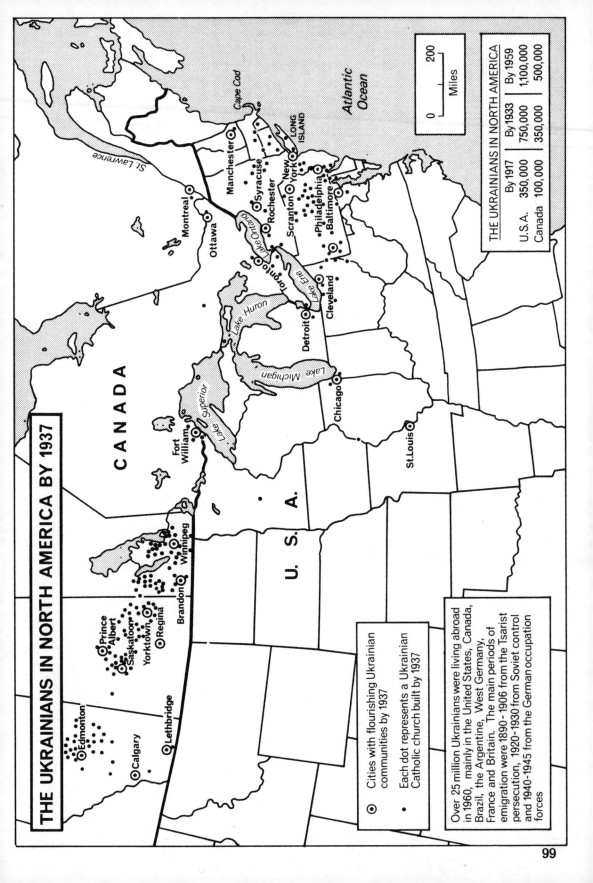

THE UKRAINIANS IN NORTH AMERICA BY 1937

THE UKRAINIANS IN NORTH AMERICA			
	By 1917	By 1933	By 1959
U.S.A.	350,000	750,000	1,100,000
Canada	100,000	350,000	500,000

0 — 200 Miles

Atlantic Ocean

St. Lawrence

CANADA

U. S. A.

Cape Cod

LONG ISLAND

Manchester
Syracuse
Rochester
New York
Scranton
Philadelphia
Baltimore
Montreal
Ottawa
Lake Ontario
Toronto
Lake Erie
Cleveland
Detroit
Lake Huron
Lake Michigan
Chicago
Lake Superior
Fort William
St. Louis

Winnipeg
Brandon
Prince Albert
Saskatoon
Yorkton
Regina
Edmonton
Calgary
Lethbridge

⊙ Cities with flourishing Ukrainian communities by 1937

•   Each dot represents a Ukrainian Catholic church built by 1937

Over 25 million Ukrainians were living abroad in 1960, mainly in the United States, Canada, Brazil, the Argentine, West Germany, France and Britain. The main periods of emigration were 1890 - 1906 from the Tsarist persecution, 1920 -1930 from Soviet control and 1940 -1945 from the German occupation forces

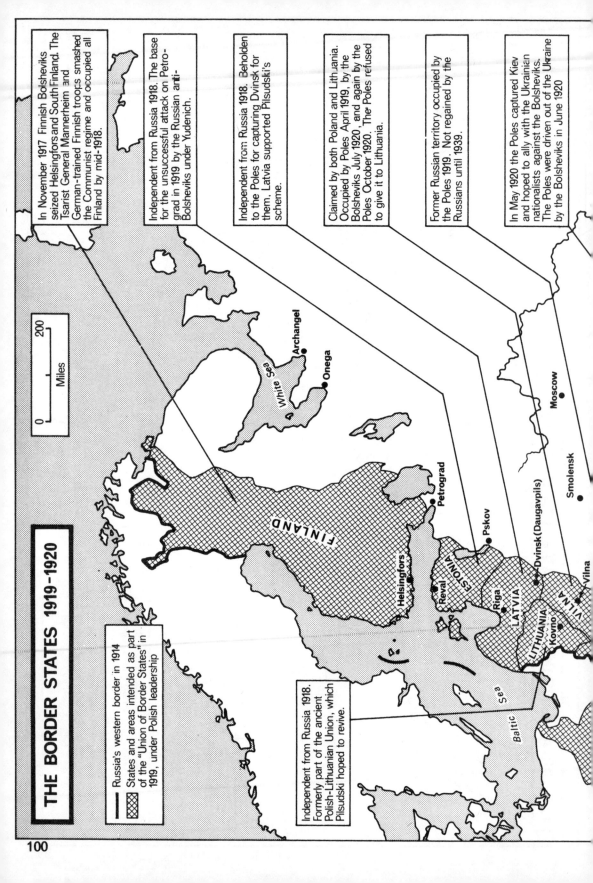

THE BORDER STATES 1919-1920

In November 1917 Finnish Bolsheviks seized Helsingfors and South Finland. The Tsarist General Mannerheim and German-trained Finnish troops smashed the Communist regime and occupied all Finland by mid-1918.

Independent from Russia 1918. The base for the unsuccessful attack on Petrograd in 1919 by the Russian anti-Bolsheviks under Yudenich.

Independent from Russia 1918. Beholden to the Poles for capturing Dvinsk for them. Latvia supported Pilsudski's scheme.

Claimed by both Poland and Lithuania. Occupied by Poles April 1919, by the Bolsheviks July 1920, and again by the Poles October 1920. The Poles refused to give it to Lithuania.

Former Russian territory occupied by the Poles 1919. Not regained by the Russians until 1939.

In May 1920 the Poles captured Kiev and hoped to ally with the Ukrainian nationalists against the Bolsheviks. The Poles were driven out of the Ukraine by the Bolsheviks in June 1920

Russia's western border in 1914

States and areas intended as part of the "Union of Border States" in 1919, under Polish leadership

Independent from Russia 1918. Formerly part of the ancient Polish-Lithuanian Union, which Pilsudski hoped to revive.

0   200
Miles

White Sea

Archangel

Onega

Petrograd

Pskov

Moscow

Smolensk

Dvinsk (Daugavpils)

Vilna

FINLAND

Helsingfors

Reval

ESTONIA

Riga

LATVIA

VILNA

LITHUANIA

Kovno

Baltic Sea

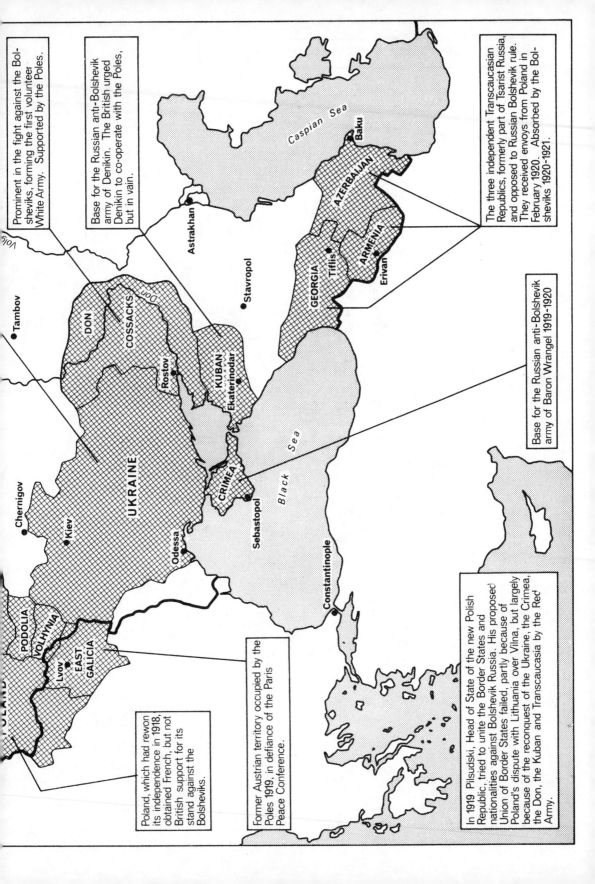

Prominent in the fight against the Bolsheviks, forming the first volunteer White Army. Supported by the Poles.

Base for the Russian anti-Bolshevik army of Denikin. The British urged Denikin to co-operate with the Poles, but in vain.

The three independent Transcaucasian Republics, formerly part of Tsarist Russia, and opposed to Russian Bolshevik rule. They received envoys from Poland in February 1920. Absorbed by the Bolsheviks 1920-1921.

Base for the Russian anti-Bolshevik army of Baron Wrangel 1919-1920

Poland, which had rewon its independence in 1918, obtained French, but not British support for its stand against the Bolsheviks.

Former Austrian territory occupied by the Poles 1919, in defiance of the Paris Peace Conference.

In 1919 Pilsudski, Head of State of the new Polish Republic, tried to unite the Border States and nationalities against Bolshevik Russia. His proposed Union of Border States failed, partly because of Poland's dispute with Lithuania over Vilna, but largely because of the reconquest of the Ukraine, the Crimea, the Don, the Kuban and Transcaucasia by the Red Army.

Volga

Tambov

Astrakhan

Caspian Sea

Baku

AZERBAIJAN

ARMENIA

GEORGIA

Tiflis

Erivan

Stavropol

DON

COSSACKS

Don

Rostov

KUBAN

Ekaterinodar

Chernigov

Kiev

UKRAINE

CRIMEA

Sebastopol

Black Sea

Odessa

PODOLIA

VOLHYNIA

Lvov

EAST GALICIA

POLAND

Constantinople

SOVIET DIPLOMACY 1920-1940

North Sea

Baltic Sea

BRITAIN

London

Bay of Biscay

Paris

F·R·A·N·C·E

NORWAY

FINLAND

Lenin grad

ESTONIA

LATVIA

Smo

FLYI
SCHO

Berlin

GERMANY

Warsaw

POLAND

CZECHO-
SLOVAKIA

AUSTRIA

RUMANIA

I·T·A·L·Y

10,000 VEHICLES

4,500 TONS MUNITIONS

200 TANKS

3,300 MACHINE GUNS

1,000 OFFICERS & MEN

San Sebastian

Madrid

Barcelona

SPAIN

1,000 OFFICERS & MEN

1,300 TRUCKS

1,300 RIFLES & GUNS

242 AEROPLANES

Mediterranean Sea

0   400

Miles

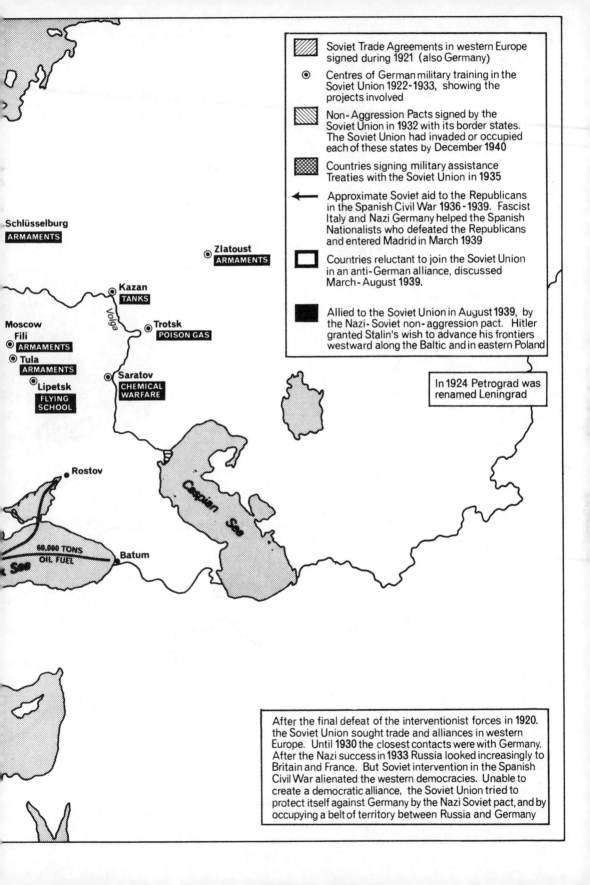

Soviet Trade Agreements in western Europe signed during 1921 (also Germany)

⊙ **Centres of German military training** in the Soviet Union 1922-1933, showing the projects involved

Non-Aggression Pacts signed by the Soviet Union in 1932 with its border states. The Soviet Union had invaded or occupied each of these states by December 1940

Countries signing military assistance Treaties with the Soviet Union in 1935

← **Approximate Soviet aid** to the Republicans in the Spanish Civil War 1936-1939. Fascist Italy and Nazi Germany helped the Spanish Nationalists who defeated the Republicans and entered Madrid in March 1939

Countries reluctant to join the Soviet Union in an anti-German alliance, discussed March-August 1939.

Allied to the Soviet Union in August 1939, by the Nazi-Soviet non-aggression pact. Hitler granted Stalin's wish to advance his frontiers westward along the Baltic and in eastern Poland

In 1924 Petrograd was renamed Leningrad

Schlüsselburg
ARMAMENTS

⊙ **Zlatoust**
ARMAMENTS

⊙ **Kazan**
TANKS

Volga

Moscow
Fili
⊙ ARMAMENTS

⊙ **Tula**
ARMAMENTS

⊙ **Lipetsk**
FLYING SCHOOL

⊙ **Trotsk**
POISON GAS

⊙ **Saratov**
CHEMICAL WARFARE

• **Rostov**

Caspian Sea

60,000 TONS OIL FUEL

Batum

...Sea

After the final defeat of the interventionist forces in 1920, the Soviet Union sought trade and alliances in western Europe. Until 1930 the closest contacts were with Germany. After the Nazi success in 1933 Russia looked increasingly to Britain and France. But Soviet intervention in the Spanish Civil War alienated the western democracies. Unable to create a democratic alliance, the Soviet Union tried to protect itself against Germany by the Nazi Soviet pact, and by occupying a belt of territory between Russia and Germany

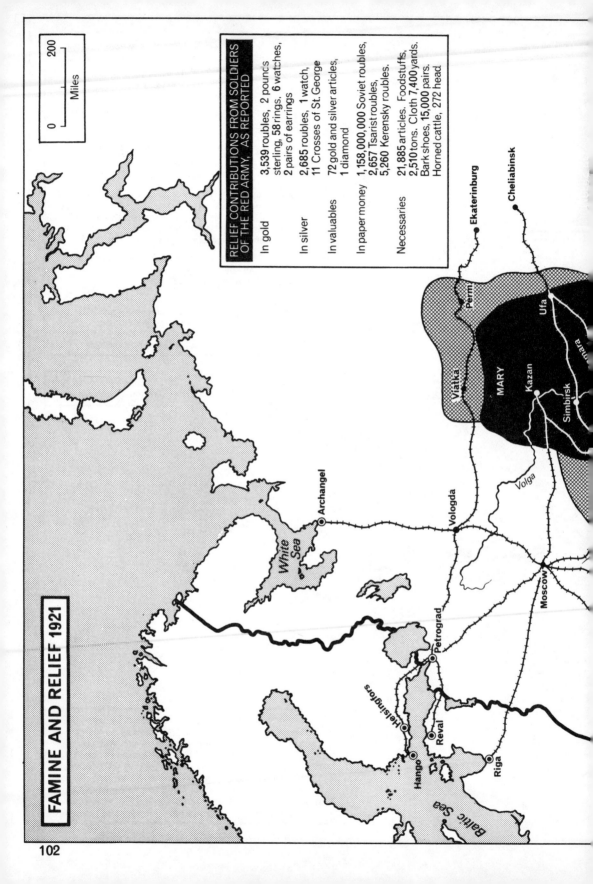

FAMINE AND RELIEF 1921

0	200
	Miles

RELIEF CONTRIBUTIONS FROM SOLDIERS OF THE RED ARMY, AS REPORTED

In gold	3,539 roubles, 2 pounds sterling, 58 rings. 6 watches, 2 pairs of earrings
In silver	2,685 roubles, 1 watch, 11 Crosses of St. George
In valuables	72 gold and silver articles, 1 diamond
In paper money	1,158,000,000 Soviet roubles, 2,657 Tsarist roubles, 5,260 Kerensky roubles.
Necessaries	21,885 articles. Foodstuffs, 2,510 tons. Cloth 7,400 yards. Bark shoes, 15,000 pairs. Horned cattle, 272 head

Ekaterinburg

Cheliabinsk

Perm

Viatka

MARY

Ufa

Kazan

Samara

Simbirsk

Archangel

White Sea

Vologda

Volga

Moscow

Petrograd

Helsingfors

Reval

Hango

Riga

Baltic Sea

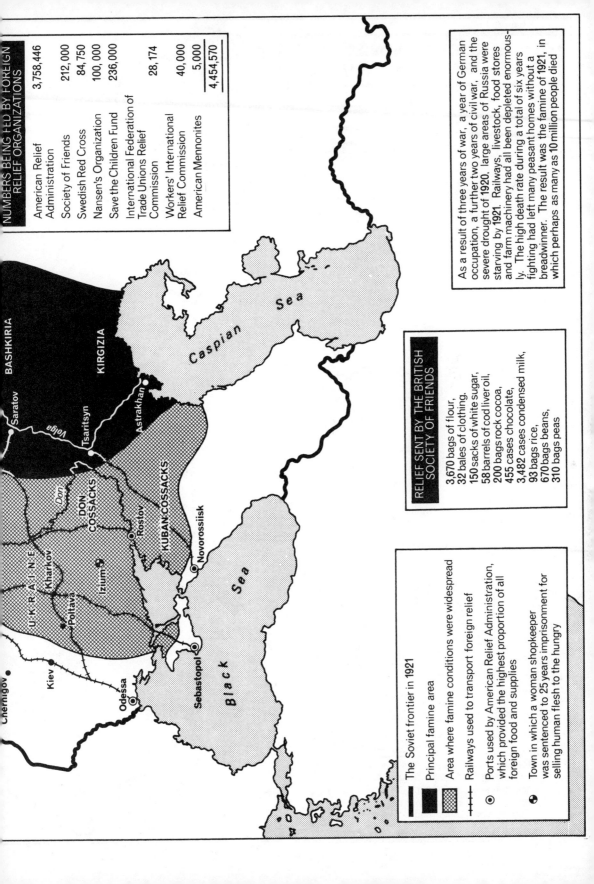

NUMBERS BEING FED BY FOREIGN RELIEF ORGANIZATIONS

American Relief Administration	3,758,446
Society of Friends	212,000
Swedish Red Cross	84,750
Nansen's Organization	100,000
Save the Children Fund	236,000
International Federation of Trade Unions Relief Commission	28,174
Workers' International Relief Commission	40,000
American Mennonites	5,000
	4,454,570

As a result of three years of war, a year of German occupation, a further two years of civil war, and the severe drought of 1920, large areas of Russia were starving by 1921. Railways, livestock, food stores and farm machinery had all been depleted enormously. The high death rate during a total of six years fighting had left many peasant homes without a breadwinner. The result was the famine of 1921, in which perhaps as many as 10 million people died

RELIEF SENT BY THE BRITISH SOCIETY OF FRIENDS

3,670 bags of flour,
32 bales of clothing.
150 sacks of white sugar,
58 barrels of cod liver oil,
200 bags rock cocoa,
455 cases chocolate,
3,482 cases condensed milk,
93 bags rice,
670 bags beans,
310 bags peas

BASHKIRIA

KIRGIZIA

Caspian Sea

Saratov

Volga

Tsaritsyn

Astrakhan

Don

DON COSSACKS

Rostov

KUBAN COSSACKS

Novorossiisk

UKRAINE

Kharkov

Izium

Poltava

Chernigov

Kiev

Odessa

Sebastopol

Black Sea

The Soviet frontier in 1921

Principal famine area

Area where famine conditions were widespread

Railways used to transport foreign relief

Ports used by American Relief Administration, which provided the highest proportion of all foreign food and supplies

Town in which a woman shopkeeper was sentenced to 25 years imprisonment for selling human flesh to the hungry

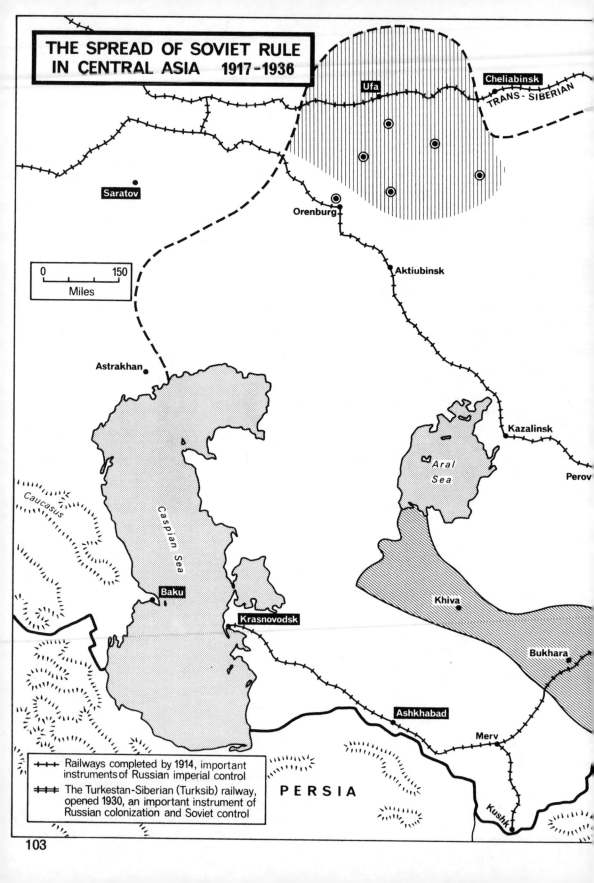

THE SPREAD OF SOVIET RULE
IN CENTRAL ASIA   1917-1936

Ufa

Cheliabinsk

TRANS - SIBERIAN

Saratov

Orenburg

Aktiubinsk

0   150

Miles

Astrakhan

Kazalinsk

*Aral
Sea*

Perov

Caucasus

*Caspian
Sea*

Baku

Khiva

Krasnovodsk

Bukhara

Ashkhabad

Merv

Railways completed by 1914, important
instruments of Russian imperial control

The Turkestan-Siberian (Turksib) railway,
opened 1930, an important instrument of
Russian colonization and Soviet control

PERSIA

Kushk

Novosibirsk

Omsk

RAILWAY

Barnaul

Semipalatinsk

Karaganda

Lake Balkhash

Verny

Pishpek

Issyk
Kul

C H I N A

(SINKIANG)

Tashkent

Kokand   Skobelev

Samarkand

Diushambe

BRITISH

AFGHANISTAN

Hindu Kush

INDIA

Tsarist rule in Central Asia was established between 1850 and 1914. In 1917 the predominantly Muslim peoples of this vast region sought independence. But by 1924 the Soviet Government had re-established Russian rule, and by 1936 the whole area was divided into Soviet Republics, bound to Moscow by direct military, political and economic ties.

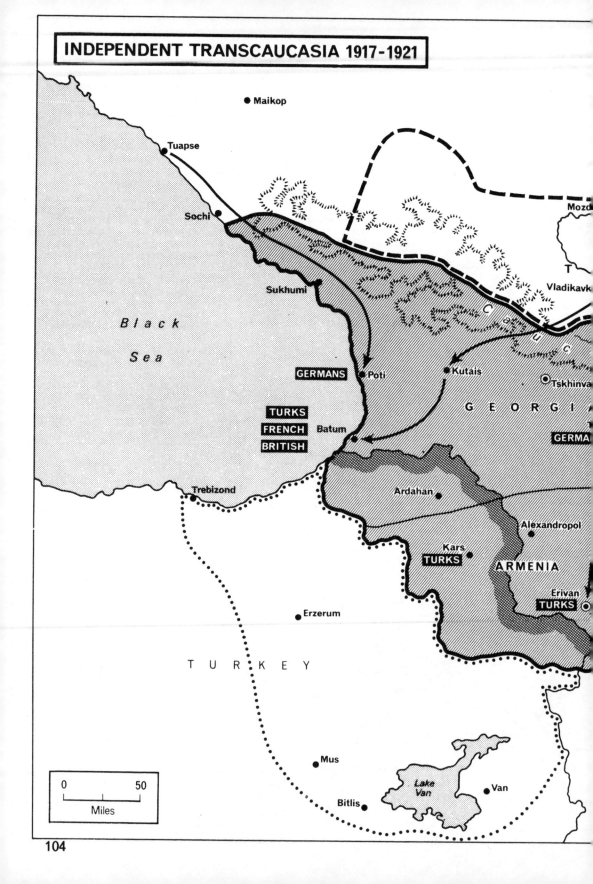

INDEPENDENT TRANSCAUCASIA 1917-1921

● Maikop

● Tuapse

● Sochi

B l a c k

S e a

Sukhumi

GERMANS   ● Poti

TURKS
FRENCH   Batum
BRITISH

● Trebizond

● Kutais

⊙ Tskhinva

G E O R G I

GERMA

Vladikavk

Mozd

T

Ardahan ●

Alexandropol ●

Kars
TURKS ●   A R M E N I A

Erivan
TURKS ⊙

● Erzerum

T U R K E Y

0   50

Miles

● Mus

*Lake
Van*

Bitlis ●   ● Van

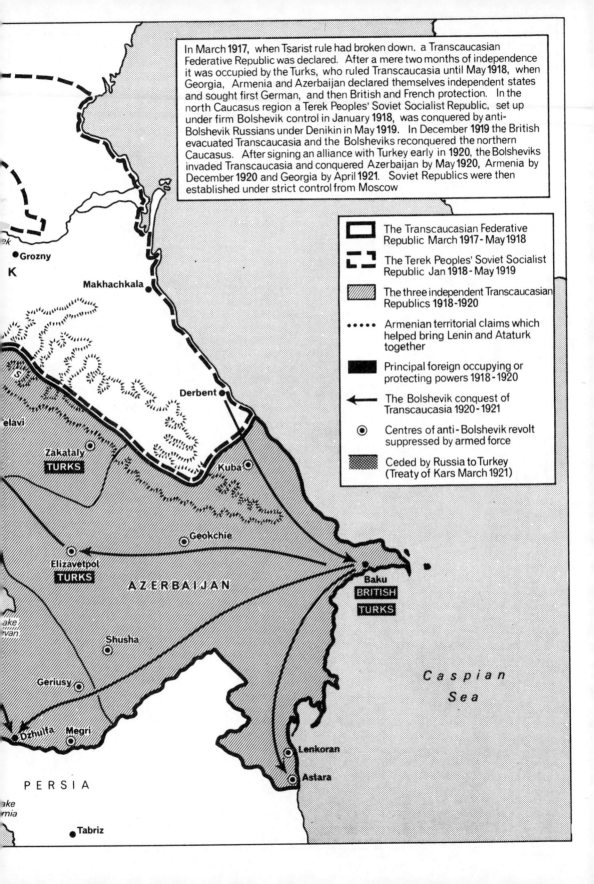

In March 1917, when Tsarist rule had broken down. a Transcaucasian Federative Republic was declared. After a mere two months of independence it was occupied by the Turks, who ruled Transcaucasia until May 1918, when Georgia, Armenia and Azerbaijan declared themselves independent states and sought first German, and then British and French protection. In the north Caucasus region a Terek Peoples' Soviet Socialist Republic, set up under firm Bolshevik control in January 1918, was conquered by anti-Bolshevik Russians under Denikin in May 1919. In December 1919 the British evacuated Transcaucasia and the Bolsheviks reconquered the northern Caucasus. After signing an alliance with Turkey early in 1920, the Bolsheviks invaded Transcaucasia and conquered Azerbaijan by May 1920, Armenia by December 1920 and Georgia by April 1921. Soviet Republics were then established under strict control from Moscow

The Transcaucasian Federative Republic March 1917 - May 1918

The Terek Peoples' Soviet Socialist Republic Jan 1918 - May 1919

The three independent Transcaucasian Republics 1918 - 1920

..... Armenian territorial claims which helped bring Lenin and Ataturk together

Principal foreign occupying or protecting powers 1918 - 1920

The Bolshevik conquest of Transcaucasia 1920 - 1921

Centres of anti - Bolshevik revolt suppressed by armed force

Ceded by Russia to Turkey (Treaty of Kars March 1921)

● Grozny

K

Makhachkala ●

Derbent ●

elavi

Zakataly ◉
TURKS

Kuba ◉

◉ Geokchie

Elizavetpol ◉
TURKS

A Z E R B A I J A N

Baku
BRITISH
TURKS

ake
van

Shusha ◉

Geriusy ◉

C a s p i a n
S e a

Dzhulfa ◉ Megri ●

Lenkoran ◉

P E R S I A

Astara ◉

ake
mia

● Tabriz

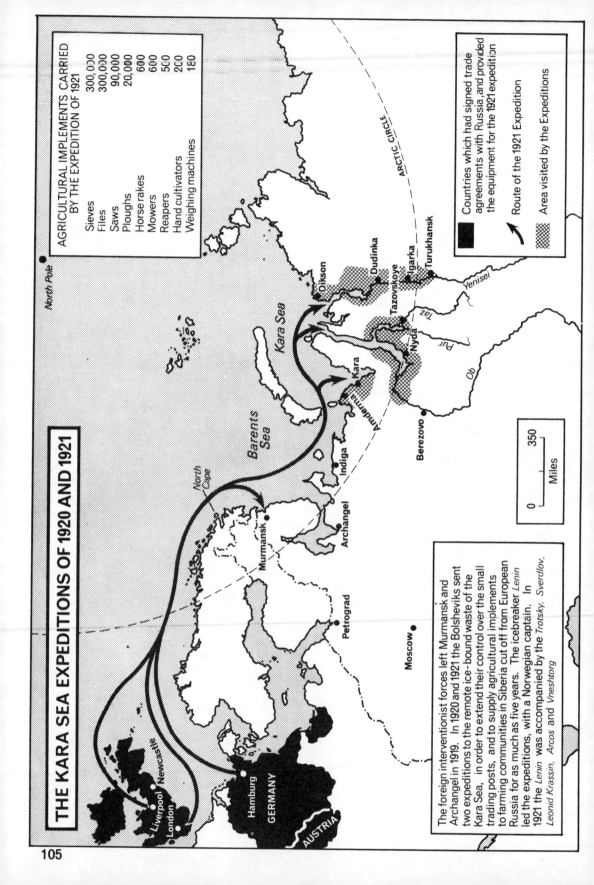

THE KARA SEA EXPEDITIONS OF 1920 AND 1921

AGRICULTURAL IMPLEMENTS CARRIED
BY THE EXPEDITION OF 1921

Sieves	300,000
Files	300,000
Saws	90,000
Ploughs	20,000
Horse rakes	600
Mowers	600
Reapers	500
Hand cultivators	200
Weighing machines	180

Countries which had signed trade
agreements with Russia, and provided
the equipment for the 1921 expedition

Route of the 1921 Expedition

Area visited by the Expeditions

North Pole

ARCTIC CIRCLE

Turukhansk
Igarka
Dudinka
Tazovskoye
Dikson
Nyda
Yenisei
Taz
Pur
Kara Sea
Kara
Amderma
Ob

Barents Sea

North Cape

Indiga
Berezovo

Murmansk

Archangel

Newcastle
Liverpool
London
Hamburg
GERMANY
AUSTRIA

Petrograd

Moscow

0 — 350
Miles

The foreign interventionist forces left Murmansk and
Archangel in 1919. In 1920 and 1921 the Bolsheviks sent
two expeditions to the remote ice-bound waste of the
Kara Sea, in order to extend their control over the small
trading posts, and to supply agricultural implements
to farming communities in Siberia cut off from European
Russia for as much as five years. The icebreaker *Lenin*
led the expeditions, with a Norwegian captain. In
1921 the *Lenin* was accompanied by the *Trotsky*, *Sverdlov*,
Leonid Krassin, *Arcos* and *Vneshtorg*

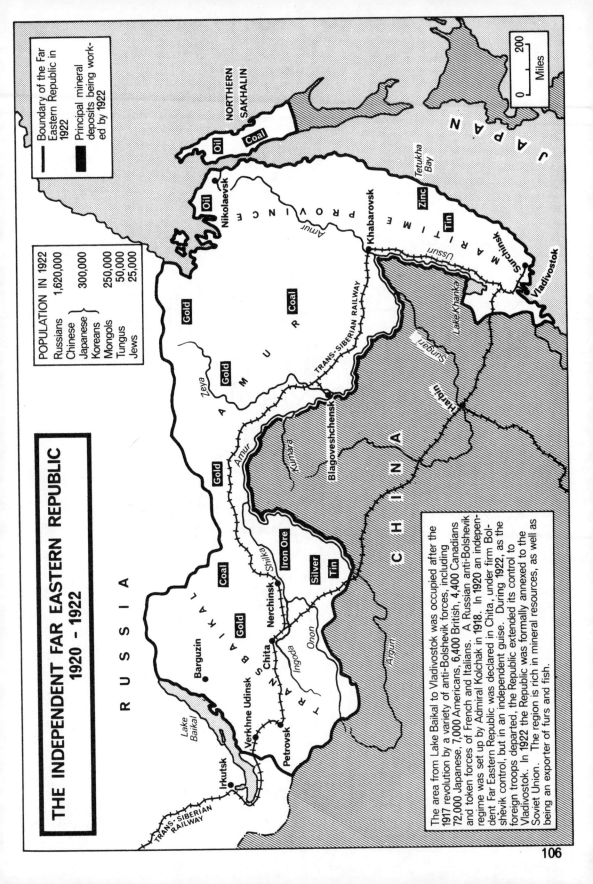

THE INDEPENDENT FAR EASTERN REPUBLIC
1920 – 1922

Boundary of the Far Eastern Republic in 1922

Principal mineral deposits being worked by 1922

POPULATION IN 1922	
Russians	1,620,000
Chinese	300,000
Japanese	
Koreans	250,000
Mongols	50,000
Tungus	25,000
Jews	

200 0 Miles

RUSSIA

Lake Baikal

Irkutsk

TRANS-SIBERIAN RAILWAY

Verkhne Udinsk

Petrovsk

Barguzin

Coal

Gold

BAIKAL

TRANSBAIKAL

Chita

Nerchinsk

Shilka

Ingoda

Onon

Iron Ore

Silver

Tin

Argun

CHINA

Gold

Gold

Zeya

Amur

AMUR

Blagoveshchensk

Kumara

Gold

Coal

TRANS-SIBERIAN RAILWAY

PROVINCE

Khabarovsk

Ussuri

Sungari

Harbin

Lake Khanka

Iman

Vladivostok

Surchinsk

MARITIME PROVINCE

Tin

Zinc

Tetukha Bay

NORTHERN SAKHALIN

Oil

Coal

Oil

Nikolaevsk

Amur

JAPAN

The area from Lake Baikal to Vladivostok was occupied after the 1917 revolution by a variety of anti-Bolshevik forces, including 72,000 Japanese, 7,000 Americans, 6,400 British, 4,400 Canadians and token forces of French and Italians. A Russian anti-Bolshevik regime was set up by Admiral Kolchak in 1918. In 1920 an independent Far Eastern Republic was declared in Chita, under firm Bolshevik control, but in an independent guise. During 1922, as the foreign troops departed, the Republic extended its control to Vladivostok. In 1922 the Republic was formally annexed to the Soviet Union. The region is rich in mineral resources, as well as being an exporter of furs and fish.

106

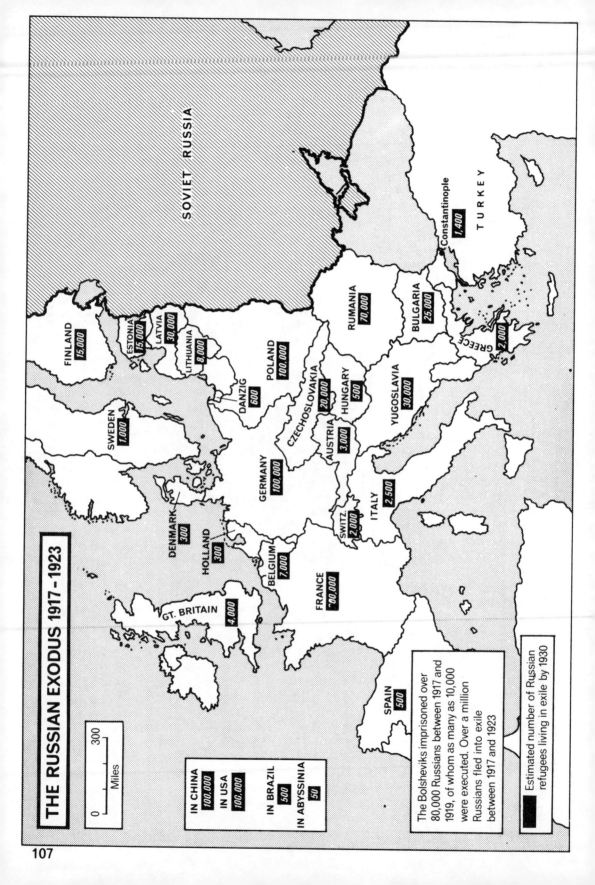

THE RUSSIAN EXODUS 1917 – 1923

Estimated number of Russian refugees living in exile by 1930

The Bolsheviks imprisoned over 80,000 Russians between 1917 and 1919, of whom as many as 10,000 were executed. Over a million Russians fled into exile between 1917 and 1923

IN CHINA *100,000*
IN USA *100,000*
IN BRAZIL *500*
IN ABYSSINIA *50*

Miles 0 300

SOVIET RUSSIA

TURKEY

Constantinople *1,400*

RUMANIA *70,000*
BULGARIA *25,000*
GREECE *2,000*

FINLAND *15,000*
ESTONIA *15,000*
LATVIA *30,000*
LITHUANIA *8,000*
POLAND *100,000*
DANZIG *600*
CZECHOSLOVAKIA *20,000*
HUNGARY *500*
AUSTRIA *3,000*
YUGOSLAVIA *30,000*
SWEDEN *1,000*
GERMANY *100,000*
SWITZ. *2,000*
ITALY *2,500*
DENMARK *300*
HOLLAND *300*
BELGIUM *7,000*
FRANCE *70,000*
GT. BRITAIN *4,000*
SPAIN *500*

107

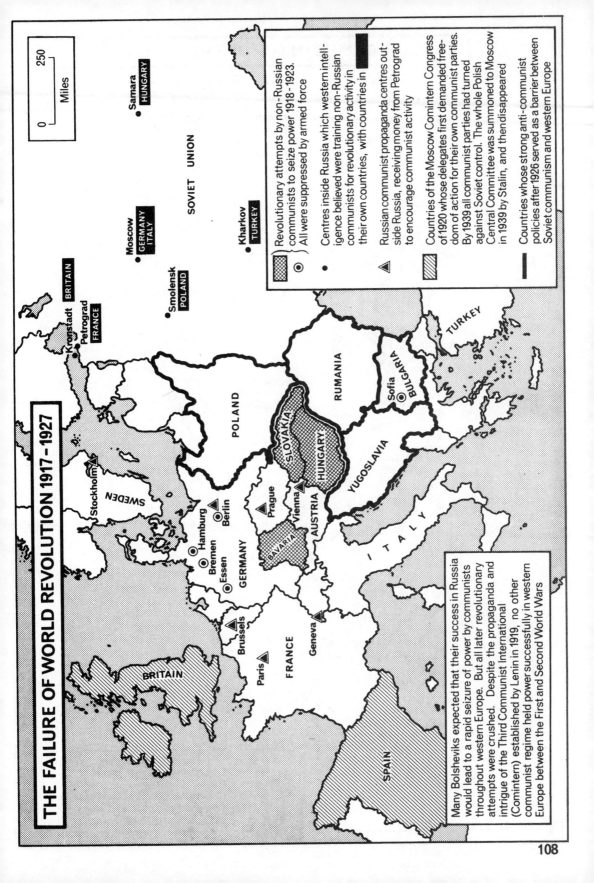

THE FAILURE OF WORLD REVOLUTION 1917-1927

Legend:

- Revolutionary attempts by non-Russian communists to seize power 1918-1923. All were suppressed by armed force

- Centres inside Russia which western intelligence believed were training non-Russian communists for revolutionary activity in their own countries, with countries in

- Russian communist propaganda centres outside Russia, receiving money from Petrograd to encourage communist activity

- Countries of the Moscow Comintern Congress of 1920 whose delegates first demanded freedom of action for their own communist parties. By 1939 all communist parties had turned against Soviet control. The whole Polish Central Committee was summoned to Moscow in 1939 by Stalin, and then disappeared

- Countries whose strong anti-communist policies after 1926 served as a barrier between Soviet communism and western Europe

Many Bolsheviks expected that their success in Russia would lead to a rapid seizure of power by communists throughout western Europe. But all later revolutionary attempts were crushed. Despite the propaganda and intrigue of the Third Communist International (Comintern) established by Lenin in 1919, no other communist regime held power successfully in western Europe between the First and Second World Wars

Scale: 0 — 250 Miles

Places labelled on map:
Samara HUNGARY, Moscow GERMANY ITALY, Kharkov TURKEY, Smolensk POLAND, SOVIET UNION, Kronstadt BRITAIN, Petrograd FRANCE, Stockholm, SWEDEN, Hamburg, Bremen, Essen, Berlin, GERMANY, Prague, Vienna, AUSTRIA, BAVARIA, SLOVAKIA, HUNGARY, POLAND, RUMANIA, Sofia BULGARIA, YUGOSLAVIA, ITALY, Brussels, Paris, FRANCE, Geneva, BRITAIN, SPAIN, TURKEY

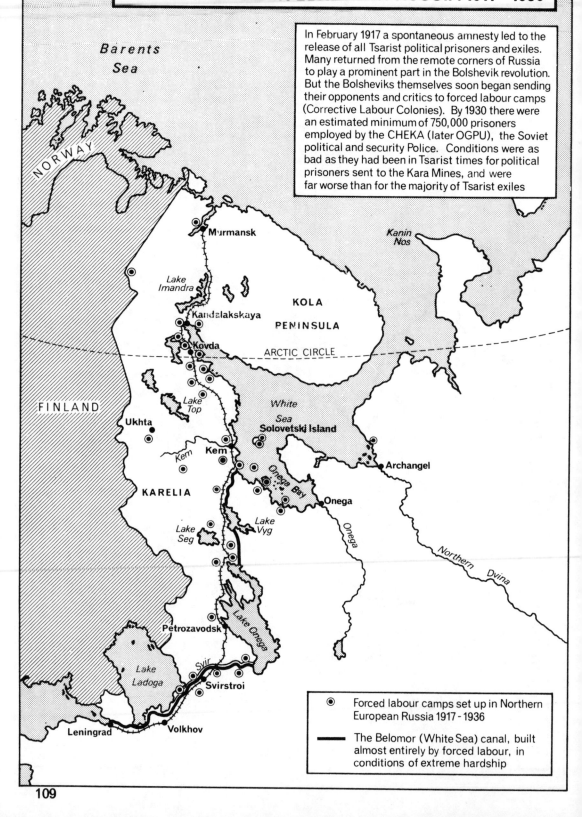

LABOUR CAMPS IN EUROPEAN RUSSIA 1917 - 1936

In February 1917 a spontaneous amnesty led to the release of all Tsarist political prisoners and exiles. Many returned from the remote corners of Russia to play a prominent part in the Bolshevik revolution. But the Bolsheviks themselves soon began sending their opponents and critics to forced labour camps (Corrective Labour Colonies). By 1930 there were an estimated minimum of 750,000 prisoners employed by the CHEKA (later OGPU), the Soviet political and security Police. Conditions were as bad as they had been in Tsarist times for political prisoners sent to the Kara Mines, and were far worse than for the majority of Tsarist exiles

Barents Sea

NORWAY

Kanin Nos

Murmansk

Lake Imandra

KOLA PENINSULA

Kandalakskaya

Kovda

ARCTIC CIRCLE

FINLAND

Lake Top

Ukhta

White Sea

Solovetski Island

Kem Kem

KARELIA

Archangel

Onega Bay

Onega

Lake Vyg

Lake Seg

Onega

Northern Dvina

Petrozavodsk

Lake Onega

Lake Ladoga

Svir

Svirstroi

Leningrad Volkhov

⊙   Forced labour camps set up in Northern European Russia 1917 - 1936

▬▬▬   The Belomor (White Sea) canal, built almost entirely by forced labour, in conditions of extreme hardship

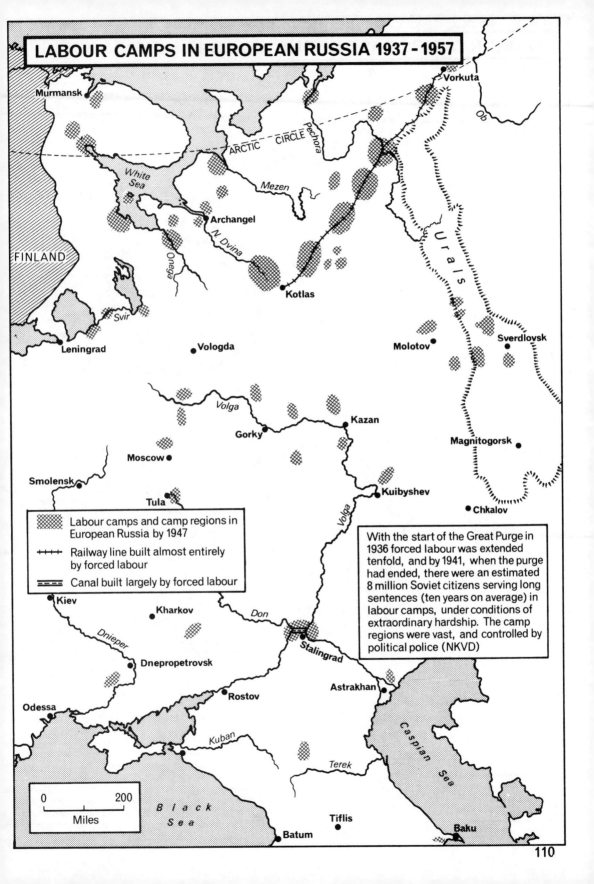

LABOUR CAMPS IN EUROPEAN RUSSIA 1937-1957

Murmansk

ARCTIC CIRCLE

Vorkuta

Ob

White Sea

Pechora

Mezen

Archangel

N. Dvina

FINLAND

Onega

Svir

Kotlas

Urals

Leningrad

Vologda

Molotov

Sverdlovsk

Volga

Kazan

Gorky

Magnitogorsk

Moscow

Smolensk

Kuibyshev

Tula

Chkalov

Labour camps and camp regions in European Russia by 1947

++++ Railway line built almost entirely by forced labour

=== Canal built largely by forced labour

With the start of the Great Purge in 1936 forced labour was extended tenfold, and by 1941, when the purge had ended, there were an estimated 8 million Soviet citizens serving long sentences (ten years on average) in labour camps, under conditions of extraordinary hardship. The camp regions were vast, and controlled by political police (NKVD)

Kiev

Kharkov

Don

Dnieper

Stalingrad

Dnepropetrovsk

Astrakhan

Odessa

Rostov

Caspian Sea

Kuban

Terek

0   200

Miles

Black Sea

Tiflis

Baku

Batum

110

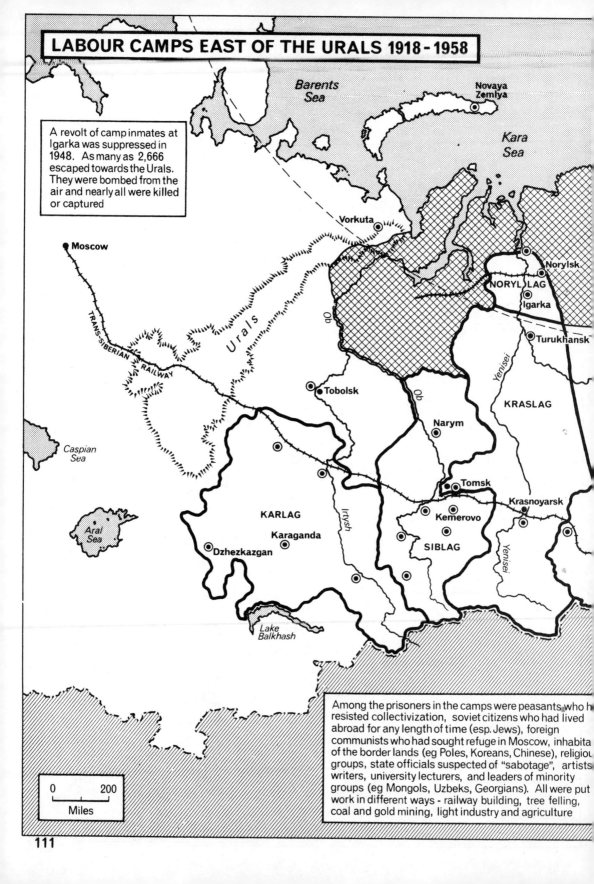

LABOUR CAMPS EAST OF THE URALS 1918-1958

Barents Sea

Novaya Zemlya

Kara Sea

A revolt of camp inmates at Igarka was suppressed in 1948. As many as 2,666 escaped towards the Urals. They were bombed from the air and nearly all were killed or captured

Vorkuta

Norylsk

NORYL LAG

Igarka

● **Moscow**

TRANS-SIBERIAN RAILWAY

Urals

Ob

Turukhansk

Yenisei

KRASLAG

● **Tobolsk**

Ob

Narym

Caspian Sea

Tomsk

Krasnoyarsk

Irtysh

KARLAG

Kemerovo

Karaganda

Aral Sea

● **Dzhezkazgan**

SIBLAG

Yenisei

Lake Balkhash

0	200

Miles

Among the prisoners in the camps were peasants who h resisted collectivization, soviet citizens who had lived abroad for any length of time (esp. Jews), foreign communists who had sought refuge in Moscow, inhabita of the border lands (eg Poles, Koreans, Chinese), religiou groups, state officials suspected of "sabotage", artists writers, university lecturers, and leaders of minority groups (eg Mongols, Uzbeks, Georgians). All were put work in different ways - railway building, tree felling, coal and gold mining, light industry and agriculture

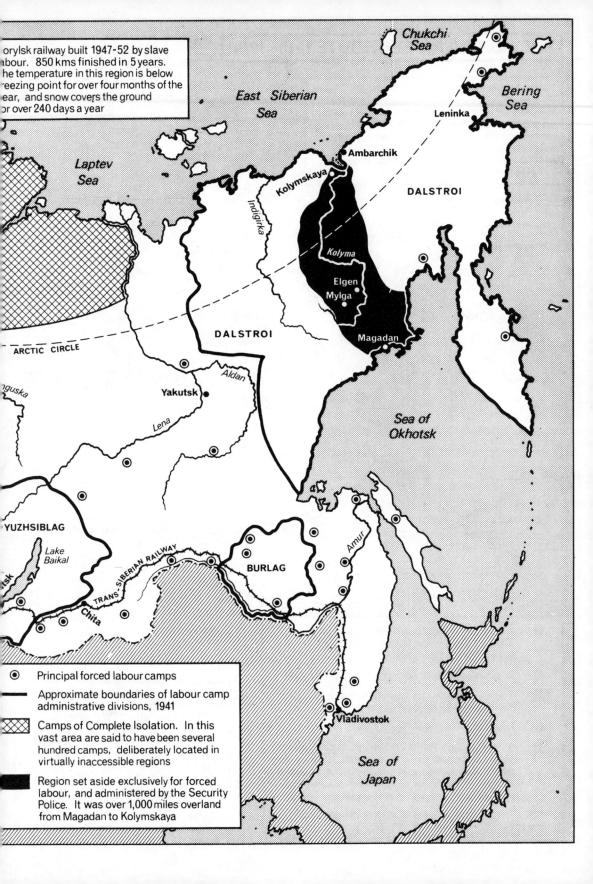

orylsk railway built 1947-52 by slave
abour. 850 kms finished in 5 years.
he temperature in this region is below
reezing point for over four months of the
ear, and snow covers the ground
or over 240 days a year

Chukchi
Sea

East Siberian
Sea

Bering
Sea

Leninka

Laptev
Sea

Kolymskaya

Ambarchik

DALSTROI

Indigirka

Kolyma

Elgen
Mylga

ARCTIC CIRCLE

DALSTROI

Magadan

Aldan

Yakutsk

Sea of
Okhotsk

Lena

nguska

YUZHSIBLAG

Lake
Baikal

Amur

TRANS SIBERIAN RAILWAY

BURLAG

sk

Chita

Vladivostok

Sea of
Japan

⊙ Principal forced labour camps

─ Approximate boundaries of labour camp
   administrative divisions, 1941

▨ Camps of Complete Isolation. In this
   vast area are said to have been several
   hundred camps, deliberately located in
   virtually inaccessible regions

■ Region set aside exclusively for forced
   labour, and administered by the Security
   Police. It was over 1,000 miles overland
   from Magadan to Kolymskaya

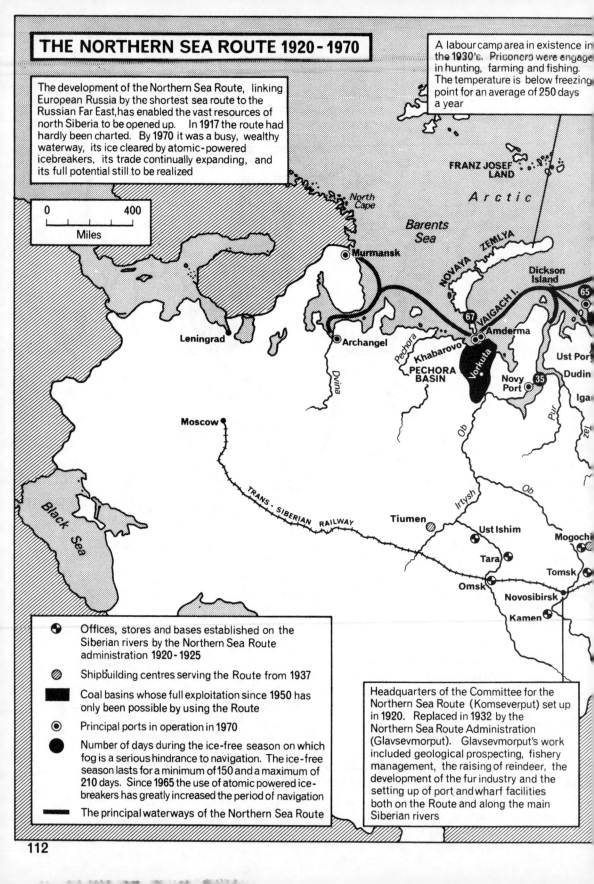

THE NORTHERN SEA ROUTE 1920 - 1970

The development of the Northern Sea Route, linking European Russia by the shortest sea route to the Russian Far East, has enabled the vast resources of north Siberia to be opened up. In 1917 the route had hardly been charted. By 1970 it was a busy, wealthy waterway, its ice cleared by atomic-powered icebreakers, its trade continually expanding, and its full potential still to be realized

A labour camp area in existence in the 1930's. Prisoners were engaged in hunting, farming and fishing. The temperature is below freezing point for an average of 250 days a year

FRANZ JOSEF LAND

Arctic

Barents Sea

North Cape

NOVAYA ZEMLYA

Murmansk

Dickson Island

65

67 VAIGACH I.

Amderma

Leningrad

Archangel

Pechora

Khabarovo

Ust Port

PECHORA BASIN

Vorkuta

Dudin

Novy Port

35

Iga

Moscow

Ob

Pur

Taz

TRANS - SIBERIAN RAILWAY

Irtysh

Ob

Tiumen

Black Sea

Ust Ishim

Mogochi

Tara

Tomsk

Omsk

Novosibirsk

Kamen

0   400

Miles

Offices, stores and bases established on the Siberian rivers by the Northern Sea Route administration 1920 - 1925

Shipbuilding centres serving the Route from 1937

Coal basins whose full exploitation since 1950 has only been possible by using the Route

Principal ports in operation in 1970

Number of days during the ice-free season on which fog is a serious hindrance to navigation. The ice-free season lasts for a minimum of 150 and a maximum of 210 days. Since 1965 the use of atomic powered ice-breakers has greatly increased the period of navigation

The principal waterways of the Northern Sea Route

Headquarters of the Committee for the Northern Sea Route (Komseverput) set up in 1920. Replaced in 1932 by the Northern Sea Route Administration (Glavsevmorput). Glavsevmorput's work included geological prospecting, fishery management, the raising of reindeer, the development of the fur industry and the setting up of port and wharf facilities both on the Route and along the main Siberian rivers

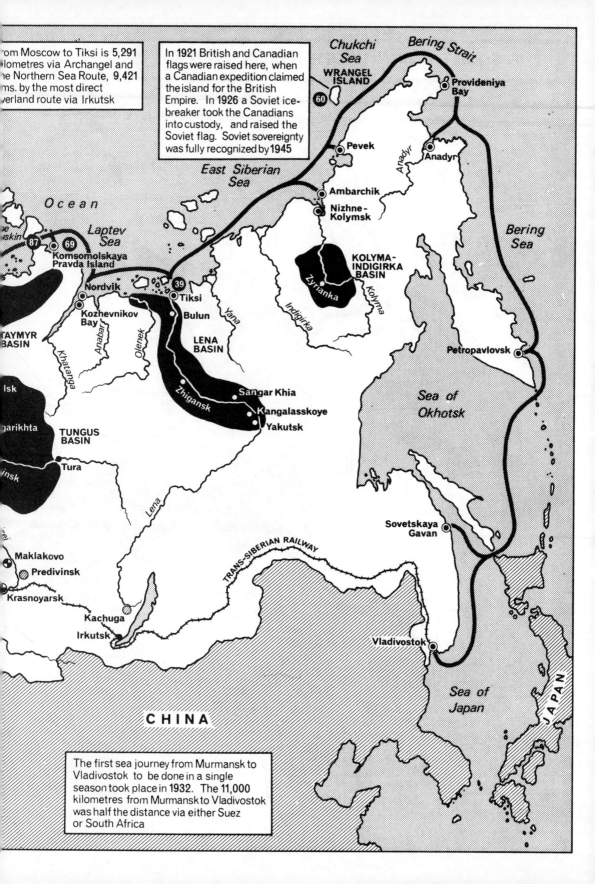

From Moscow to Tiksi is 5,291 kilometres via Archangel and the Northern Sea Route, 9,421 kms. by the most direct overland route via Irkutsk

In 1921 British and Canadian flags were raised here, when a Canadian expedition claimed the island for the British Empire. In 1926 a Soviet ice-breaker took the Canadians into custody, and raised the Soviet flag. Soviet sovereignty was fully recognized by 1945

Chukchi Sea

Bering Strait

WRANGEL ISLAND

60

Provideniya Bay

East Siberian Sea

Pevek

Anadyr

Anadyr

Bering Sea

Ocean

skin

Laptev Sea

Ambarchik

Nizhne-Kolymsk

87

69

Komsomolskaya Pravda Island

KOLYMA-INDIGIRKA BASIN

Zyrianka

Kolyma

Nordvik

39

Tiksi

Indigirka

Kozhevnikov Bay

TAYMYR BASIN

Anabar

Olenek

Yana

Bulun

LENA BASIN

Petropavlovsk

Khatanga

Isk

Zhigansk

Sangar Khia

Kangalasskoye

Sea of Okhotsk

garikhta

TUNGUS BASIN

Yakutsk

Tura

Lena

insk

Sovetskaya Gavan

Maklakovo

Predivinsk

TRANS-SIBERIAN RAILWAY

Krasnoyarsk

Kachuga

Irkutsk

Vladivostok

CHINA

Sea of Japan

JAPAN

The first sea journey from Murmansk to Vladivostok to be done in a single season took place in 1932. The 11,000 kilometres from Murmansk to Vladivostok was half the distance via either Suez or South Africa

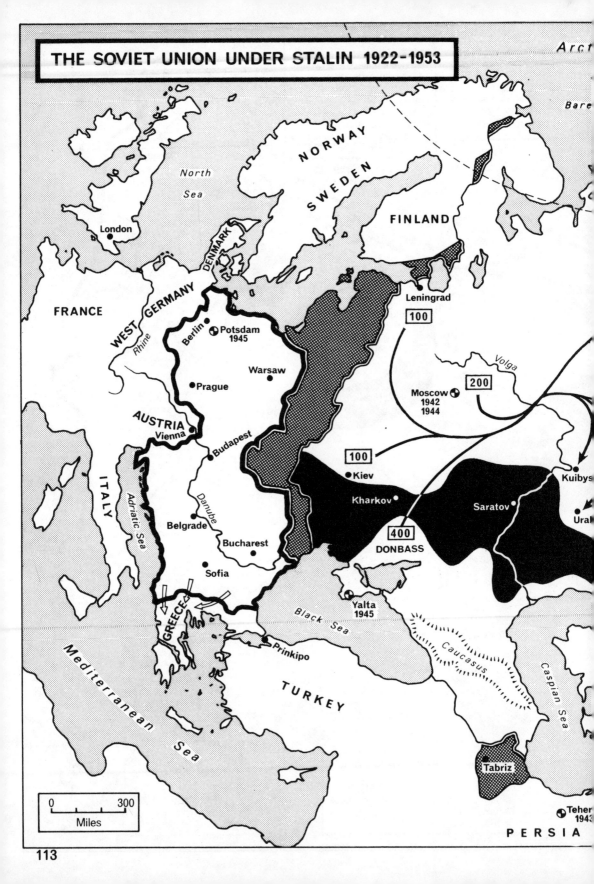

THE SOVIET UNION UNDER STALIN 1922-1953

Arct

Bare

North Sea

NORWAY

SWEDEN

FINLAND

London

DENMARK

Leningrad

100

FRANCE

WEST GERMANY

Rhine

Berlin

Potsdam 1945

Warsaw

Prague

Volga

Moscow 1942 1944

200

AUSTRIA

Vienna

Budapest

100

Kiev

Kharkov

Saratov

Kuibys

Danube

ITALY

Adriatic Sea

Belgrade

Bucharest

400

DONBASS

Ural

Sofia

GREECE

Yalta 1945

Black Sea

Prinkipo

Caucasus

Caspian Sea

Mediterranean Sea

TURKEY

Tabriz

Teher 1943

0   300

Miles

PERSIA

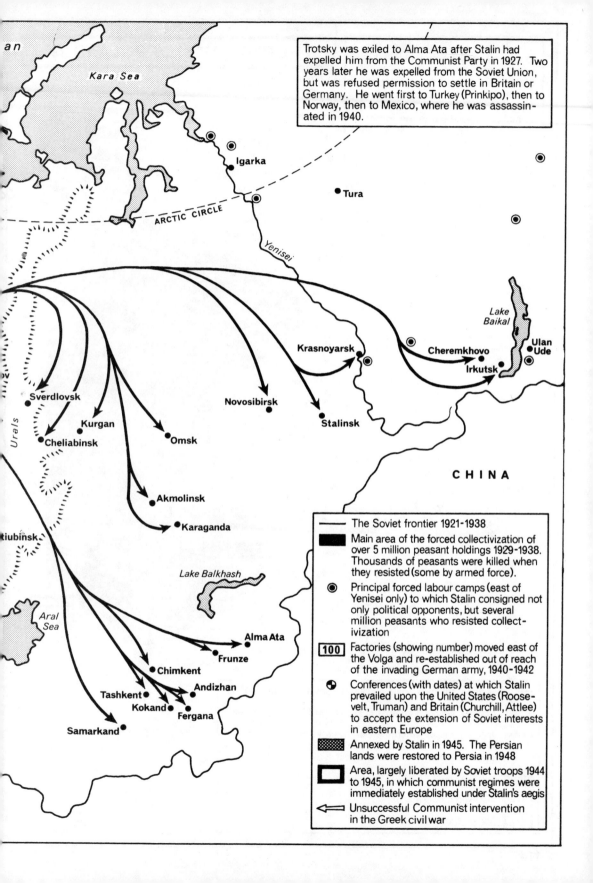

Trotsky was exiled to Alma Ata after Stalin had expelled him from the Communist Party in 1927. Two years later he was expelled from the Soviet Union, but was refused permission to settle in Britain or Germany. He went first to Turkey (Prinkipo), then to Norway, then to Mexico, where he was assassinated in 1940.

Kara Sea

Igarka

ARCTIC CIRCLE

Yenisei

• Tura

Lake Baikal

Krasnoyarsk   Cheremkhovo   Ulan Ude

Irkutsk

• Sverdlovsk

Novosibirsk

• Kurgan

• Cheliabinsk   • Omsk   • Stalinsk

Urals

• Akmolinsk

• Karaganda

C H I N A

Kiubinsk

Lake Balkhash

Aral Sea

Alma Ata

Frunze

• Chimkent

Andizhan

Tashkent •   Kokand •   Fergana

Samarkand •

— The Soviet frontier 1921-1938

■ Main area of the forced collectivization of over 5 million peasant holdings 1929-1938. Thousands of peasants were killed when they resisted (some by armed force).

◉ Principal forced labour camps (east of Yenisei only) to which Stalin consigned not only political opponents, but several million peasants who resisted collectivization

[100] Factories (showing number) moved east of the Volga and re-established out of reach of the invading German army, 1940-1942

⊕ Conferences (with dates) at which Stalin prevailed upon the United States (Roosevelt, Truman) and Britain (Churchill, Attlee) to accept the extension of Soviet interests in eastern Europe

▨ Annexed by Stalin in 1945. The Persian lands were restored to Persia in 1948

▭ Area, largely liberated by Soviet troops 1944 to 1945, in which communist regimes were immediately established under Stalin's aegis

⇐ Unsuccessful Communist intervention in the Greek civil war

THE PARTITION OF POLAND 1939

The destruction of Poland was principally a German action. 1,700,000 German troops soon defeated the 600,000 Polish soldiers. German air attack destroyed the centres of the main Polish cities. The Poles hoped to make a final stand in the Pripet marsh area, but the Russian advance destroyed all chance of further Polish resistance

Baltic   Sea

Königsberg

EAST

PRUSSIA

LITHUANIA

Vilna

Suvalki

Augustov

Grodno

Lomza

Bialystok

Minsk

RUSSIA

Posnan

Warsaw

Brest-
Litovsk

Pinsk

Pripet

Marshes

Lodz

P   O   L   A   N   D

Lublin

Lutsk

Rovno

SOVIET

Sokal

GERMANY

Tarnov

Yaroslav

Lvov

Cracow

Tarnopol

Przemysl

Stanislavov

Kamenets
Podolsk

SLOVAKIA

HUNGARY

RUMANIA

⟹ German advance against Poland from 3 September 1939

⟸ Russian advance against Poland from 17 September 1939

▬ Dividing line between the German and Russian zones
of occupation,   agreed upon in advance by the
Russo-German Pact of 23 August 1939

■ Annexed by the Soviet Union in October 1939

▨ Annexed by Germany

▧ Annexed by Lithuania

0		100

Miles

114

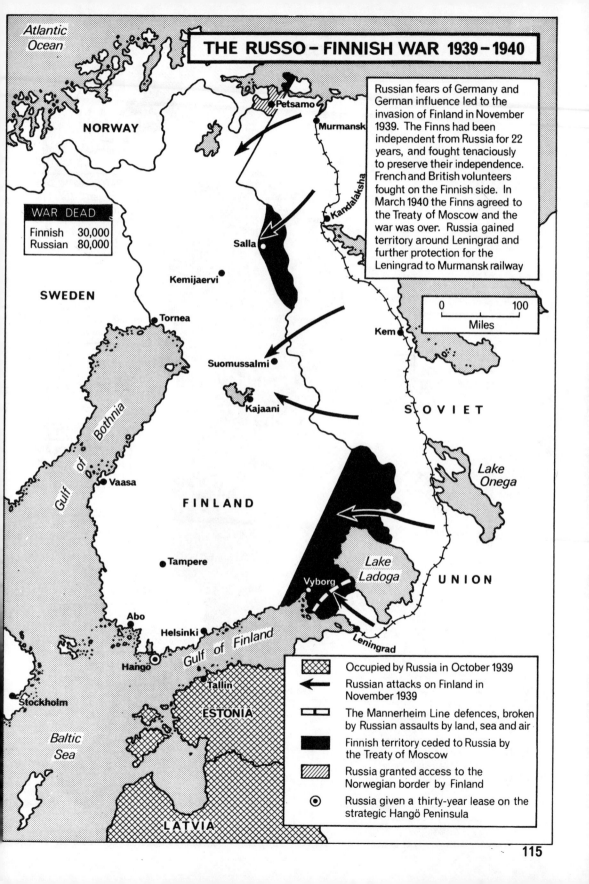

THE RUSSO – FINNISH WAR 1939 – 1940

Atlantic
Ocean

NORWAY

Russian fears of Germany and German influence led to the invasion of Finland in November 1939. The Finns had been independent from Russia for 22 years, and fought tenaciously to preserve their independence. French and British volunteers fought on the Finnish side. In March 1940 the Finns agreed to the Treaty of Moscow and the war was over. Russia gained territory around Leningrad and further protection for the Leningrad to Murmansk railway

Petsamo
Murmansk
Kandalaksha

WAR DEAD
Finnish 30,000
Russian 80,000

Salla

Kemijaervi

SWEDEN

Tornea

0   100
Miles

Kem

Suomussalmi

S O V I E T

Kajaani

Gulf of Bothnia

Vaasa

FINLAND

Lake
Onega

Tampere

Lake
Ladoga

U N I O N

Vyborg

Abo

Helsinki

Gulf of Finland

Leningrad

Hango

Stockholm

Tallin

Baltic
Sea

ESTONIA

⬩⬩⬩⬩ Occupied by Russia in October 1939

◄── Russian attacks on Finland in November 1939

▭▭ The Mannerheim Line defences, broken by Russian assaults by land, sea and air

■ Finnish territory ceded to Russia by the Treaty of Moscow

▨ Russia granted access to the Norwegian border by Finland

⊙ Russia given a thirty-year lease on the strategic Hangö Peninsula

LATVIA

115

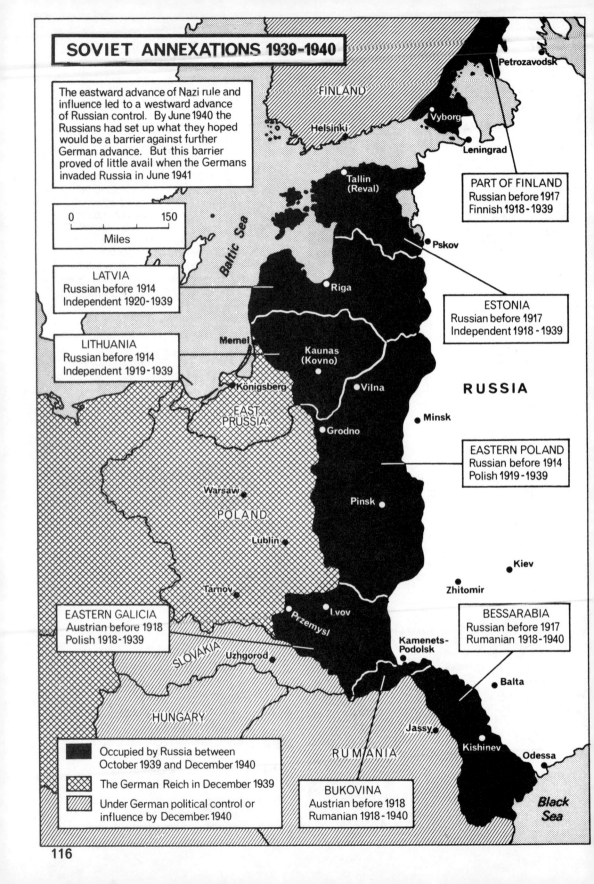

SOVIET ANNEXATIONS 1939-1940

The eastward advance of Nazi rule and influence led to a westward advance of Russian control. By June 1940 the Russians had set up what they hoped would be a barrier against further German advance. But this barrier proved of little avail when the Germans invaded Russia in June 1941

0 — 150
Miles

FINLAND

Petrozavodsk

Vyborg

Helsinki

Leningrad

Tallin (Reval)

PART OF FINLAND
Russian before 1917
Finnish 1918-1939

Pskov

Baltic Sea

LATVIA
Russian before 1914
Independent 1920-1939

Riga

ESTONIA
Russian before 1917
Independent 1918-1939

LITHUANIA
Russian before 1914
Independent 1919-1939

Memel

Kaunas (Kovno)

RUSSIA

Königsberg

EAST PRUSSIA

Vilna

Minsk

Grodno

EASTERN POLAND
Russian before 1914
Polish 1919-1939

Warsaw

POLAND

Pinsk

Lublin

Kiev

Zhitomir

Tarnov

Przemysl

Lvov

EASTERN GALICIA
Austrian before 1918
Polish 1918-1939

Kamenets-Podolsk

BESSARABIA
Russian before 1917
Rumanian 1918-1940

SLOVAKIA

Uzhgorod

Balta

HUNGARY

Jassy

RUMANIA

Kishinev

Odessa

Black Sea

Legend:

- ■ Occupied by Russia between October 1939 and December 1940
- ▨ The German Reich in December 1939
- ▨ Under German political control or influence by December 1940

BUKOVINA
Austrian before 1918
Rumanian 1918-1940

EUROPE ON 22 JUNE 1941

Archangel

NORWAY

SWEDEN

FINLAND

Hango

Leningrad

BRITAIN

EIRE

DENMARK

Riga

Kovno

Moscow

Vilna

HOLLAND

London

Danzig

SOVIET UNION

Berlin

Cologne

GREATER GERMANY

Warsaw

Brest-Litovsk

BELGIUM

Prague

Cracow

Lvov

FRANCE

Munich

Vienna

SLOVAKIA

Kishinev

SWITZ.

HUNGARY

Odessa

RUMANIA

SPAIN

YUGOSLAVIA

BULGARIA

ITALY

ALBANIA

GREECE

TURKEY

The German Reich on 22 June 1941, the day of the German invasion of Russia

Countries under German rule or influence by June 1941

Neutral countries

Great Britain, the only state at war with Germany on 21 June 1941; and the Soviet Union, to whom Britain immediately offered all possible help and alliance in the fight against Nazism

0   300

Miles

117

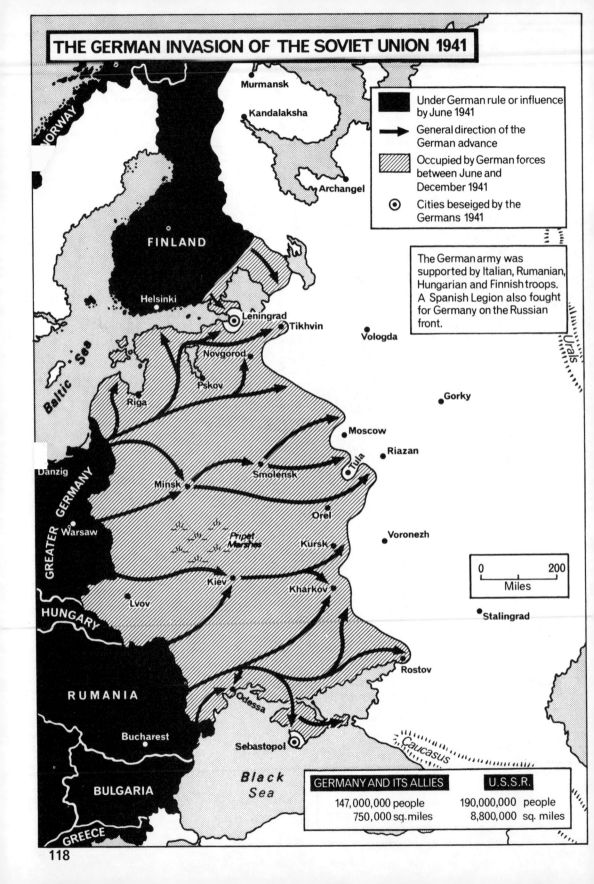

THE GERMAN INVASION OF THE SOVIET UNION 1941

Under German rule or influence by June 1941

→ General direction of the German advance

Occupied by German forces between June and December 1941

⊙ Cities beseiged by the Germans 1941

The German army was supported by Italian, Rumanian, Hungarian and Finnish troops. A Spanish Legion also fought for Germany on the Russian front.

NORWAY

Murmansk

Kandalaksha

Archangel

FINLAND

Helsinki

Leningrad Tikhvin

Vologda

Urals

Baltic Sea

Novgorod

Pskov

Riga

Gorky

Danzig

Moscow

Riazan

GREATER GERMANY

Warsaw

Minsk

Smolensk

Tula

Orel

Voronezh

Pripet Marshes

Kursk

0   200
Miles

Kiev

Kharkov

HUNGARY

Lvov

Stalingrad

RUMANIA

Rostov

Odessa

Caucasus

Bucharest

Sebastopol

BULGARIA

Black Sea

GREECE

GERMANY AND ITS ALLIES	U.S.S.R.
147,000,000 people	190,000,000 people
750,000 sq. miles	8,800,000 sq. miles

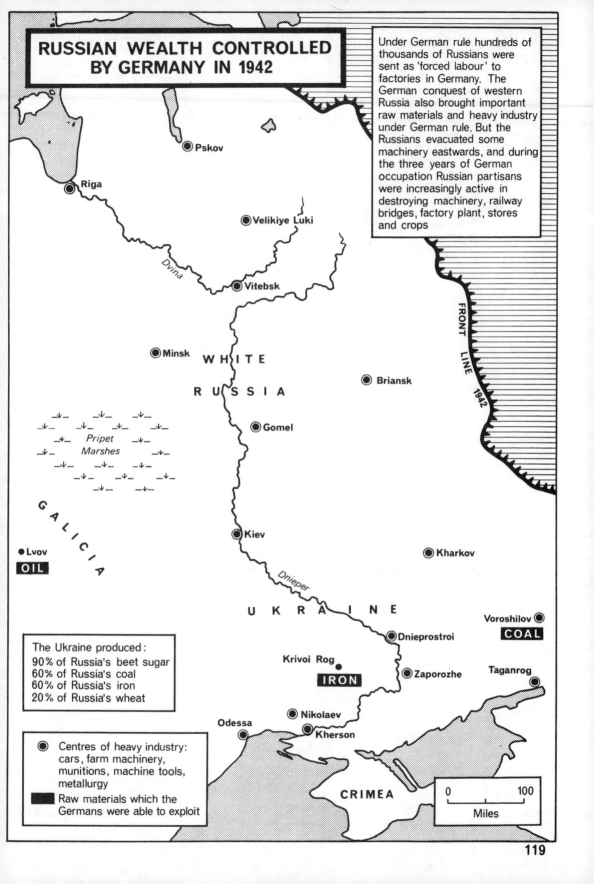

RUSSIAN WEALTH CONTROLLED BY GERMANY IN 1942

Under German rule hundreds of thousands of Russians were sent as 'forced labour' to factories in Germany. The German conquest of western Russia also brought important raw materials and heavy industry under German rule. But the Russians evacuated some machinery eastwards, and during the three years of German occupation Russian partisans were increasingly active in destroying machinery, railway bridges, factory plant, stores and crops

Pskov

Riga

Velikiye Luki

Dvina

Vitebsk

Minsk

W H I T E

R U S S I A

Briansk

FRONT LINE 1942

Gomel

Pripet Marshes

G A L I C I A

Kiev

•Lvov

OIL

Kharkov

Dnieper

U K R A I N E

Voroshilov

COAL

Dnieprostroi

Krivoi Rog

IRON

Zaporozhe

Taganrog

The Ukraine produced:
90% of Russia's beet sugar
60% of Russia's coal
60% of Russia's iron
20% of Russia's wheat

Nikolaev

Odessa

Kherson

⊙ Centres of heavy industry: cars, farm machinery, munitions, machine tools, metallurgy

▬ Raw materials which the Germans were able to exploit

CRIMEA

0   100

Miles

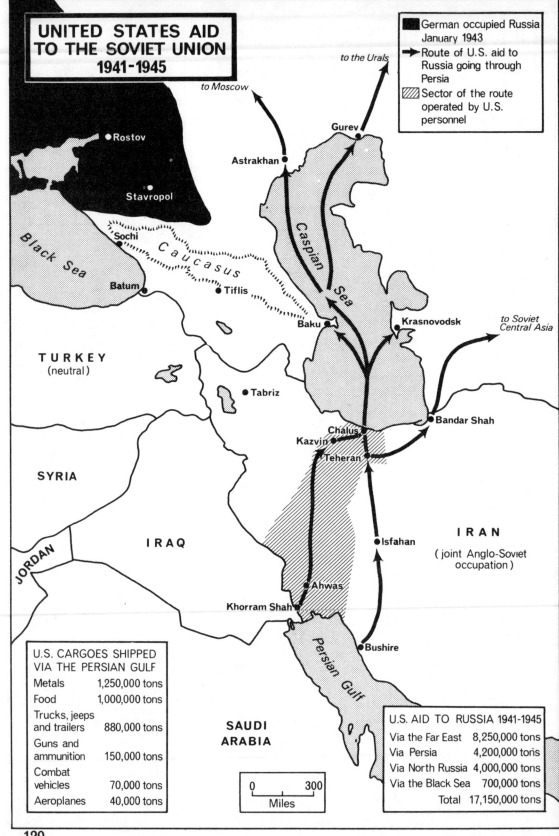

UNITED STATES AID TO THE SOVIET UNION 1941-1945

Legend:
- German occupied Russia January 1943
- Route of U.S. aid to Russia going through Persia
- Sector of the route operated by U.S. personnel

to Moscow

to the Urals

Gurev

Astrakhan

Rostov

Stavropol

Sochi

Caucasus

Black Sea

Batum

Tiflis

Baku

Caspian Sea

Krasnovodsk

to Soviet Central Asia

TURKEY (neutral)

Tabriz

Chalus

Kazvin

Teheran

Bandar Shah

SYRIA

JORDAN

IRAQ

Isfahan

IRAN (joint Anglo-Soviet occupation)

Ahwas

Khorram Shah

Bushire

Persian Gulf

SAUDI ARABIA

0   300
Miles

U.S. CARGOES SHIPPED VIA THE PERSIAN GULF

Metals	1,250,000 tons
Food	1,000,000 tons
Trucks, jeeps and trailers	880,000 tons
Guns and ammunition	150,000 tons
Combat vehicles	70,000 tons
Aeroplanes	40,000 tons

U.S. AID TO RUSSIA 1941-1945

Via the Far East	8,250,000 tons
Via Persia	4,200,000 tons
Via North Russia	4,000,000 tons
Via the Black Sea	700,000 tons
Total	17,150,000 tons

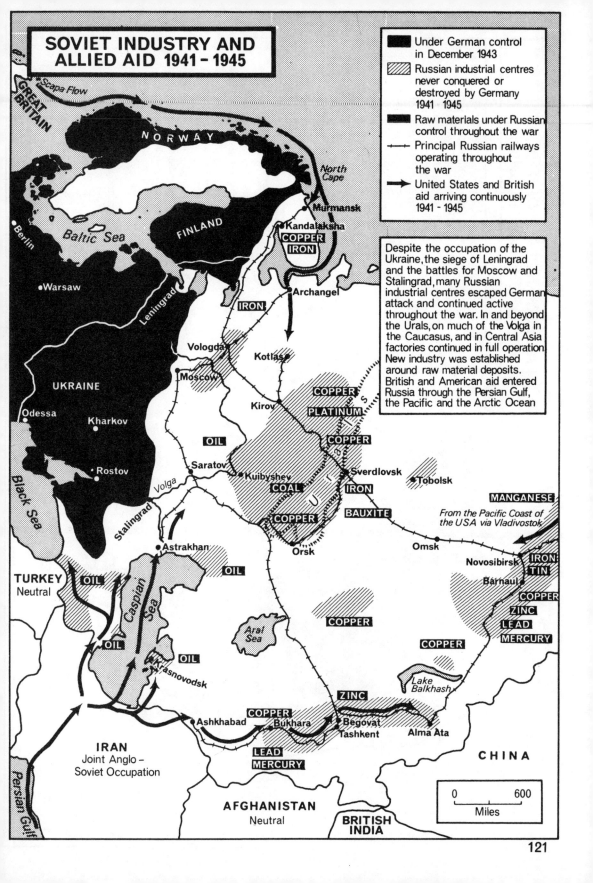

SOVIET INDUSTRY AND ALLIED AID 1941 – 1945

Legend:
- ■ Under German control in December 1943
- ▨ Russian industrial centres never conquered or destroyed by Germany 1941 – 1945
- ■ Raw materials under Russian control throughout the war
- ┼┼┼ Principal Russian railways operating throughout the war
- ➜ United States and British aid arriving continuously 1941 – 1945

Despite the occupation of the Ukraine, the siege of Leningrad and the battles for Moscow and Stalingrad, many Russian industrial centres escaped German attack and continued active throughout the war. In and beyond the Urals, on much of the Volga in the Caucasus, and in Central Asia factories continued in full operation. New industry was established around raw material deposits. British and American aid entered Russia through the Persian Gulf, the Pacific and the Arctic Ocean

GREAT BRITAIN

Scapa Flow

NORWAY

North Cape

Baltic Sea

FINLAND

•Berlin

•Warsaw

Leningrad

Murmansk

Kandalaksha
COPPER
IRON

Archangel

IRON

Vologda

Kotlas

•Moscow

UKRAINE

•Odessa

Kharkov

Kirov

COPPER
PLATINUM

COPPER

•Rostov

OIL

Saratov

Kuibyshev

COAL

COPPER

Sverdlovsk

IRON

•Tobolsk

MANGANESE

From the Pacific Coast of the USA via Vladivostok

Black Sea

Volga

Stalingrad

Orsk

BAUXITE

Omsk

Novosibirsk

IRON
TIN

•Astrakhan

OIL

TURKEY
Neutral

OIL

Caspian Sea

OIL

Aral Sea

COPPER

Barnaul

COPPER
ZINC
LEAD
MERCURY

OIL

Krasnovodsk

OIL

COPPER

Lake Balkhash

ZINC

COPPER
Bukhara

Begovat

•Ashkhabad

Tashkent

Alma Ata

IRAN
Joint Anglo –
Soviet Occupation

LEAD
MERCURY

CHINA

Persian Gulf

AFGHANISTAN
Neutral

BRITISH INDIA

0   600
Miles

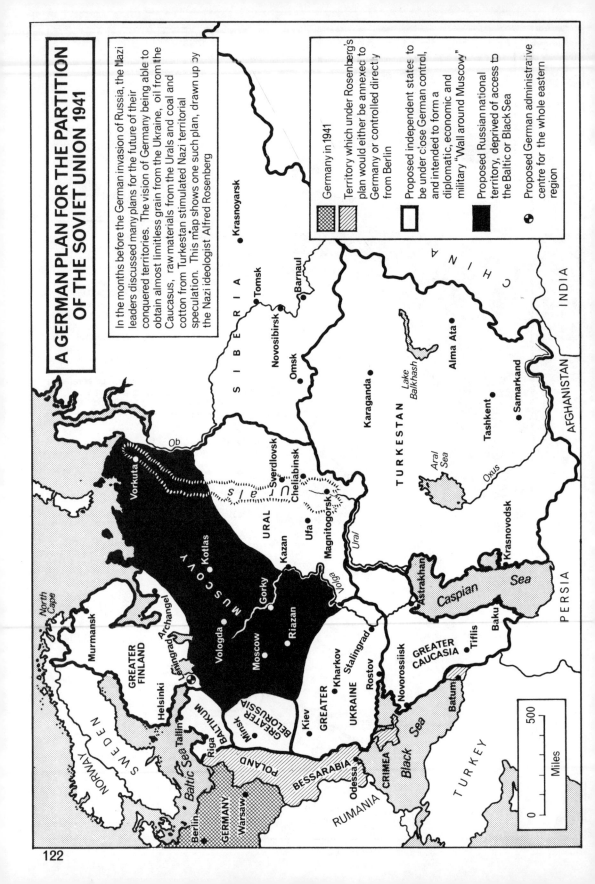

A GERMAN PLAN FOR THE PARTITION OF THE SOVIET UNION 1941

In the months before the German invasion of Russia, the Nazi leaders discussed many plans for the future of their conquered territories. The vision of Germany being able to obtain almost limitless grain from the Ukraine, oil from the Caucasus, raw materials from the Urals and coal and cotton from Turkestan stimulated Nazi territorial speculation. This map shows one such plan, drawn up by the Nazi ideologist Alfred Rosenberg

Germany in 1941

Territory which under Rosenberg's plan would either be annexed to Germany or controlled directly from Berlin

Proposed independent states to be under close German control, and intended to form a diplomatic, economic and military "Wall around Muscovy"

Proposed Russian national territory, deprived of access to the Baltic or Black Sea

Proposed German administrative centre for the whole eastern region

NORWAY

SWEDEN

North Cape

Murmansk

GREATER FINLAND

Helsinki

Archangel

Leningrad

Baltic Sea

BALTIKUM

Tallinn

Riga

GREATER BELORUSSIA

Minsk

GERMANY

Berlin

Warsaw

POLAND

RUMANIA

BESSARABIA

Odessa

CRIMEA

GREATER UKRAINE

Kiev

Kharkov

Black Sea

TURKEY

Rostov

Stalingrad

Novorossiisk

Batumi

GREATER CAUCASIA

Tiflis

Batum

Baku

Caspian Sea

Astrakhan

Krasnovodsk

PERSIA

Vorkuta

Ob

Urals

URAL

Sverdlovsk

Chelliabinsk

Kotlas

Vologda

MUSCOVY

Gorky

Moscow

Riazan

Kazan

Ufa

Magnitogorsk

Volga

Ural

Aral Sea

Oxus

TURKESTAN

Karaganda

Lake Balkhash

Alma Ata

Tashkent

Samarkand

AFGHANISTAN

INDIA

CHINA

SIBERIA

Omsk

Novosibirsk

Barnaul

Tomsk

Krasnoyarsk

Miles

0   500

122

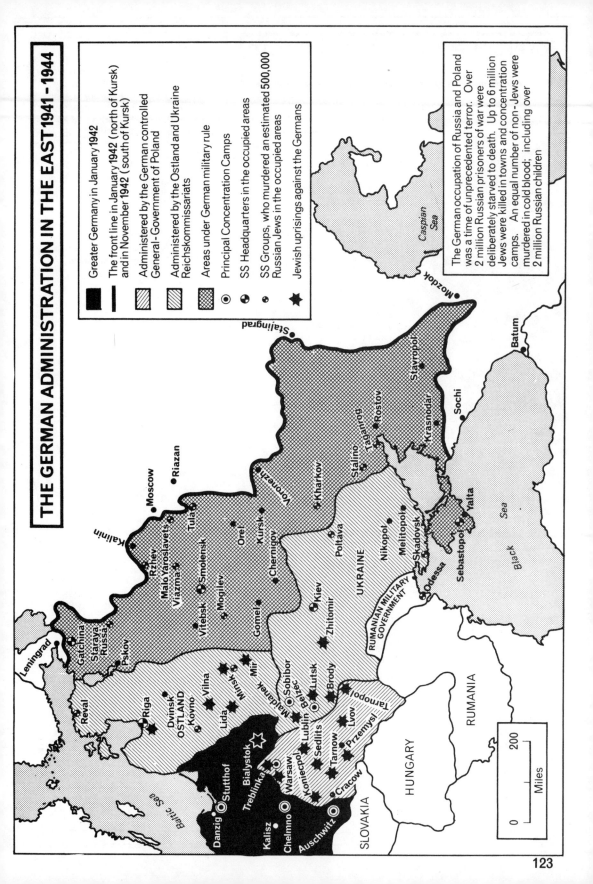

THE GERMAN ADMINISTRATION IN THE EAST 1941 – 1944

Greater Germany in January 1942

The front line in January 1942 (north of Kursk) and in November 1942 (south of Kursk)

Administered by the German controlled General-Government of Poland

Administered by the Ostland and Ukraine Reichskommissariats

Areas under German military rule

Principal Concentration Camps

SS Headquarters in the occupied areas

SS Groups, who murdered an estimated 500,000 Russian Jews in the occupied areas

Jewish uprisings against the Germans

The German occupation of Russia and Poland was a time of unprecedented terror. Over 2 million Russian prisoners of war were deliberately starved to death. Up to 6 million Jews were killed in towns and concentration camps. An equal number of non-Jews were murdered in cold blood; including over 2 million Russian children

123

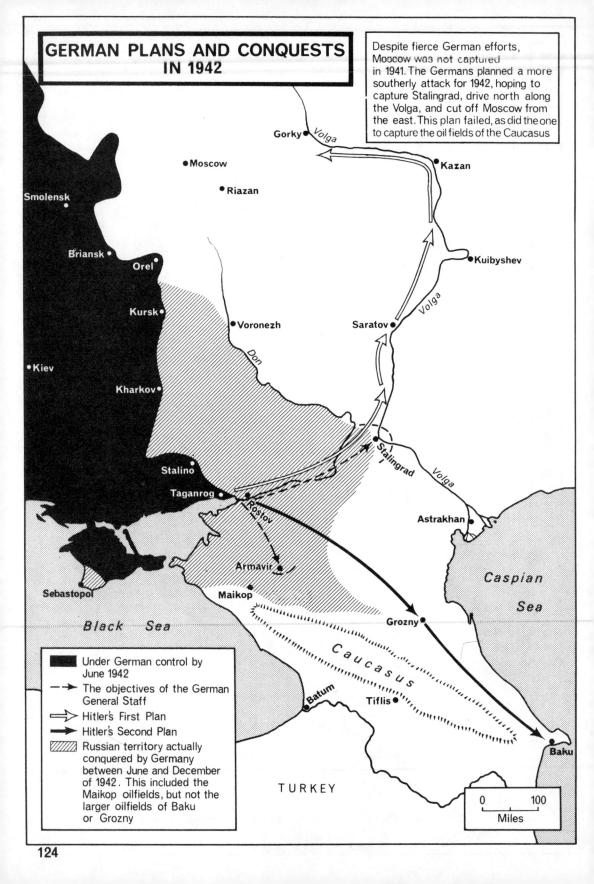

GERMAN PLANS AND CONQUESTS IN 1942

Despite fierce German efforts, Moscow was not captured in 1941. The Germans planned a more southerly attack for 1942, hoping to capture Stalingrad, drive north along the Volga, and cut off Moscow from the east. This plan failed, as did the one to capture the oil fields of the Caucasus

Smolensk

Gorky

Volga

Kazan

Moscow

Riazan

Kuibyshev

Brⁱansk

Orel

Kursk

Voronezh

Volga

Saratov

Don

Kiev

Kharkov

Stalingrad

Volga

Stalino

Astrakhan

Taganrog

Rostov

Caspian Sea

Armavir

Maikop

Sebastopol

Grozny

Black Sea

Caucasus

Batum

Tiflis

Baku

TURKEY

■	Under German control by June 1942
– ➤	The objectives of the German General Staff
▷	Hitler's First Plan
➤	Hitler's Second Plan
▨	Russian territory actually conquered by Germany between June and December of 1942. This included the Maikop oilfields, but not the larger oilfields of Baku or Grozny

```
0        100
      Miles
```

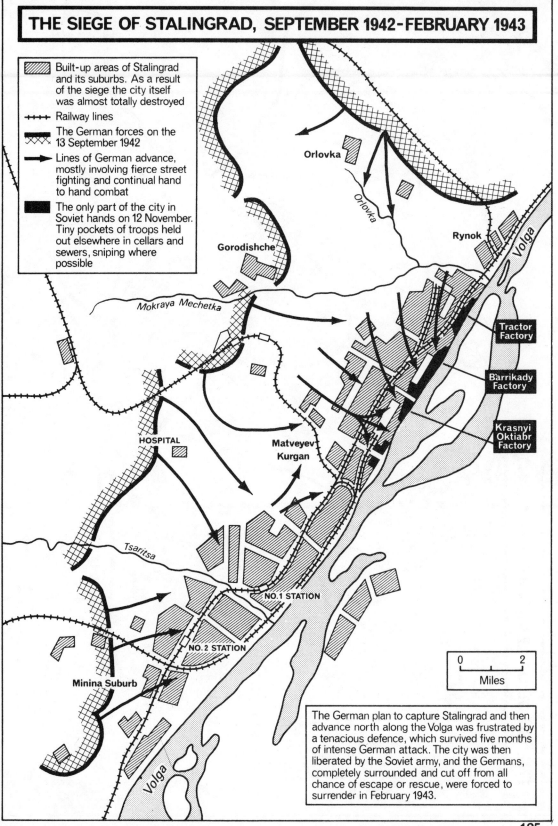

THE SIEGE OF STALINGRAD, SEPTEMBER 1942–FEBRUARY 1943

Built-up areas of Stalingrad and its suburbs. As a result of the siege the city itself was almost totally destroyed

Railway lines

The German forces on the 13 September 1942

Lines of German advance, mostly involving fierce street fighting and continual hand to hand combat

The only part of the city in Soviet hands on 12 November. Tiny pockets of troops held out elsewhere in cellars and sewers, sniping where possible

Orlovka

Orlovka

Rynok

Volga

Gorodishche

Mokraya Mechetka

Tractor Factory

Barrikady Factory

Krasnyi Oktiabr Factory

HOSPITAL

Matveyev Kurgan

Tsaritsa

NO.1 STATION

NO.2 STATION

0   2
Miles

Minina Suburb

Volga

The German plan to capture Stalingrad and then advance north along the Volga was frustrated by a tenacious defence, which survived five months of intense German attack. The city was then liberated by the Soviet army, and the Germans, completely surrounded and cut off from all chance of escape or rescue, were forced to surrender in February 1943.

125

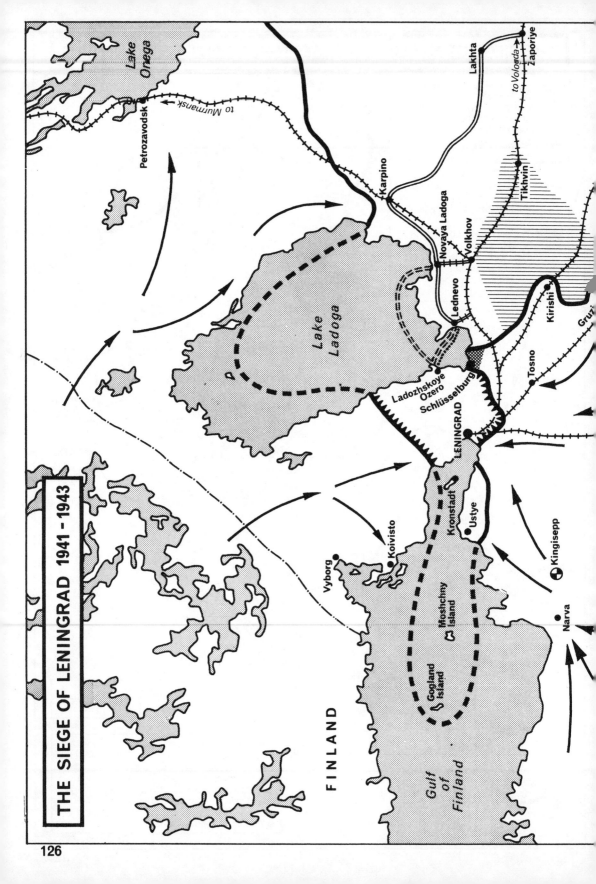

THE SIEGE OF LENINGRAD 1941 – 1943

Lake Onega

Petrozavodsk

to Murmansk

Karpino

Novaya Ladoga

Lakhta

Zaporiye

to Vologda

Tikhvin

Volkhov

Lednevo

Kirishi

Gruz

Lake Ladoga

Ladozhskoye Ozero

Schlüsselburg

LENINGRAD

Tosno

FINLAND

Vyborg

Koivisto

Kronstadt

Ustye

Kingisepp

Moshchny Island

Gogland Island

Narva

Gulf of Finland

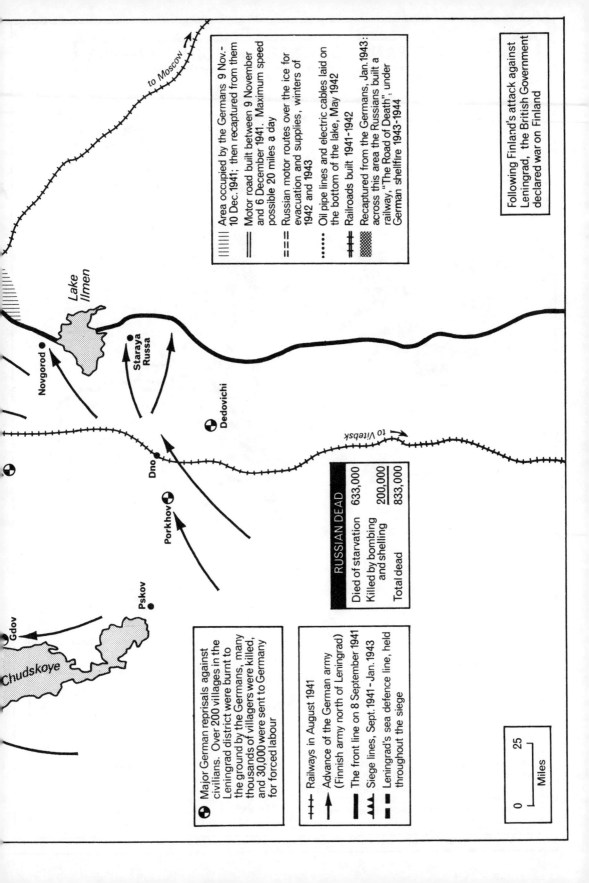

to Moscow

Lake
Ilmen

Novgorod

Staraya
Russa

Dedovichi

Dno

Porkhov

to Vitebsk

Pskov

Gdov

Chudskoye

Area occupied by the Germans 9 Nov.-
10 Dec. 1941; then recaptured from them

Motor road built between 9 November
and 6 December 1941. Maximum speed
possible 20 miles a day

Russian motor routes over the ice for
evacuation and supplies, winters of
1942 and 1943

Oil pipe lines and electric cables laid on
the bottom of the lake, May 1942

Railroads built 1941-1942

Recaptured from the Germans, Jan.1943:
across this area the Russians built a
railway, "The Road of Death", under
German shellfire 1943-1944

Following Finland's attack against
Leningrad, the British Government
declared war on Finland

RUSSIAN DEAD	
Died of starvation	633,000
Killed by bombing and shelling	200,000
Total dead	833,000

Major German reprisals against
civilians. Over 200 villages in the
Leningrad district were burnt to
the ground by the Germans, many
thousands of villagers were killed,
and 30,000 were sent to Germany
for forced labour

Railways in August 1941

Advance of the German army
(Finnish army north of Leningrad)

The front line on 8 September 1941

Siege lines, Sept. 1941 – Jan. 1943

Leningrad's sea defence line, held
throughout the siege

0   25
Miles

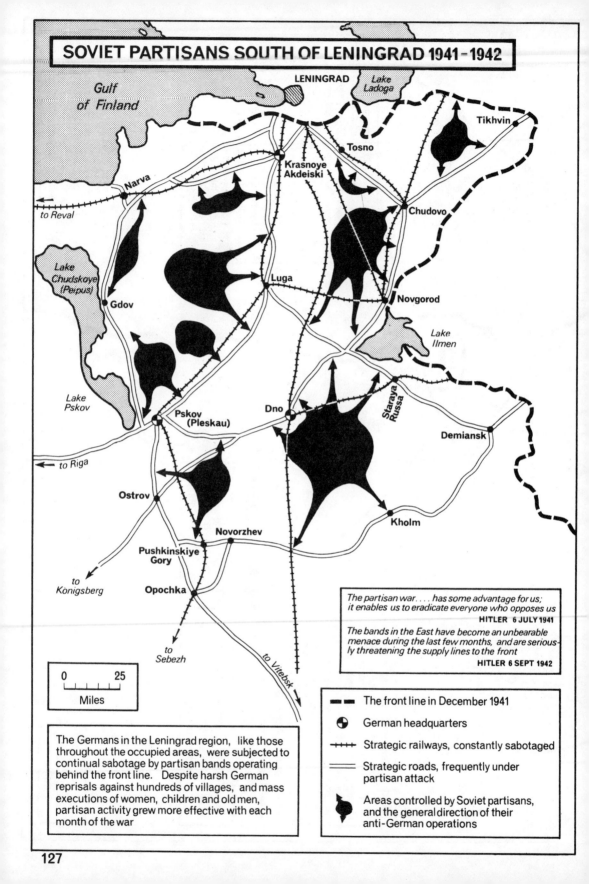

SOVIET PARTISANS SOUTH OF LENINGRAD 1941-1942

Gulf
of Finland

LENINGRAD

Lake
Ladoga

Tikhvin

Tosno

to Reval

Narva

Krasnoye
Akdeiski

Chudovo

Lake
Chudskoye
(Peipus)

Gdov

Luga

Novgorod

Lake
Ilmen

Lake
Pskov

Pskov
(Pleskau)

Dno

Staraya
Russa

to Riga

Demiansk

Ostrov

Novorzhev

Kholm

Pushkinskiye
Gory

to
Königsberg

Opochka

to
Sebezh

to Vitebsk

0   25
Miles

*The partisan war. . . . has some advantage for us;
it enables us to eradicate everyone who opposes us*
HITLER 6 JULY 1941

*The bands in the East have become an unbearable
menace during the last few months, and are serious-
ly threatening the supply lines to the front*
HITLER 6 SEPT 1942

The Germans in the Leningrad region, like those
throughout the occupied areas, were subjected to
continual sabotage by partisan bands operating
behind the front line.   Despite harsh German
reprisals against hundreds of villages, and mass
executions of women, children and old men,
partisan activity grew more effective with each
month of the war

- - -   The front line in December 1941

⬒   German headquarters

+++   Strategic railways, constantly sabotaged

═══   Strategic roads, frequently under
        partisan attack

         Areas controlled by Soviet partisans,
         and the general direction of their
         anti-German operations

THE GERMAN DRIVE TO THE CAUCASUS 1941-1943

Russians ahead,
Russians behind,
And in between
Shooting
GERMAN SOLDIERS DITTY

Saratov

VOLGA
GERMANS

Kharkov

Don

Stalino

Nikolayev

Stalingrad

Berdiansk

Rostov

Manych

Sea of
Azov

Volga

CRIMEAN
TATARS

Krasnodar

Kuban

Astrakhan

Anapa

KALMYKS

Novorossiisk

Stavropol

Tuapse

Maikop

Kuma

Black Sea

KARACHAIS

Terek

Caspian Sea

Grozny

Ordzhonikidze

Poti

CHECHEN-
INGUSH

Makachkala

Batum

Caucasus

Trabzon

Tiflis

TURKEY

Kars

Erivan

Baku

Legend

- The high peaks of the Caucasus (over 3000 metres)
- Soviet territory conquered by the Germans before 5 December 1941
- Directions of main German advance
- Furthest southern advance of German troops by November 1942
- Furthest eastward point reached by German advanced units
- Autonomous groups, deported by Stalin for having thought to have welcomed the German advance
- ◉ Principal areas of Soviet partisan activity
- ✚ Major oil wells, urgently needed by the Germans for their war effort. Only the smallest (at Maikop) fell into their hands. They were driven out of the Caucasus during 1943

Tabriz

PERSIA

0   200
Miles

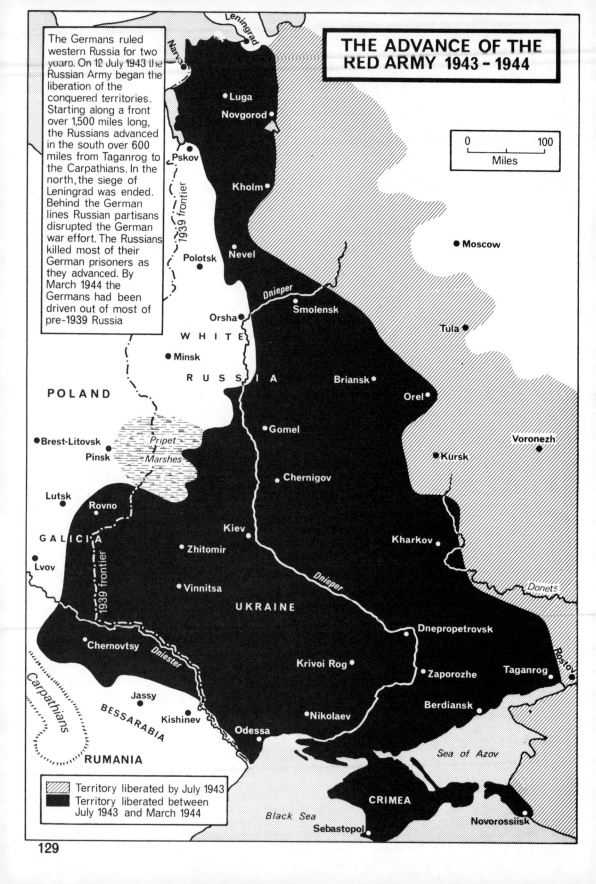

THE ADVANCE OF THE RED ARMY 1943 - 1944

The Germans ruled western Russia for two years. On 12 July 1943 the Russian Army began the liberation of the conquered territories. Starting along a front over 1,500 miles long, the Russians advanced in the south over 600 miles from Taganrog to the Carpathians. In the north, the siege of Leningrad was ended. Behind the German lines Russian partisans disrupted the German war effort. The Russians killed most of their German prisoners as they advanced. By March 1944 the Germans had been driven out of most of pre-1939 Russia

0   100
Miles

Leningrad

Narva

Luga
Novgorod

Pskov

1939 frontier

Kholm

Moscow

Nevel

Polotsk

Dnieper

Smolensk

Orsha

Tula

WHITE

Minsk

RUSSIA

Briansk

Orel

POLAND

Voronezh

Brest-Litovsk

Pripet

Gomel

Pinsk

Marshes

Kursk

Chernigov

Lutsk

Rovno

GALICIA

Kiev

Kharkov

Zhitomir

1939 frontier

Lvov

Dnieper

Donets

Vinnitsa

UKRAINE

Dnepropetrovsk

Chernovtsy

Dniester

Rostov

Krivoi Rog

Zaporozhe

Taganrog

Jassy

Berdiansk

BESSARABIA

Kishinev

Nikolaev

Odessa

Sea of Azov

Carpathians

RUMANIA

Territory liberated by July 1943
Territory liberated between
July 1943 and March 1944

CRIMEA

Black Sea

Sebastopol

Novorossiisk

THE DEFEAT OF GERMANY
1944 – 1945

EUROPEAN WAR DEAD 1939-1945

CIVILIANS	approx.
Jews	6,000,000
Russians	3,000,000
Yugoslavs	1,280,000
Poles	1,000,000
Germans	800,000
Hungarians	280,000
Rumanians	260,000
Dutch	200,000
Greeks	140,000
French	107,000
Austrians	104,000
British	62,000
Belgians	16,000

Total civilian
dead over 13 million

EUROPEAN WAR DEAD 1939-1945

SOLDIERS	approx.
Russians	7,500,000
Germans	3,500,000
Hungarians	410,000
Yugoslavs	410,000
British	400,000
Italians	330,000
Polish	320,000
Rumanians	300,000
Americans (U.S.A.)	290,000
French	210,000
Finns	85,000
Belgians	12,000
Dutch	12,000

Total military
dead over 13 million

Liberated by Soviet troops before May 1944
Liberated by British and American troops before May 1944
→ Soviet advances from May 1944 to May 1945
⇒ Other Allied advances, May 1944 to May 1945
■ Territory still in German hands when Germany surrendered unconditionally on 8 May 1945
Neutral countries

130

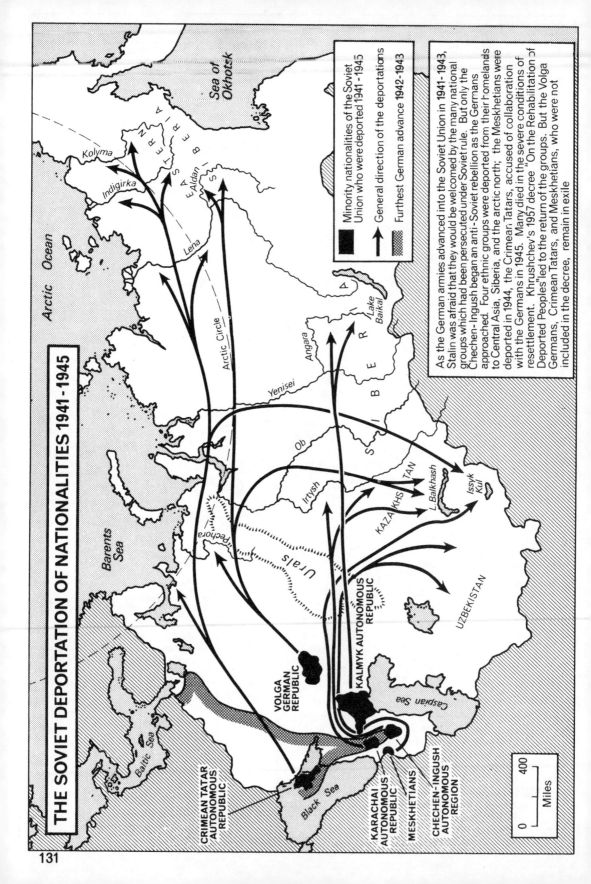

THE SOVIET DEPORTATION OF NATIONALITIES 1941 - 1945

Legend:

■ Minority nationalities of the Soviet Union who were deported 1941 - 1945

↑ General direction of the deportations 1941 - 1945

▨ Furthest German advance 1942 - 1943

As the German armies advanced into the Soviet Union in 1941 - 1943, Stalin was afraid that they would be welcomed by the many national groups which had been persecuted under Soviet rule. But only the Chechen - Ingush began an anti-Soviet rebellion as the Germans approached. Four ethnic groups were deported from their homelands to Central Asia, Siberia, and the arctic north; the Meskhetians were deported in 1944, the Crimean Tatars, accused of collaboration with the Germans in 1945. Many died in the severe conditions of resettlement. Khrushchev's 1957 decree "On the Rehabilitation of Deported Peoples" led to the return of the groups. But the Volga Germans, Crimean Tatars, and Meskhetians, who were not included in the decree, remain in exile

Map labels:

Arctic Ocean
Barents Sea
Sea of Okhotsk
Baltic Sea
Black Sea
Caspian Sea
Lake Baikal
Issyk Kul
L. Balkhash

Kolyma
Indigirka
Lena
Aldan
Yenisei
Angara
Ob
Irtysh
Pechora
Urals

EASTERN SIBERIA
SIBERIA
KAZAKHSTAN
UZBEKISTAN

Arctic Circle

VOLGA GERMAN REPUBLIC
KALMYK AUTONOMOUS REPUBLIC
CRIMEAN TATAR AUTONOMOUS REPUBLIC
KARACHAI AUTONOMOUS REPUBLIC
MESKHETIANS
CHECHEN - INGUSH AUTONOMOUS REGION

0   400
Miles

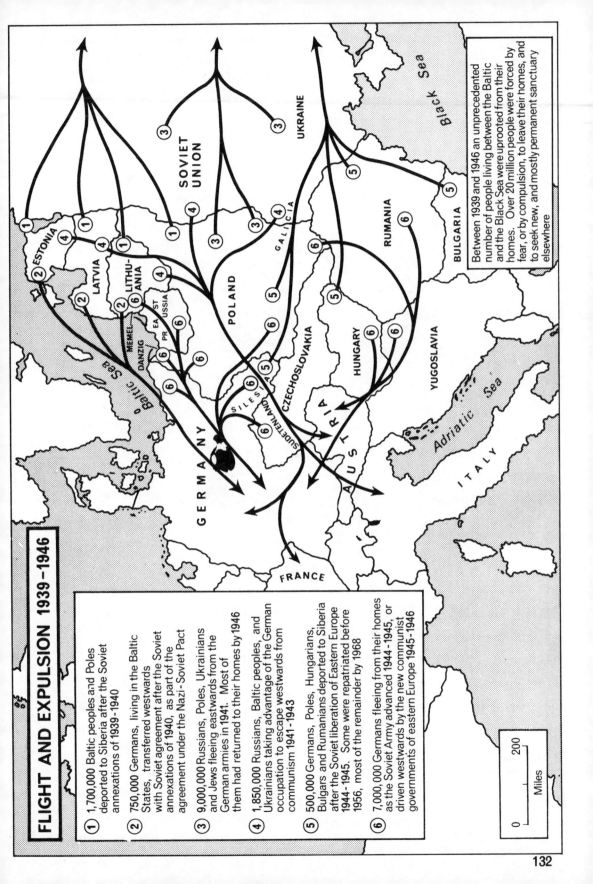

FLIGHT AND EXPULSION 1939-1946

Between 1939 and 1946 an unprecedented number of people living between the Baltic and the Black Sea were uprooted from their homes. Over 20 million people were forced by fear, or by compulsion, to leave their homes, and to seek new, and mostly permanent sanctuary elsewhere

① 1,700,000 Baltic peoples and Poles deported to Siberia after the Soviet annexations of 1939-1940

② 750,000 Germans, living in the Baltic States, transferred westwards with Soviet agreement after the Soviet annexations of 1940, as part of the agreement under the Nazi-Soviet Pact

③ 9,000,000 Russians, Poles, Ukrainians and Jews fleeing eastwards from the German armies in 1941. Most of them had returned to their homes by 1946

④ 1,850,000 Russians, Baltic peoples, and Ukrainians taking advantage of the German occupation to escape westwards from communism 1941-1943

⑤ 500,000 Germans, Poles, Hungarians, Bulgars and Rumanians deported to Siberia after the Soviet liberation of Eastern Europe 1944-1945. Some were repatriated before 1956, most of the remainder by 1968

⑥ 7,000,000 Germans fleeing from their homes as the Soviet Army advanced 1944-1945, or driven westwards by the new communist governments of eastern Europe 1945-1946

0   200
Miles

132

THE SOVIET UNION IN EASTERN EUROPE 1945-1948

Territory annexed by Russia 1939-1940, and re-incorporated in Russia in 1945

Former German and Czechoslovak territory annexed by Russia in 1945

States liberated by the Soviet army, and in which Communist regimes came to power between 1945 and 1948

Russian occupation zones in Austria (evacuated 1950) and Germany

British, French and American occupation zones

The 'Iron Curtain' in 1948

North Sea

SWEDEN

FINLAND

Baltic Sea

Vyborg

Leningrad

Reval

ESTONIA

Pskov

Riga

LATVIA

Memel

LITHUANIA

Königsberg

EAST PRUSSIA

Kovno

Vilna

Minsk

Bremen

Stettin

annexed by Poland from Germany

Bialystok

S O V I E T

Berlin

Posnan

Warsaw

Pinsk

G E R M A N Y

Erfurt

POLAND

U N I O N

Bonn

Dresden

Breslau

SILESIA

Cracow

Prague

Przemysl

Lvov

GALICIA

Chernovtsy

Nuremburg

CZECHOSLOVAKIA

FRANCE

Munich

Vienna

Uzhgorod

Jassy

BESSARABIA

Kishinev

SWITZ.

AUSTRIA

Budapest

HUNGARY

Trieste

RUMANIA

ITALY

Adriatic Sea

Belgrade

YUGOSLAVIA

Bucharest

Sofia

BULGARIA

Black Sea

ALBANIA

Tirana

GREECE

Ægean Sea

TURKEY

The Russian liberation of Eastern Europe was quickly followed by the establishment of communist regimes, and an 'Iron Curtain' from the Baltic to the Adriatic. Communist rule brought national subservience to Russian policy, and the subordination of personal liberty. The cities of Berlin and Vienna were divided into Russian, British, French and American sectors

0   200
Miles

THE SOVIET UNION IN EASTERN EUROPE 1949-1968

0   200
Miles

FINLAND

Vyborg

Leningrad

Tallin (Reval)

Riga

SWEDEN

North Sea

Baltic Sea

Klaypeda (Memel)

Kaliningrad

SOVIET UNION

Rostock

East Berlin

EAST GERMANY

Halle

Dresden

Gdansk

Szczecin

POLAND

Posnan

Warsaw

Lodz

Wroclaw

Lublin

Cracow

Przemysl

Lvov

Kiev

WEST GERMANY

Prague

CZECHOSLOVAKIA

Brno

Kosice

FRANCE

SWITZ.

AUSTRIA

Bratislava

Debrecen

Györ

Budapest

HUNGARY

Pécs

Zagreb

Rijeka

Arad

Cluj

Jassy

Odessa

RUMANIA

Constanza

Belgrade

Bucharest

YUGOSLAVIA

Split

Nish

Varna

ITALY

Adriatic Sea

Kotor

BULGARIA

Sofia

Burgas

Black Sea

Tirana

Durres

ALBANIA

Vlone

TURKEY

GREECE

Aegean Sea

Frontiers of communist states since 1945

Only European communist state entirely free from Soviet direction of foreign, economic and domestic policy since 1949

Only communist state within the Soviet bloc pursuing a relatively independent foreign policy since 1968

Only communist state in Europe aligned with China and refusing all contact with the Soviet Union since 1961

Only European communist state to accept Soviet guidance with equanimity

Principal areas of anti-Soviet protest and revolt 1953-1968, crushed by Soviet military intervention (East Germany, Hungary, Czechoslovakia) and by strong political pressure (Poland)

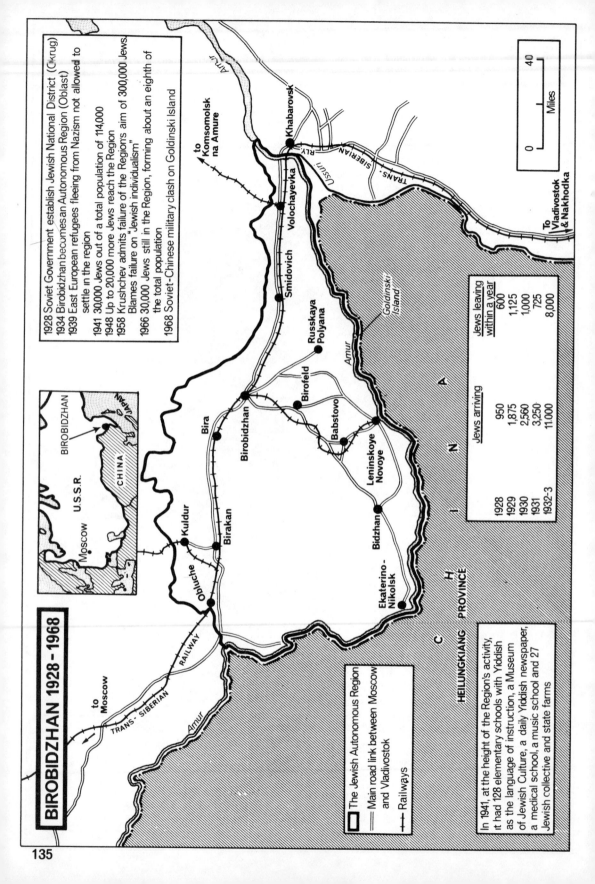

BIROBIDZHAN 1928–1968

1928 Soviet Government establish Jewish National District (Okrug)
1934 Birobidzhan becomes an Autonomous Region (Oblast)
1939 East European refugees fleeing from Nazism not allowed to settle in the region
1941 30,000 Jews out of a total population of 114,000
1948 Up to 20,000 more Jews reach the Region
1958 Krushchev admits failure of the Region's aim of 300,000 Jews. Blames failure on "Jewish individualism"
1966 30,000 Jews still in the Region, forming about an eighth of the total population
1968 Soviet-Chinese military clash on Goldinski Island

	Jews arriving	Jews leaving within a year
1928	950	600
1929	1,875	1,125
1930	2,560	1,000
1931	3,250	725
1932-3	11,000	8,000

In 1941, at the height of the Region's activity, it had 128 elementary schools with Yiddish as the language of instruction, a Museum of Jewish Culture, a daily Yiddish newspaper, a medical school, a music school and 27 Jewish collective and state farms

□ The Jewish Autonomous Region

═ Main road link between Moscow and Vladivostok

┼┼┼ Railways

to Moscow
TRANS-SIBERIAN RAILWAY
Amur
Obluche
Kuldur
Birakan
Ekaterino-Nikolsk
Bidzhan
Bira
Birobidzhan
Birofeld
Babstovo
Leninskoye
Novoye
Russkaya Polyana
Smidovich
Volochayevka
Khabarovsk
Ussuri
TRANS-SIBERIAN RLY.
to Komsomolsk na Amure
Amur
Goldinski Island
C H I N A
HEILUNGKIANG PROVINCE
To Vladivostok & Nakhodka

U.S.S.R.
Moscow
CHINA
JAPAN
BIROBIDZHAN

0   40
Miles

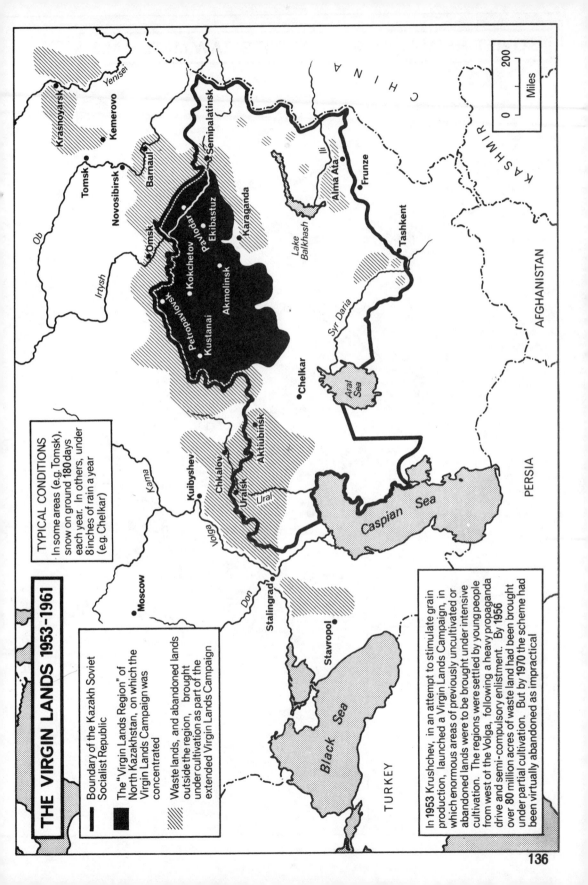

THE VIRGIN LANDS 1953-1961

Legend:

▬ Boundary of the Kazakh Soviet Socialist Republic

■ The "Virgin Lands Region" of North Kazakhstan, on which the Virgin Lands Campaign was concentrated

▨ Waste lands, and abandoned lands outside the region, brought under cultivation as part of the extended Virgin Lands Campaign

TYPICAL CONDITIONS

In some areas (e.g. Tomsk), snow on ground 180 days each year. In others, under 8 inches of rain a year (e.g. Chelkar)

In 1953 Krushchev, in an attempt to stimulate grain production, launched a Virgin Lands Campaign, in which enormous areas of previously uncultivated or abandoned lands were to be brought under intensive cultivation. The regions were settled by young people from west of the Volga, following a heavy propaganda drive and semi-compulsory enlistment. By 1956 over 80 million acres of waste land had been brought under partial cultivation. But by 1970 the scheme had been virtually abandoned as impractical

CHINA

KASHMIR

AFGHANISTAN

PERSIA

TURKEY

Krasnoyarsk

Kemerovo

Tomsk

Novosibirsk

Barnaul

Semipalatinsk

Omsk

Pavlodar

Ekibastuz

Karaganda

Kokchetov

Petropavlovsk

Akmolinsk

Kustanai

Alma Ata

Frunze

Tashkent

Lake Balkhash

Syr Darria

Aral Sea

Chelkar

Aktiubinsk

Chkalov

Uralsk

Kuibyshev

Moscow

Stalingrad

Stavropol

Caspian Sea

Black Sea

Yenisei

Ob

Irtysh

Kama

Volga

Don

Ural

0   200 Miles

SOVIET HEAVY INDUSTRY AND ITS RAW MATERIALS

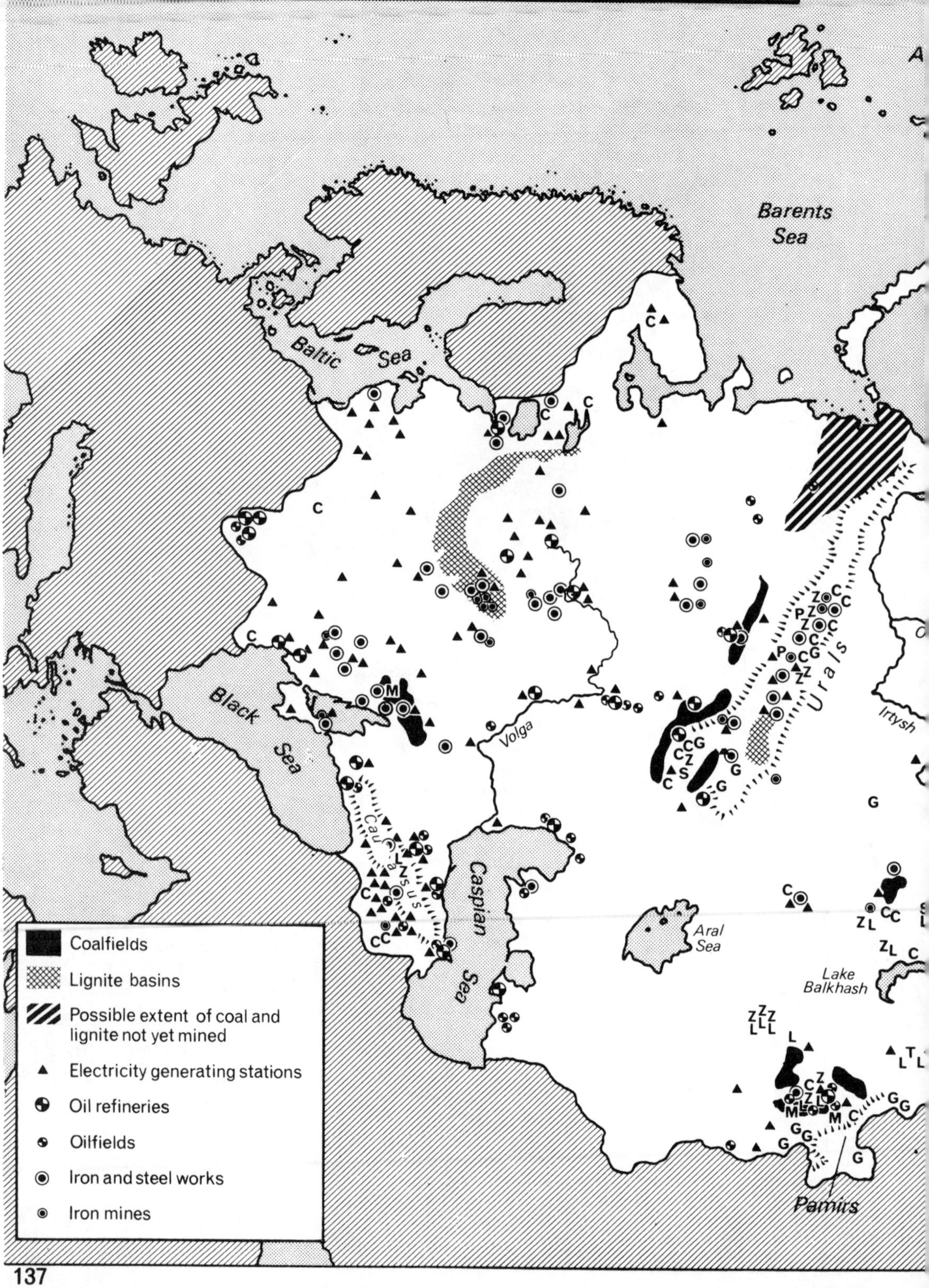

Barents Sea

Baltic Sea

Black Sea

Volga

Caucasus

Caspian Sea

Urals

Irtysh

Aral Sea

Lake Balkhash

Pamirs

Legend:

- ■ Coalfields
- ▨ Lignite basins
- ▨ Possible extent of coal and lignite not yet mined
- ▲ Electricity generating stations
- ☯ Oil refineries
- ◉ Oilfields
- ◉ Iron and steel works
- ◉ Iron mines

137

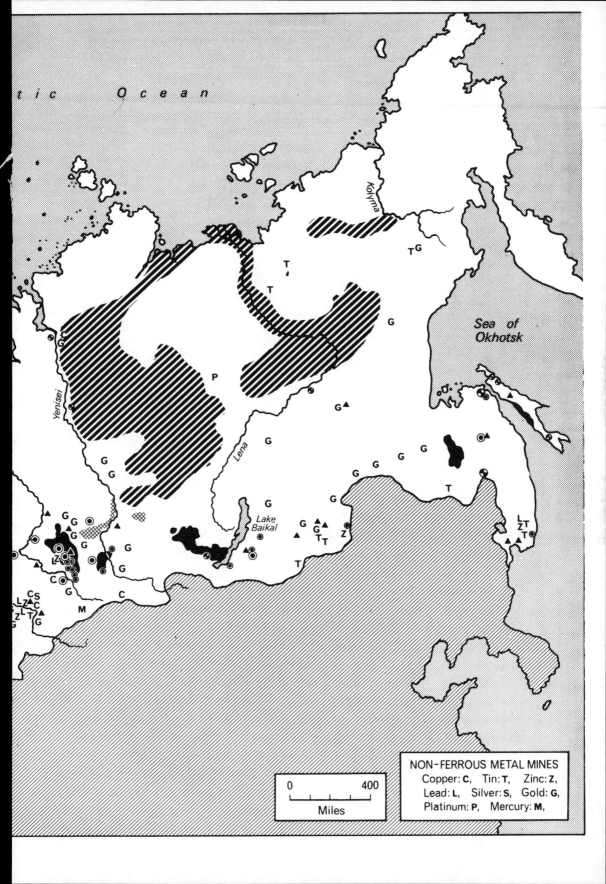

Arctic Ocean

Kolyma

Sea of Okhotsk

Yenisei

Lena

Lake Baikal

NON-FERROUS METAL MINES
Copper: **C**, Tin: **T**, Zinc: **Z**,
Lead: **L**, Silver: **S**, Gold: **G**,
Platinum: **P**, Mercury: **M**,

0   400
Miles

CITIES AND RAILWAYS IN THE SOVIET UNION 1917-1959

In 1959 there were 22 cities with over 500,000 inhabitants, and 3 with over one million. All these cities were west of Lake Baikal (which is itself 2,000 miles from the most easterly point of the Soviet Union). Five cities all east of the Urals, had increased tenfold since 1926. But vast areas of Siberia and Central Asia remain largely uninhabited, being arid desert or frozen waste

London

Paris

Brussels

Berlin

Prague

Vienna

Rome

Belgrade

Sofia

Bucharest

Ankara

Baltic Sea

Warsaw

Riga

Helsinki

FINLAND

Minsk

Kiev

1 million

Odessa

Kharkov

Stalino

Dnepropetrovsk

Rostov

Stalingrad

Black Sea

TURKEY

Barents Sea

Archangel

Leningrad
3 million

Moscow
5 million

Gorky

Kazan

Molotov

Sverdlovsk

Saratov

Kuibyshev

Ufa

Volga

Magnitogorsk

Cheliabinsk

Omsk

Irtysh

Ural

Karaganda

Aral Sea

Lake Balkash

Tiflis

Erivan

Baku

Caspian Sea

Oxus

Tashkent

Teheran

PERSIA

AFGHANISTAN

⊕ Cities with over one million inhabitants (census of 1959)

⊙ Cities with over half a million inhabitants

⊚ Cities of over 250,000 inhabitants whose population had increased tenfold since 1926

⊛ Towns east of Lake Baikal with a population of over 100,000

▨ Sparsely settled areas with less than 3 inhabitants per square mile

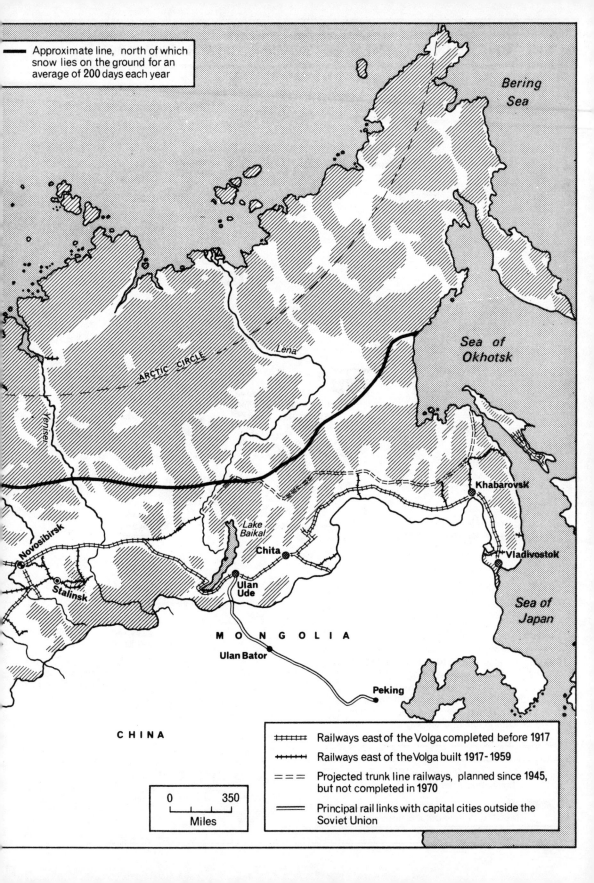

Approximate line, north of which snow lies on the ground for an average of 200 days each year

Bering Sea

Sea of Okhotsk

ARCTIC CIRCLE

Lena

Yenisei

Khabarovsk

Novosibirsk

Lake Baikal

Chita

Vladivostok

Stalinsk

Ulan Ude

Sea of Japan

M O N G O L I A

Ulan Bator

Peking

C H I N A

0   350

Miles

┼┼┼┼┼ Railways east of the Volga completed before 1917

┼─┼─┼ Railways east of the Volga built 1917-1959

= = = Projected trunk line railways, planned since 1945, but not completed in 1970

═══ Principal rail links with capital cities outside the Soviet Union

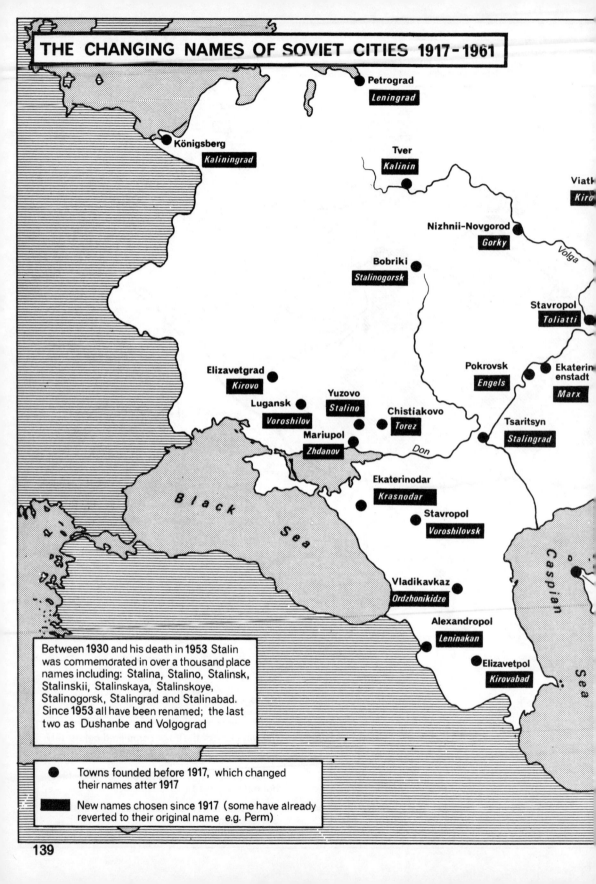

THE CHANGING NAMES OF SOVIET CITIES 1917-1961

Petrograd
Leningrad

Königsberg
Kaliningrad

Tver
Kalinin

Viatk
Kiro

Nizhnii-Novgorod
Gorky

Volga

Bobriki
Stalinogorsk

Stavropol
Toliatti

Elizavetgrad
Kirovo

Lugansk
Voroshilov

Yuzovo
Stalino

Chistiakovo
Torez

Pokrovsk
Engels

Ekaterin
enstadt
Marx

Mariupol
Zhdanov

Don

Tsaritsyn
Stalingrad

Ekaterinodar
Krasnodar

Stavropol
Voroshilovsk

Black Sea

Caspian Sea

Vladikavkaz
Ordzhonikidze

Alexandropol
Leninakan

Elizavetpol
Kirovabad

Between **1930** and his death in **1953** Stalin was commemorated in over a thousand place names including: Stalina, Stalino, Stalinsk, Stalinskii, Stalinskaya, Stalinskoye, Stalinogorsk, Stalingrad and Stalinabad. Since **1953** all have been renamed; the last two as Dushanbe and Volgograd

● Towns founded before 1917, which changed their names after 1917

■ New names chosen since 1917 (some have already reverted to their original name e.g. Perm)

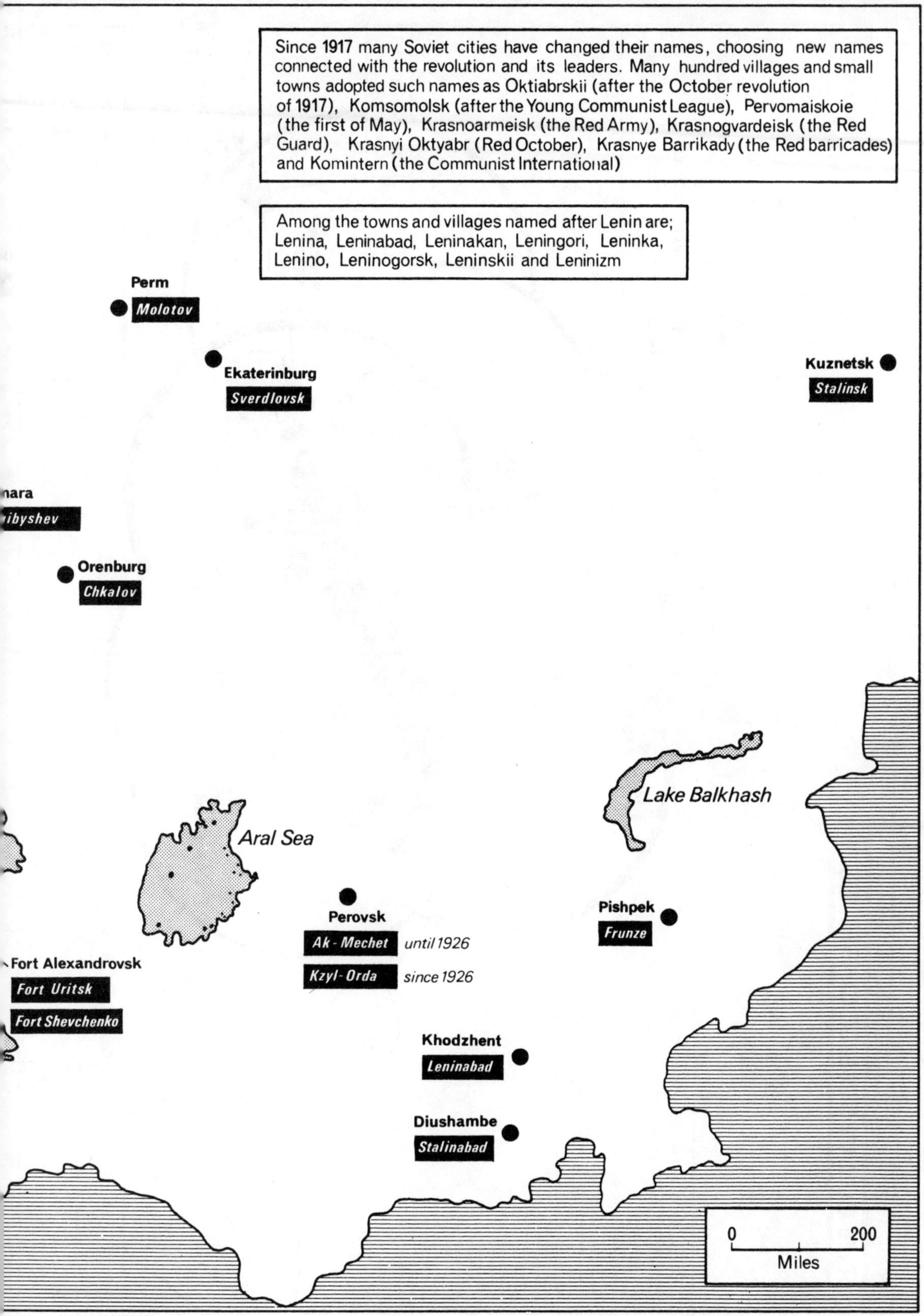

Since 1917 many Soviet cities have changed their names, choosing new names connected with the revolution and its leaders. Many hundred villages and small towns adopted such names as Oktiabrskii (after the October revolution of 1917), Komsomolsk (after the Young Communist League), Pervomaiskoie (the first of May), Krasnoarmeisk (the Red Army), Krasnogvardeisk (the Red Guard), Krasnyi Oktyabr (Red October), Krasnye Barrikady (the Red barricades) and Komintern (the Communist International)

Among the towns and villages named after Lenin are; Lenina, Leninabad, Leninakan, Leningori, Leninka, Lenino, Leninogorsk, Leninskii and Leninizm

Perm
Molotov

Ekaterinburg
Sverdlovsk

Kuznetsk
Stalinsk

nara
ibyshev

Orenburg
Chkalov

Lake Balkhash

Aral Sea

Perovsk
Ak - Mechet until 1926
Kzyl- Orda since 1926

Pishpek
Frunze

Fort Alexandrovsk
Fort Uritsk
Fort Shevchenko

Khodzhent
Leninabad

Diushambe
Stalinabad

0   200
Miles

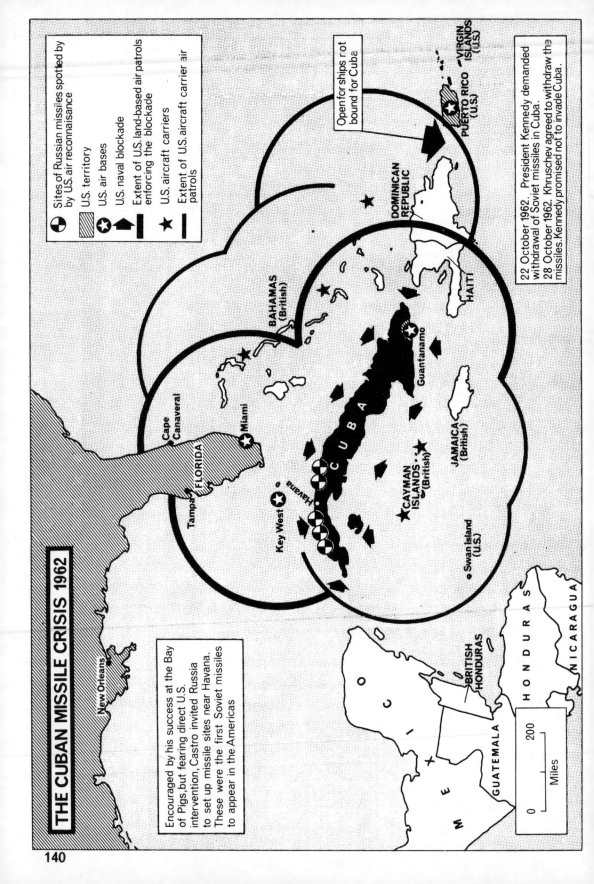

THE CUBAN MISSILE CRISIS 1962

Legend

- ◐ Sites of Russian missiles spotted by U.S. air reconnaissance
- ▨ U.S. territory
- ✪ U.S. air bases
- ▲ U.S. naval blockade
- | Extent of U.S. land-based air patrols enforcing the blockade
- ★ U.S. aircraft carriers
- | Extent of U.S. aircraft carrier air patrols

Encouraged by his success at the Bay of Pigs, but fearing direct U.S. intervention, Castro invited Russia to set up missile sites near Havana. These were the first Soviet missiles to appear in the Americas

Open for ships not bound for Cuba.

22 October 1962. President Kennedy demanded withdrawal of Soviet missiles in Cuba.
28 October 1962. Khruschev agreed to withdraw the missiles. Kennedy promised not to invade Cuba.

New Orleans

FLORIDA

Cape Canaveral

Tampa

Miami

Key West

Havana

C U B A

Guantanamo

BAHAMAS (British)

DOMINICAN REPUBLIC

HAITI

PUERTO RICO (U.S.)

VIRGIN ISLANDS (U.S.)

CAYMAN ISLANDS (British)

JAMAICA (British)

Swan Island (U.S.)

M E X I C O

GUATEMALA

BRITISH HONDURAS

H O N D U R A S

NICARAGUA

0   200

Miles

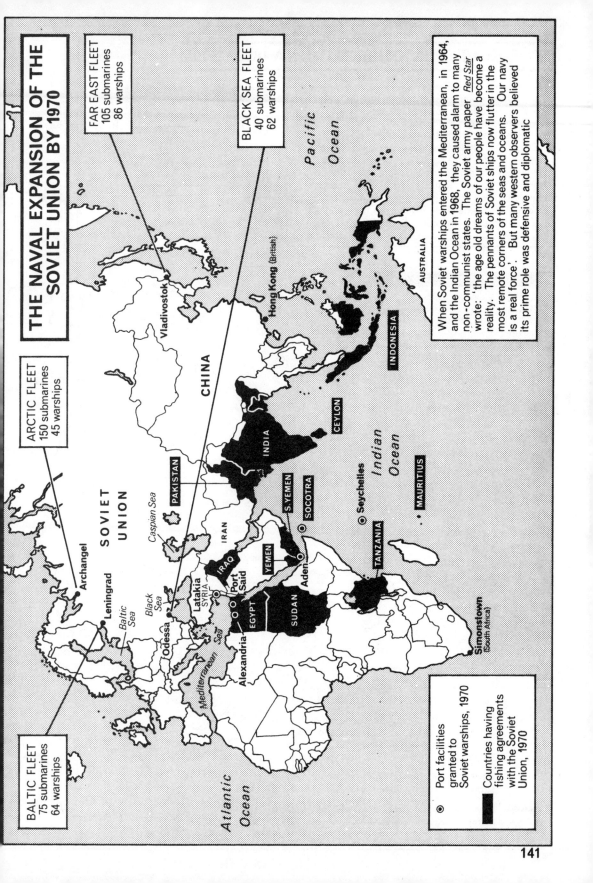

THE NAVAL EXPANSION OF THE SOVIET UNION BY 1970

FAR EAST FLEET
105 submarines
86 warships

BLACK SEA FLEET
40 submarines
62 warships

ARCTIC FLEET
150 submarines
45 warships

BALTIC FLEET
75 submarines
64 warships

When Soviet warships entered the Mediterranean, in 1964, and the Indian Ocean in 1968, they caused alarm to many non-communist states. The Soviet army paper _Red Star_ wrote: "the age old dreams of our people have become a reality. The pennants of Soviet ships now flutter in the most remote corners of the seas and oceans. Our navy is a real force". But many western observers believed its prime role was defensive and diplomatic

Pacific Ocean

Indian Ocean

Atlantic Ocean

Caspian Sea

Mediterranean Sea

Black Sea

Baltic Sea

SOVIET UNION

CHINA

IRAN

INDIA

PAKISTAN

CEYLON

AUSTRALIA

INDONESIA

SOCOTRA

S.YEMEN

YEMEN

IRAQ

EGYPT

SUDAN

TANZANIA

Seychelles

MAURITIUS

Hong Kong (British)

Vladivostok

Archangel

Leningrad

Odessa

Latakia

SYRIA

Port Said

Alexandria

Aden

Simonstown
(South Africa)

⊚ Port facilities
granted to
Soviet warships, 1970

■ Countries having
fishing agreements
with the Soviet
Union, 1970

THE SOVIET UNION AND CHINA 1860-1970

The Chinese Communist Party was founded in 1921. But the Soviet Union preferred to support the Kuomintang under Chiang Kai Shek, to which it gave substantial military aid to establish its power 1923-1927, and to fight the Japanese 1937-1941 (when Stalin formed a Non-Aggression pact with Japan). In 1945 Soviet troops drove the Japanese from Northern China. In 1949 the Chinese Communists came to power. From a policy of considerable Soviet aid to China in the 1950's, the two nations became increasingly hostile. By 1960 the rift was open, and soon led to armed skirmishes on the frontier

TANNU TUVA

1914	Russian protectorate
1921	Independent "Peoples' Republic" allied with the Soviet Union
1944	Annexed by the Soviet Union

SINKIANG

1760-1920	Chinese
1921-1949	Under Soviet influence and partial occupation
Since 1949	Chinese. Heavily colonized by Chinese settlers

SOVIET UNION

Irkut

TANNU TUVA

MONGO

Lake Balkhash

Alma Ata

Urumchi

Hami

Tashkent

Kashgar

SINKIANG

Lop Nor

Yarkand

Khotan

AFGHANISTAN

Gilgit

Kabul

KASHMIR

C H

Lahore

PAKISTAN

TIBET

INDIA

Lhasa

NEPAL

SIKKIM

BHUTAN

INDIA

INDIA

EAST PAKISTAN

BURMA

Territory annexed by Russia 1858-1860

⊙ Communist Party cells established under Moscow's instructions 1920-1924 and urged to collaborate with the Kuomintang (nationalists)

☯ Soviet air units defending Kuomintang strongholds against Japan 1941

→ Soviet military advances across China in the war against Japan 1945

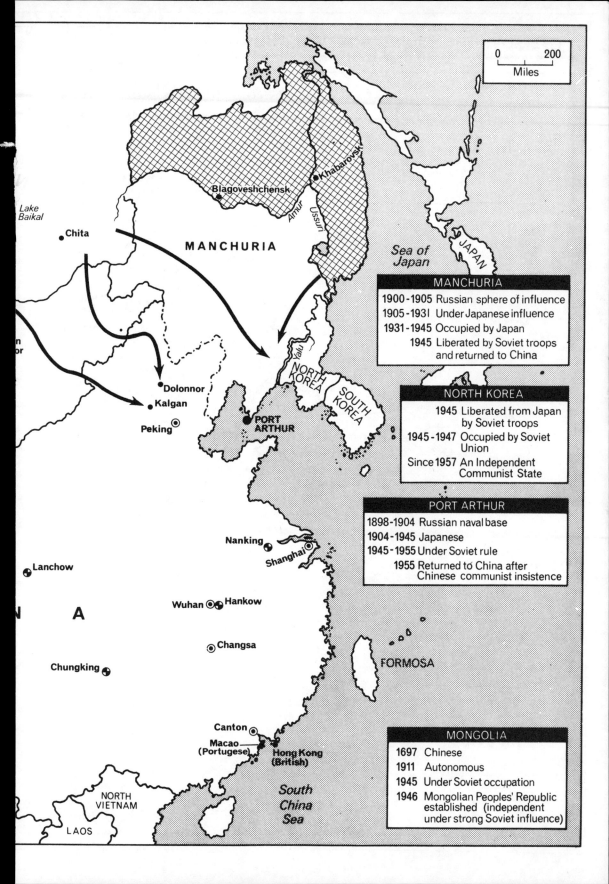

0   200
Miles

Lake Baikal

• Chita

MANCHURIA

• Blagoveshchensk

Khabarovsk

Amur

Ussuri

Sea of Japan

JAPAN

Yalu

NORTH KOREA

SOUTH KOREA

• Dolonnor

• Kalgan

Peking ⊙

● PORT ARTHUR

• Lanchow

Nanking ⊕

Shanghai ⊙

N   A

Wuhan ⊙● Hankow

⊙ Changsa

Chungking ⊙

FORMOSA

Canton ⊙

Macao (Portugese)

Hong Kong (British)

South China Sea

NORTH VIETNAM

LAOS

MANCHURIA
1900-1905	Russian sphere of influence
1905-1931	Under Japanese influence
1931-1945	Occupied by Japan
1945	Liberated by Soviet troops and returned to China

NORTH KOREA
1945	Liberated from Japan by Soviet troops
1945-1947	Occupied by Soviet Union
Since 1957	An Independent Communist State

PORT ARTHUR
1898-1904	Russian naval base
1904-1945	Japanese
1945-1955	Under Soviet rule
1955	Returned to China after Chinese communist insistence

MONGOLIA
1697	Chinese
1911	Autonomous
1945	Under Soviet occupation
1946	Mongolian Peoples' Republic established (independent under strong Soviet influence)

THE SOVIET-CHINESE BORDERLANDS 1970

————	The Soviet-Chinese border
—·—·—	Other international borders
⊢⊢⊢⊢⊢⊢⊢	Soviet, Mongolian and Chinese railways in the border area
▨	Land over 2000 metres (6562 feet)
⊕	Main airfields

Caspian Sea

Aral Sea

S O V I E T

to Moscow

Omsk

TRANS - SIBERIAN RAILWAY

Novosibirsk ⊕

Achinsk ⊕

Karaganda ⊕

Barnaul

Krasnoyarsk ⊕

Rubtsovsk

Biisk

Semipalatinsk ⊕

Leninogorsk

Abakan

PERSIA

Lake Balkash

Aktogai

Lake Zaisan

Lake Markakol

Tashkent ⊕

Lugovoi

Urdzhar

Samarkand

Diushambe

Frunze

Panfilov

L. Alakol

Zaisan

Tahcheng

Ulyungur Nor

Dzhalal Abad

Rybachiye

⊕ Alma Ata

Ebi Nor

Osh

Issyk Kul

Kuldja

Diushambe ⊕

AFGHANISTAN

Kashgar

Aksu

Urumchi ⊕

M

PAKISTAN

KASHMIR

Lop Nor

INDIA

C H I

Lanchow

0	250

Miles

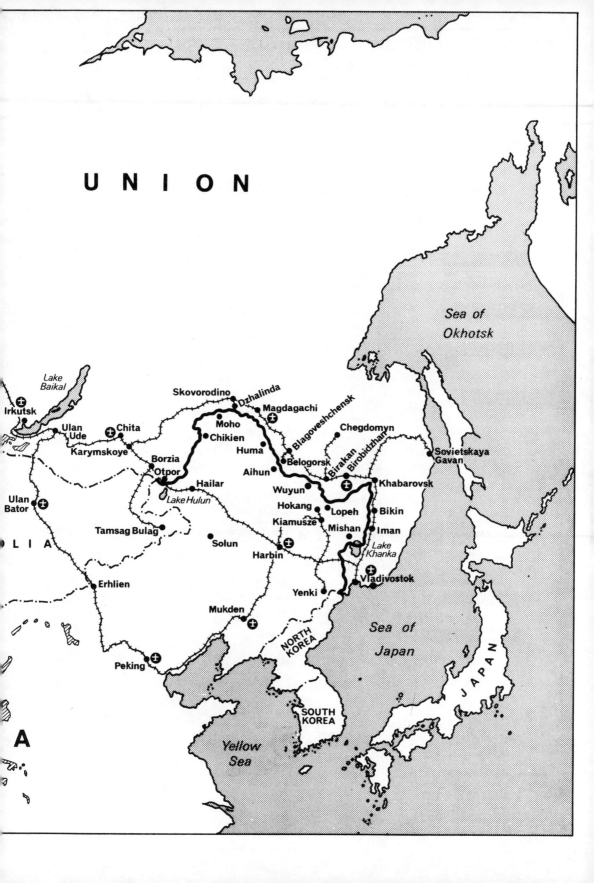

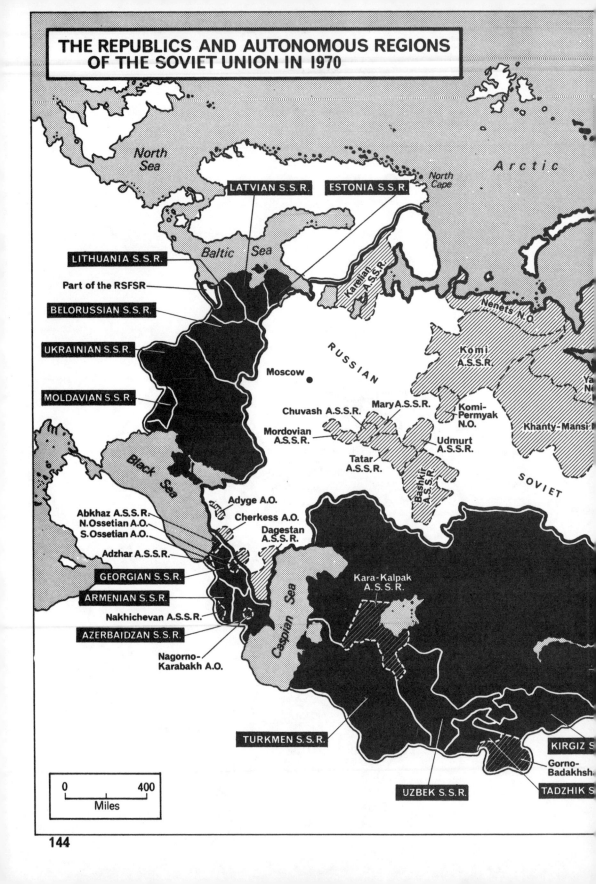

THE REPUBLICS AND AUTONOMOUS REGIONS OF THE SOVIET UNION IN 1970

North Sea

Arctic

LATVIAN S.S.R.

ESTONIA S.S.R.

North Cape

Baltic Sea

LITHUANIA S.S.R.

Part of the RSFSR

BELORUSSIAN S.S.R.

UKRAINIAN S.S.R.

MOLDAVIAN S.S.R.

Karelian A.S.S.R.

Nenets N.O.

RUSSIAN

Komi A.S.S.R.

Moscow

Ya Ne

Chuvash A.S.S.R.

Mary A.S.S.R.

Komi-Permyak N.O.

Mordovian A.S.S.R.

Udmurt A.S.S.R.

Khanty-Mansi

Tatar A.S.S.R.

Bashkir A.S.S.R.

SOVIET

Black Sea

Adyge A.O.

Abkhaz A.S.S.R.
N.Ossetian A.O.
S.Ossetian A.O.

Cherkess A.O.

Dagestan A.S.S.R.

Adzhar A.S.S.R.

GEORGIAN S.S.R.

ARMENIAN S.S.R.

Nakhichevan A.S.S.R.

AZERBAIDZAN S.S.R.

Nagorno-Karabakh A.O.

Kara-Kalpak A.S.S.R.

Caspian Sea

TURKMEN S.S.R.

KIRGIZ S

Gorno-Badakhsh

UZBEK S.S.R.

TADZHIK S

0 — 400
Miles

Chukchi A.S.S.R.

Koriak N.O.

Bering Sea

Ocean

Taimyr N.O.

REPUBLIC

Yakut A.S.S.R.

Sea of Okhotsk

Evenki N.O.

SOCIALIST

Jewish A.O.

FEDERATIVE

Ust-Orda Buriat-Mongol N.O.

Buriat-Mongol A.S.S.R.

Aga-Buriat Mongol A.O.

kass O.

orno-ltai A.O.

Tuva A.S.S.R.

Sea of Japan

ZAKH S.S.R.

───── Boundary of the Union of Soviet Socialist Republics (USSR)

☐ The Russian Soviet Federative Socialist Republic (RSFSR)

■ The 14 other Soviet Republics forming, with the RSFSR the USSR or Soviet Union

▨ Principal areas within the Soviet Union
▨ containing ethnic groups which have been granted autonomous status. The size of the areas depends upon the area of settlement of each group. The largest have been given Autonomous Soviet Socialist Republics, Autonomous Oblasts, and National Okrugs

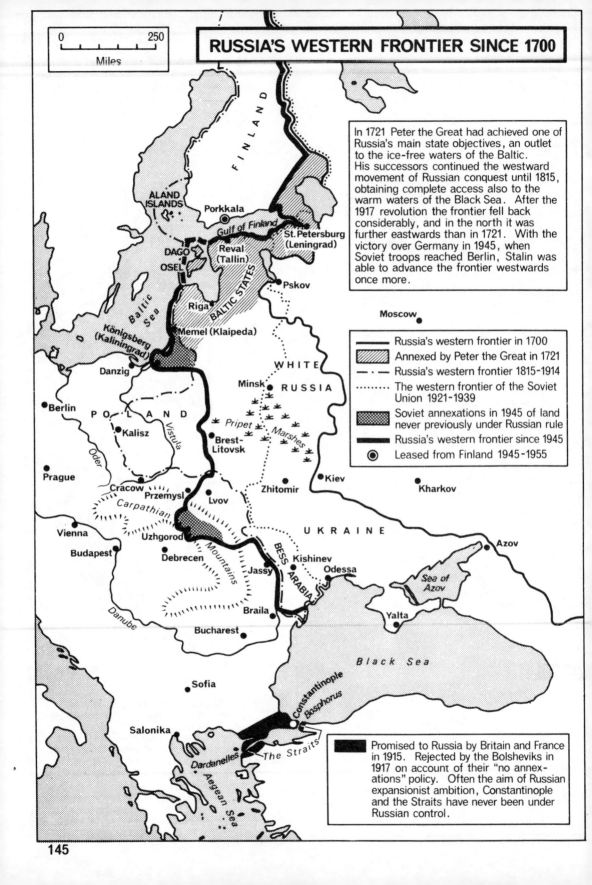

RUSSIA'S WESTERN FRONTIER SINCE 1700

0 — 250
Miles

In 1721 Peter the Great had achieved one of Russia's main state objectives, an outlet to the ice-free waters of the Baltic. His successors continued the westward movement of Russian conquest until 1815, obtaining complete access also to the warm waters of the Black Sea. After the 1917 revolution the frontier fell back considerably, and in the north it was further eastwards than in 1721. With the victory over Germany in 1945, when Soviet troops reached Berlin, Stalin was able to advance the frontier westwards once more.

—————— Russia's western frontier in 1700

▨▨▨ Annexed by Peter the Great in 1721

— · — Russia's western frontier 1815-1914

· · · · · · The western frontier of the Soviet Union 1921-1939

▦▦▦ Soviet annexations in 1945 of land never previously under Russian rule

▬▬▬ Russia's western frontier since 1945

◉ Leased from Finland 1945-1955

Promised to Russia by Britain and France in 1915. Rejected by the Bolsheviks in 1917 on account of their "no annexations" policy. Often the aim of Russian expansionist ambition, Constantinople and the Straits have never been under Russian control.

Map labels

FINLAND
ALAND ISLANDS
Porkkala
Gulf of Finland
St. Petersburg (Leningrad)
DAGO
Reval (Tallin)
OSEL
Pskov
Baltic Sea
Riga
BALTIC STATES
Königsberg (Kaliningrad)
Memel (Klaipeda)
Moscow
Danzig
WHITE RUSSIA
Minsk
Berlin
POLAND
Kalisz
Vistula
Pripet Marshes
Brest-Litovsk
Oder
Kiev
Kharkov
Prague
Cracow
Przemysl
Lvov
Zhitomir
Carpathian
Vienna
Uzhgorod
UKRAINE
Azov
Budapest
Debrecen
Mountains
BESSARABIA
Kishinev
Odessa
Sea of Azov
Jassy
Braila
Yalta
Danube
Bucharest
Black Sea
Sofia
Constantinople
Bosphorus
Salonika
Dardanelles
The Straits
Aegean Sea

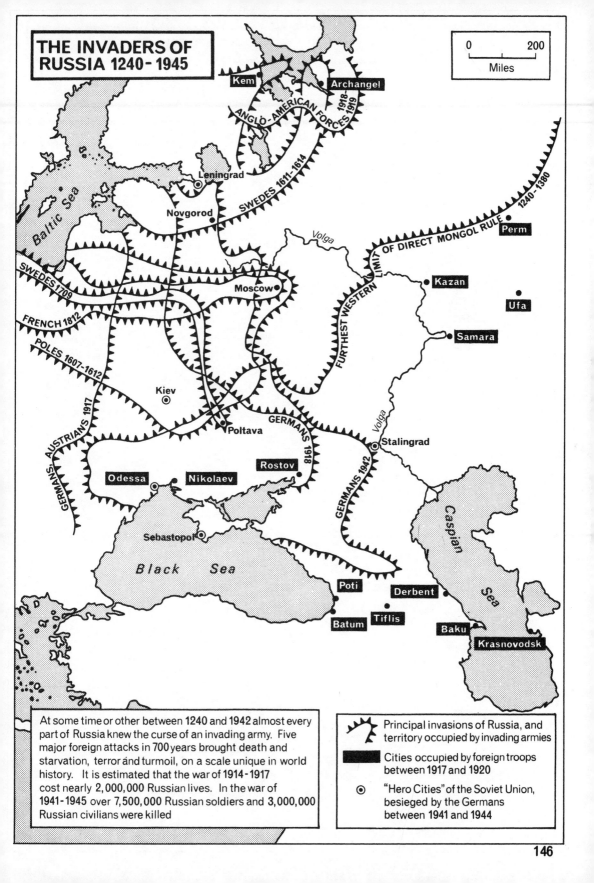

THE INVADERS OF RUSSIA 1240-1945

Kem

Archangel

ANGLO-AMERICAN FORCES 1918-1919

SWEDES 1611-1614

Leningrad

Novgorod

Volga

1240-1380

LIMIT OF DIRECT MONGOL RULE

Perm

SWEDES 1709

Moscow

FURTHEST WESTERN

Kazan

Ufa

FRENCH 1812

Samara

POLES 1607-1612

Kiev

AUSTRIANS 1917

GERMANS 1918

Poltava

GERMANS

Volga

Stalingrad

GERMANS 1942

Odessa Nikolaev

Rostov

Sebastopol

Caspian Sea

Black Sea

Poti

Derbent

Batum **Tiflis**

Baku

Krasnovodsk

Baltic Sea

0   200
Miles

At some time or other between **1240** and **1942** almost every part of Russia knew the curse of an invading army. Five major foreign attacks in 700 years brought death and starvation, terror and turmoil, on a scale unique in world history. It is estimated that the war of **1914-1917** cost nearly **2,000,000** Russian lives. In the war of **1941-1945** over **7,500,000** Russian soldiers and **3,000,000** Russian civilians were killed

Principal invasions of Russia, and territory occupied by invading armies

Cities occupied by foreign troops between 1917 and 1920

"Hero Cities" of the Soviet Union, besieged by the Germans between 1941 and 1944

146

Bibliography of Works Consulted

(i) ATLASES

Baratov, R. B. (and others), *Atlas Tadzhikskoi Sovetskoi Sotsialisticheskoi Respubliki* (Dushanbe and Moscow, 1968)

Bartholomew, John (ed), *The Times Atlas of the World*, 5 vols (London, 1959)

Bazilevich, K. V., Golubtsov, I. A. and Zinoviev, M. A., *Atlas Istorii SSSR*, 3 vols (Moscow, 1949–54)

Beloglazova, O. A. (ed), *Atlas SSSR* (Moscow, 1954)

Czapliński, Wladislaw and Ladogórski, Tadeusz, *Atlas Historyczny Polski* (Warsaw, 1968)

Droysens, G., *Historischer Handatlas* (Bielefeld and Leipzig, 1886)

Durov, A. G. (General editor), *Atlas Leningradskoi Oblasti* (Moscow, 1967)

Engel, Joseph, *Grosser Historischer Weltatlas* (Munich, 1962)

Grosier, L'Abbé, *Atlas Générale de la Chine* (Paris 1785)

Hudson, G. F. and Rajchman, Marthe, *An Atlas of Far Eastern Politics* (London, 1938)

Kalesnik, S. V. (and others), *Peterburg–Leningrad* (Leningrad, 1957)

Kosev, Dimiter (and others), *Atlas Po Bulgarska Istoriya* (Sofia, 1963)

Kubijovyć, Volodymyr, *Atlas of Ukraine and Adjoining Countries* (Lvov, 1937)

Kudriàshov, K. V., *Russkii Istoricheskii Atlas* (Leningrad, 1928)

Kovalevsky, Pierre, *Atlas Historique et Culturel de la Russie et du Monde Slave* (Paris, 1961)

McEvedy, Colin, *The Penguin Atlas of Medieval History* (London, 1961)

Penkala, Maria, *A Correlated History of the Far East* (The Hague and Paris, 1966)

Oxford Regional Economic Atlas: The USSR and Eastern Europe (Oxford, 1956)

Sochava, V. B. (Principal ed), *Atlas Zabaikalia* (Moscow and Irkutsk, 1967)

Taaffe, Robert N. and Kingsbury, Robert C., *An Atlas of Soviet Affairs* (London, 1965)

Terekhov, N. M. (senior editor), *Atlas Volgogradskoi Oblasti* (Moscow, 1967)

Toynbee, Arnold J. and Myers, Edward D., *Historical Atlas and Gazetteer* (London, 1959)

Voznesenski (and others), *Atlas Razvitiya Khoziastva i Kultury SSSR* (Moscow, 1967)

Westermann, Georg, *Atlas zur Weltgeschichte* (Braunschweig, 1956)

Zamyslovski, Igor E., *Uchebnii Atlas po Russkoi Istorii* (St Petersburg, 1887)

(ii) MAPS

Atanasiu, A. D., *La Bessarabie* (Paris, 1919)

Bazewicz, J. M., *Polska w Trzech Zaborach* (Warsaw, n.d.)

Bazileva, Z. P., *Rossiiskaya Imperia 1801–1861* (Moscow, 1960)

British G.H.Q., Constantinople, *Ethnographical Map of Caucasus* (Constantinople, 1920)

Fedorovskaya, G. P. (publisher), *Promyshlennost Rossii 1913; Promyshlennost Soyuza SSR 1940* (Moscow, 1962)

Filonenko, W. J., *Volkstumkarte der Krim* (Vienna, 1932)

Kuchborskaya, E. P., *Rossiiskaya Imperia 1725–1801* (Moscow, 1959)

Stanford, Edward, *Sketch of the Acquisitions of Russia* (London, 1876)

Wyld, James, *Wyld's Military Staff Map of Central Asia, Turkistan and Afghanistan* (London, 1878)

(iii) ENCYCLOPAEDIAS, REFERENCE BOOKS AND GENERAL WORKS

Baedeker, Karl, *Russland* (Leipzig, 1912)
Cole, J. P., *Geography of the USSR* (London, 1967)
Florinsky, Michael T. (ed), *Encyclopaedia of Russia and the Soviet Union* (New York, 1961)
Katzenelson, Y. L. and Gintsburg, D. G. (eds), *Evreiskaya Entsiklopediya,* 16 vols (St Petersburg, 1906–13)
Kubijovyć, Volodymyr (ed), *Ukraine: A Concise Encyclopaedia* (Toronto, 1963)
Pares, Bernard, *A History of Russia* (London, 1926)
Parker, W. H., *An Historical Georgraphy of Russia* (London, 1968)
Sumner, B. H., *Survey of Russian History* (London, 1944)
Utechin, S. V., *Everyman's Concise Encyclopaedia of Russia* (London, 1961)
Zhukov, E. M. (ed), *Sovetskaya Istoricheskaya Entsiklopediya,* vols 1–12 (Moscow, 1961–69)

(iv) BOOKS ON SPECIAL TOPICS

Allen, W. E. D., *The Ukraine: A History* (Cambridge, 1940)
Allen, W. E. D. and Muratov, P., *Caucasian Battlefields: A History of the Wars on the Turco-Caucasian Border 1828–1921* (London, 1953)
Allilueva, A. S., *Iz Vospominanii* (Moscow, 1946)
Armstrong, John A. (ed), *Soviet Partisans in World War II* (Madison, 1964)
Armstrong, Terence E., *The Northern Sea Route* (Cambridge, 1952)
Avalishvili, Zourab, *The Independence of Georgia in International Politics 1918–1921* (London, 1940)
Baddeley, John F., *The Russian Conquest of the Caucasus* (London, 1908)
Baddeley, John F., *Russia, Mongolia, China,* 2 vols (London, 1919)
Caroe, Olaf, *Soviet Empire: The Turks of Central Asia and Stalinism* (London, 1953)
Chamberlin, William Henry, *The Russian Revolution 1917–1921,* 2 vols (New York, 1935)
Clark, Alan, *Barbarossa: The Russo-German Conflict 1941–1945* (London, 1965)
Conquest, Robert, *The Soviet Deportation of Nationalities* (London, 1960)
Cresson, W. P., *The Cossacks, their History and Country* (New York, 1919)
Dallin, Alexander, *German Rule in Russia 1941–1945* (London, 1957)
Dallin, David J., *The Rise of Russia in Asia* (London, 1950)
Dallin, David J. and Nicolaevsky, Boris I., *Forced Labour in Soviet Russia* (London, 1948)
Dixon, C. Aubrey and Heilbrunn, Otto, *Communist Guerilla Warfare* (London, 1954)
Dubnow, S. M., *History of the Jews in Russia and Poland* (Philadelphia, 1916–20)
Eudin, X. J. and Fisher, H. H., *Soviet Russia and the West 1920–1927: A Documentary Survey* (Stanford, 1957)
Fennell, J. L. I., *Ivan the Great of Moscow* (London, 1963)
Fennell, J. L. I., *The Emergence of Moscow 1304–1359* (London, 1968)
Fischer, Louis, *The Soviets in World Affairs,* 2 vols (London, 1930)
Fischer, Louis, *The Life of Lenin* (London, 1964)
Freund, Gerald, *Unholy Alliance: Russian-German relations from the Treaty of Brest-Litovsk to the Treaty of Berlin* (London, 1957)
Futrell, Michael, *Northern Underground: Episodes of Russian Revolutionary Transport and Communications through Scandinavia and Finland 1863–1917* (London, 1963)
Greenberg, Louis, *The Jews in Russia: The Struggle For Emancipation,* 2 vols (New Haven, 1944, 1951)

Höhne, Heinz, *The Order of the Death's Head: The Story of Hitler's S.S.* (London, 1969)

Indian Officer, An (anon), *Russia's March Towards India*, 2 vols (London, 1894)

Jackson, W. A. Douglas, *Russo-Chinese Borderlands* (Princeton, 1962)

Joll, James, *The Anarchists* (London, 1964)

Kamenetsky, Ihor, *Hitler's Occupation of Ukraine 1941–1944: A study of Totalitarian imperialism* (Milwaukee, 1956)

Kazemzadeh, F., *The Struggle for Transcaucasia* (New York, 1951)

Katkov, George, *Russia 1917: The February Revolution* (London, 1967)

Kennan, George, *Siberia and the Exile System* (New York, 1891)

Kerner, Robert J., *The Urge to the Sea: The Course of Russian History* (Berkeley and Los Angeles, 1946)

Kirchner, Walther, *Commercial Relations Between Russia and Europe 1400 to 1800* (Bloomington, Indiana, 1966)

Klyuchevskii, Vasilii Osipovich, *Peter the Great* (London, 1958)

Kochan, Lionel, *Russia in Revolution 1890–1918* (London, 1966)

Kolarz, Walter, *Russia and her Colonies* (London, 1952)

Krypton, Constantine, *The Northern Sea Route* (New York, 1953)

Lang, D. M., *A Modern History of Georgia* (London, 1962)

Leslie, R. F., *Reform and Insurrection in Russian Poland* (London, 1963)

Lias, Godfrey, *Kazak Exodus* (London, 1956)

Liubavskii, M. K., *Ocherk Istorii Litovsko-Russkovo Gosudarstva* (Moscow, 1910; Russian Reprint Series, The Hague, 1966)

Lorimer, F., *The Population of the Soviet Union: History and Prospects* (Geneva, 1946)

Lyashchenko, Peter I., *History of the National Economy of Russia to the 1917 Revolution* (New York, 1949)

Maksimov, S., *Sibir i Katorga,* 3 vols (St Petersburg, 1871)

Malozemoff, A., *Russian Far-Eastern Policy 1881–1904* (Los Angeles, 1958)

Manning, Clarence A., *Twentieth-Century Ukraine* (New York, 1951)

Mazour, Anatole G., *The First Russian Revolution, 1825: the Decembrist movement* (Stanford, 1961)

Mikhailov, V., *Pamiatnaya Knizhka Sotsialista-Revoliutsionera*, 2 vols (Paris, 1911, 1914)

Miller, Margaret, *The Economic Development of Russia 1905–1914* (London, 1926)

Mora, Sylvestre and Zwierniak, Pierre, *La Justice Sovietique* (Rome, 1945)

Nasonov, A. N., *Russkaya Zemlia* (Moscow, 1951)

Nikitin, M. N. and Vagin, P. I., *The Crimes of the German Fascists in the Leningrad Region: Materials and Documents* (London, 1947)

Nosenko, A. K. (ed), *V. I. Lenin 1870–1924* (Kiev, n.d.). A collection of photographs, with 2 maps

Obolenski, Prince Eugene, *Souvenirs D'Un Exilé en Sibérie* (Leipzig, 1862)

Owen, Launcelot A., *The Russian Peasant Movement 1906–17* (London, 1937)

Park, Alexander G., *Bolshevism in Turkestan 1917–1927* (New York, 1957)

Philippi, Alfred and Heim, Ferdinand, *Der Feldzug gegen Sowjetrussland 1941–1945* (Stuttgart, 1962)

Pierce, Richard A., *Russian Central Asia 1867–1917* (Berkeley and Los Angeles, 1960)

Pipes, Richard, *The Formation of the Soviet Union: Communism and Nationalism 1917–1923* (Cambridge, Massachusetts, 1954)

Platonov, S. F., *Ocherki Po Istorii Smuti v Moskovskom Gosudarstve* (Moscow, 1937)

Pospelov, P. N., *Istoriya Kommunisticheskoi Partii Sovetskovo Soyuza,* 6 vols (Moscow, 1964–68)

Pounds, Norman J. G., *Poland Between East and West* (Princeton, 1964)
Radkey, Oliver H., *The Agrarian Foes of Bolshevism* (New York, 1958)
Rapport du Parti Socialiste Revolutionnaire de Russie au Congres Socialiste International de Stuttgart (Ghent, 1907)
Reddaway, W. R., Penson, J. H., Halecki, O. and Dyboski, R. (eds), *Cambridge History of Poland*, 2 vols (Cambridge, 1941, 1950)
Reitlinger, Gerald, *The House Built on Sand: The Conflicts of German Policy in Russia 1939–1945* (London, 1960)
Riasanovsky, Nicholas V., *A History of Russia* (New York, 1963)
Rosen, Baron A., *Russian Conspirators in Siberia* (London, 1872)
Rostovtzeff, M., *The Iranians and Greeks in South Russia* (Oxford, 1922)
Salisbury, Harrison E., *The Siege of Leningrad* (London, 1969)
Schuyler, Eugene, *Peter the Great: Emperor of Russia,* 2 vols (London, 1844)
Schwarz, Solomon M., *The Russian Revolution of 1905* (Chicago, 1967)
Serge, Victor, *Memoirs of a Revolutionary 1901–1941* (London, 1963)
Seton-Watson, Hugh, *The Russian Empire 1801–1917* (London, 1967)
Shukman, Harold, *Lenin and the Russian Revolution* (London, 1966)
Simpson, Sir John Hope, *The Refugee Problem* (London, 1939)
Skazkin, S. D. (and others), *Istoriya Vizantii*, 3 vols (Moscow, 1967)
Slusser, Robert M. and Triska Jan F., *A Calendar of Soviet Treaties 1917–1957* (Stanford, 1959)
Squire, P. S., *The Third Department: The establishment and practices of the political police in the Russia of Nicholas I* (Cambridge, 1968)
Stephan, John J., *Sakhalin* (Oxford, 1971)
Sullivant, Robert S., *Soviet Politics and the Ukraine 1917–1957* (New York, 1962)
Sumner, B. H., *Peter the Great and the Ottoman Empire* (Oxford, 1949)
Sumner, B. H., *Peter the Great and the Emergence of Russia* (London, 1950)
Suprunenko, M. I. (and others), *Istoria Ukrainskoi RSR* (Kiev, 1958)
Tikhonov, Nikolai (and others), *The Defence of Leningrad: Eye-witness Accounts of the Siege* (London, 1944)
Treadgold, Donald W., *The Great Siberian Migration* (Princeton, 1957)
Trotsky, Leon, *My Life* (London, 1930)
Vernadsky, George, *The Mongols and Russia* (London, 1953)
Wheeler, G., *The Modern History of Soviet Central Asia* (London, 1964)
Woodward, David, *The Russians at Sea* (London, 1965)
Yarmolinski, Avram, *The Road to Revolution: A Century of Russian Radicalism* (London, 1957)
Yaroslavsky, E., *History of Anarchism in Russia* (London, 1937)
Zimin, A. A., *Reformy Ivana Groznovo* (Moscow, 1960)

(v) ARTICLES

Anon, 'How the Bear Learned to Swim', *The Economist* (London, 24–30 October 1970)
Bealby, John Thomas, Kropotkin, Prince Peter Alexeivitch, Philips, Walter Alison and Wallace, Sir Donald Mackenzie, 'Russia', *The Encyclopaedia Britannica* (Eleventh edition, London and New York, 1910)
Carsten, F. L., 'The Reichswehr and the Red Army 1920–1933', *Survey* (London, 1962)
Dziewanowski, M. K., 'Pilsudski's Federal Policy 1919–21', *Journal of Central European Affairs* (London, 1950)
Footman, David, 'Nestor Makno', *St Antony's Papers No. 6: Soviet Affairs No. 2* (Oxford, 1959)

Lobanov-Rostovsky, A., 'Anglo-Russian Relations through the Centuries', *Russian Review*, vol 7 (New York, 1948)

Parkes, Harry, 'Report on the Russian Caravan Trade with China', *Journal of the Royal Geographic Society*, vol 25 (London, 1854)

Stanhope, Henry, 'Soviet Strength at Sea', *The Times* (London, 25 January 1971)

Sullivan, Joseph L., 'Decembrists in Exile', *Harvard Slavic Studies,* vol 4 (The Hague, 1954)

Wildes, Harry Emerson, 'Russia's Attempts to Open Japan', *Russian Review,* vol 5 (New York, 1945)

Yakunskiy, V. K. 'La Révolution Industrielle en Russie', *Cahiers du Monde Russe et Sovietique* (The Hague, 1961)

Index

Compiled by the Author

camps near, 110; allied aid enters the Soviet Union through (1941–45), 120, 121; a German plan for (1941), 122; Germans fail to reach (1941–43), 128

Atatürk, Kemal: his rejection of Armenian territorial claims gives him common cause with Lenin, 104

Athens: 3; raided by the Goths, 5; under Roman Catholic control, 24

Athos: raided by the Goths, 5

Attila the Hun: extends rule of the Huns to the Rhine, 6

Augustow: Germans occupy (1914), 81; Soviet Union annexes (1939), 114

Aurora (Russian cruiser): fires blanks at the Winter Palace, Petrograd (1917), 90

Auschwitz: German concentration camp at, 123

Austerlitz: Napoleon defeats the Russians at (1805), 49

Austria: Catherine the Great gives Russia a common frontier with, 41; a party to two partitions of Poland (1772, 1795), 42; Russia suppresses Hungarian revolt in (1849), 51; helps Russia suppress Polish revolt (1860), 53; signs trade agreement with Bolshevik Russia (1921), 101; helps to equip the Kara Sea Expedition (1921), 105; Russian refugees in (by 1930), 107; Soviet occupation zone in (1945–50), 133

Austria–Hungary: and European diplomacy (1872–1907), 63, 64; and Russian policy in the Balkans (1876–1914), 78, 79; Lenin allowed to leave (1914), 87

Avars: their European conquests, 8; their demise, 9; settled along the middle Danube, 10

Azef; exposed as a police spy, 72

Azerbaijan: and the proposed Union of Border States (1919–20), 100; its brief independence (1918–20), 104; a Soviet Socialist Republic, 144

Azov: principal town of the Crimean Khanate, 25; a principal town of the Don Cossacks, 35; Don Cossacks defeated at (1708), 37; battle of (1736), 46

Azov, Sea of: Greek and Scythian settlements on shores of, 3; river routes across Russia from, 27; naval battle in (1737), 46; anarchist headquarters on the shore of (1918–20), 95; German occupation forces driven from (1943–44), 129

Babylon: area of Assyrian settlement in 800 BC, 1; reached by nomads from central Asia, 2

Bagdad: part of the Islamic world, 10, 15

Bahrein: comes under British control (1867), 61

Baibert: battle of (1829), 46

Baikal, Lake: largely within the Mongol dominions, 21; early Russian settlements on, 33; Chinese territory extended towards (1720–60), 40; and the Siberian exile system (1648–1917), 54; and Russian trade with China (1850–70), 59; and the Trans-Siberian railway, 62; forms the western boundary of the Far Eastern Republic (1920–22), 106; Soviet labour camp near, 111; industry in the region of (1970), 137

Bakhchisaray: unsuccessful Russian attack on (1556–59), 26; battle of (1736), 46

Baku: Viking settlers reach, 11; temporarily annexed by Russia from Persia (1723–25), 37; large German community in (by 1914), 39; annexed by Russia (1806), 48; anarchists active in (1905–06), 55; industrial growth of (by 1860), 56; strikes in (before 1905), 68; industry in (by 1900), 71; political assassinations in, 72; secret Bolshevik printing press in, 73; revolutionary outbreak at (1905), 76; occupied by the Turks (1917–18), 85, 91; occupied by the British (1918–19), 92, 103, 104, 146; Soviet labour camps near, 110; United States aid reaches (1941–45), 120; a German plan for (1941), 122; its oilfields a major German military objective (1942), 124, 128; over half a million inhabitants (1959), 138

Bakunin, Mikhail Alexandrovich: exiled to Siberia, 54; his view of anarchism, 55

Balkans: raided by the Slavs, 8; Slav settlements in, 9; Turkish rule of, 49; Bismarck demarcates Austro-Russian line of influence in, 63

Balkhash, Lake: on the eastern boundary of the lands of the Golden Horde, 21; and Russian trade with China (1850–70),

59; Ukrainian settlements in the region of (by 1937), 98; anti-Bolshevik revolt in region of (1917–20), 103; Stalinist deportation of national groups to (1941–45), 131; industry to the north of (1970), 137

Balta. annexed by Russia (1793), 43; anti-Jewish violence in, 69

Baltic Sea: Goths settle along, 4; Goths extend their control to the Black Sea from, 5; reached by the Huns, 6; reached by the Slavs, 7; reached by the Avars, 8; Slav control established along part of southern shore of, 9; Kievan Russian trade across, 14; extension of German control along southern shore of, 20; Lithuanians rule from shore of, to Black Sea, 23; its shores entirely controlled by Roman Catholic rulers, 24; Tsar Fedor re-establishes Russian control on, 26; river routes across Russia from, 27; Russian trade in, 34; Russian westward expansion along (1721–1945), 35, 47; Jews expelled from the coastline of (1828, 1830), 51

Baltimore (USA): Ukrainians at, 99

Balts: their area of settlement by 800 BC, 1; by 200 AD, 4; increasingly discontented with Russian rule (by 1905), 68, 76; four million in Russia (1897), 74

Bandar Shah (Persia): United States aid enters Soviet Union through (1941–45), 120

Bar: Jews murdered in (1648–52), 31

Baranovichi: annexed by Russia (1795), 43

Barguzin: founded (1648), 33; and the Siberian exiles, 54; in the Far Eastern Republic (1920–22), 106

Barnaul: Ukrainians at (by 1937), 98; industry at (1941–45), 121; a German plan for (1941), 122; Virgin Lands campaign extended to (after 1953), 136 ·

Bashkirs: revolt against Russian rule (1708–11), 37; famine in homeland of (1921), 102; anti-Bolshevik uprising in (1917–20), 103; form an Autonomous Soviet Socialist Republic, 144

Basidu: British island near possible Russian railhead on Indian Ocean, 61

Batum: ceded to Russia by Turkey (1878), 48; anarchists active in (1905–06), 55; strikes in (before 1905), 68; Bolsheviks active in (1903–14), 73; revolution in (1905), 76; Turks advance on (1917), 85; Turks occupy (1918), 91; British occupy (1918–19), 92, 104, 146; Soviet aid to Republican Spain leaves from (1936–39), 101; a German plan to control (1941), 122

Baturin: revolt against Peter the Great in (1708), 37

Bavaria: German communists fail to seize power in, 108

Bayazit: occupied by Russia (1829), 46

Begovat: industry at (1941–45), 121

Belgium: Russian refugees from Bolshevism in (by 1930), 107

Belgorod: within area of peasants' revolt (1606–07), 29; trade fair at, 34; revolutionary outbreak at (1905), 76

Belgrade: Treaty of (1739), 46; and the defeat of Germany (1944–45), 130

Belogorsk: and the Soviet-Chinese border (1970), 143

Belomor Canal: largely built by forced labour, 109

Belozersk: within Kievan Russia, 13; Orthodox monastery established at, 16; Ivan IV seizes land in region of, 28

Belzec (Belzhets): German concentration camp at, 123

Bender: proposed Russian railway to Persian Gulf at, 61

Bendery: siege of (1770), 46

Berdiansk: attacked by anarchists (1918–20), 95; occupied by the Germans (1941–43), 128; Germans driven from (1943), 129

Berdichev: Jewish political activity in, 70

Berezov: founded (1593), 33

Bering Sea: Soviet labour camps on the shore of, 111

Berlin: colonized by the Germans, 20; Protocols of Zion published in (1911), 69; Russian students in, 70; Lenin in exile in (1907, 1912), 73; Treaty of (1878), 78; Lenin returns to Russia through (1917), 87; German communists try to seize power, but suppressed in, 108; entered by Soviet troops (1945), 113, 130; divided in Soviet, British, French and United States sectors (1945), 133

Berne (Switzerland): Lenin in exile in (1913–17), 73, 87

Bessarabia: annexed by Russia from Turkey (1812), 46, 50; peasant uprising in province of (1905), 75; Rumanian (from 1918), annexed by the Soviet Union (1940), 116; a German plan

18; river routes across Russia from, 27; Ivan IV seizes lands to the south and east of, 28; Swedish conquests in region of, 30; a Soviet labour camp established at, 109; and the siege of Leningrad (1941–43), 126

Ladozhskoye Ozero: a lakeside town, crucial for the defence of Leningrad (1941–43), 126

Laibach: conference of, 50

Lakhta: and the siege of Leningrad (1941–42), 126

Lampozhnia: town founded by the Republic of Novgorod, 19

Lanchow (China): and Russian trade with China (1850–70), 59; defended by Soviet air units (1941), 142

Lapland: a Roman Catholic region (by 1300), 24; part of, annexed by Russia from Sweden (1809), 47

Laptev Sea: Soviet labour camp region borders on, 111; Northern Sea Route passes through, 112

Latakia (Syria): Soviet naval facilities at (1970), 141

Latvia: taken by Russia from Sweden (1721), 36; the growing national aspirations of (1917), 89; intervenes against the Bolsheviks (1918–19), 92; and the proposed Union of Border States (1919), 100; signs non-aggression Pact with Soviet Union (1932), 101; Russian refugees in (by 1930), 107; annexed by the Soviet Union (1939), 115, 116; population movements from (1943–46), 132; reincorporated into the Soviet Union (1945), 133; a Soviet Republic (since 1945), 144

Lausanne (Switzerland): Lenin in, 73

Laz: their settlement by 800 BC, 1

Lednovo: and the siege of Leningrad (1941–43), 126

Leipzig (Germany): Russian students in, 70; Bolshevik activity in (1903–14), 73

Lemnos: raided by the Goths, 5

Lena, River: early Russian settlements along, 33; and the Siberian exile system, 54; Soviet labour camps on, 111; coal basin along the lower reaches of, 112, 137; Stalinist deportation of national groups to (1941–45), 131

Lenin, Vladimir Ilich: his political activity (before 1917), 73; returns to Russia from exile (1917), 86, 87, 88; goes into hiding in Finland (1917), 89; returns to Petrograd (Oct 1917), 90; established Third Communist International (1919), 108; towns and villages named after, 139

Lenin (Russian icebreaker); leads Kara Sea Expeditions (1920, 1921), 105

Leningrad: Soviet aid to Republican Spain leaves from (1936–39), 101; factories evacuated from (1940–41), 113; besieged by Germany (1941–43), 118, 126; a German plan for (1941), 122; Soviet partisans south of (1941–42), 127; three million inhabitants (by 1959), 138; Soviet naval forces based on (1970), 141; a 'Hero City' of the Soviet Union, 146

Lenkoran: annexed by Russia (1813), 48, 61; anti-Bolshevik revolt in (1920–21), 104

Lethbridge (Canada): Ukrainians at, 99

Lhasa (Tibet): conquered by China (1780), 40; British troops enter (1904), 65

Libau: taken by Russia from Poland (1795), 36, 42, 43; industrial growth of (after 1860), 56; Jewish political activity in, 70; revolution at (1905), 76; and German war aims (1914), 80; German army occupies (1914–15), 82

Lida: annexed by Russia (1795), 43; annexed by Germany (1941), 123

Liegnitz: attacked by the Mongols, 22

Lindisfarne: Viking settlers reach, 11

Lipetsk: Germans train pilots secretly at (1922–33), 101

Lisbon: Viking settlers reach, 11

Lithuania: Russian monasteries in, 16; controls Russian province of Polotsk, 17; attacks Republic of Novgorod, 18; extends its rule to Black Sea, 23; a Roman Catholic kingdom, 24; peasants flee from serfdom in, to become Cossacks, 35; annexed by Russia (1795), 41, 43; intervenes against the Bolsheviks (1918–19), 92; and the proposed Union of Border States (1919), 100; Russian refugees in (by 1930), 107; annexed to the Soviet Union (1940), 116; population movements from (1939–46), 132; reincorporated into the Soviet Union (1945), 133; a Soviet Republic (since 1945), 144

Litvinov, Maksim Maksimovich: in London at the time of the revolution (1917), 88

Liubech: a town in Kievan Russia, 13

Livonia: peasant uprising in Province of (1905), 75

Lodz: Polish town, annexed by Prussia (1793), 42; part of Russia, and anti-Jewish violence in, 69, 75; Jewish political activity in, 70; revolution in (1905), 76; and German war aims (1914), 80; Germans defeat Russians at (1914), 81; Polish (from 1918), occupied by Germany (1939), 114; part of Poland, and anti-Soviet revolt in (1956), 134

Lomza: Polish town annexed by the Soviet Union (1939), 114

London: Russian Jews flee to (1880–1905), 70; Lenin in exile in (1907), 73; Lenin plans to return to Russia through (1917), 87; Russian Bolshevik leaders in (1917), 88

Lovat, River: a highway of trade in Kievan Russia, 14

Lozovaya: attacked by anarchists (1918–20), 95

Lublin: Jews murdered in (1648–52), 31; annexed by Austria from Poland (1795), 42, 43; Russian (after 1815), and a centre of Polish revolt against Russia (1860), 53; revolution in (1905), 76; and German war aims (1914), 80; Russian army advances into Austria from (1914), 81; Polish (since 1918), Red Army fails to capture (1920), 96; occupied by Germany (1939), 114, 116; Jewish uprising against Germans in, 123

Luga: Tsarist troops disarmed at (1917), 86; occupied by anti-Bolshevik forces (1919), 93; German reprisals against Russian civilians in (1941–43), 126; Soviet partisans active near, 127; Germans driven from (1943–44), 129

Lugansk: large German community in (by 1914), 39; industry in (by 1900), 71; annexed to the Independent Ukraine (1918), 97; name changed to Voroshilov, 139; *for further index entries see* Voroshilov

Lunacharsky, Anatoli Vasilevich: in Switzerland at the time of the revolution (1917), 88

Lüneburg: a Hansa town, 20

Lutsk: becomes part of Russia (1795), 41, 43; a Polish town (since 1921), annexed by the Soviet Union (1939), 114; annexed by Germany (1941), 123

Lvov (Lemberg): a principal town of the Kingdom of Poland, 23; under Roman Catholic control, 24; Jews murdered in (1648–52), 31; annexed by Austria from Poland (1772), 42, 43; Bolshevik propaganda enters Russia through (1903–14), 73; Russians occupy (1914), 81; Russians driven from (1915), 82; Russians fail to retake (1916), 83; second Russian offensive against, unsuccessful (1917), 89; Red Army fails to capture (1920), 96; part of the West Ukrainian Republic (1918), 97; occupied by the Poles (1919), 100; annexed by the Soviet Union (1939), 114, 116; occupied by the Germans (1941), 118, 119; Jewish uprising against the Germans in, 123; Germans driven from (1944), 130; reincorporated into the Soviet Union (1945), 133

Macedonia: and Russian policy in the Balkans (1876–85), 78

Magadan: principal town of the Kolyma River forced labour area, 111

Magdagachi: and the Soviet-Chinese border (1970), 143

Magnitogorsk: many Ukrainians settled at (by 1937), 98; a German plan for (1941), 122; over a quarter of a million inhabitants (1959), 138

Magyars: settle along the middle Danube, 12; converted to Roman Catholicism, 15

Maikop: annexed by Russia (1864), 48; revolutionary outbreak at (1905), 76; occupied by the Germans (1942), 124, 128

Maimaichin: under Chinese control, 40; and Russian trade with China (1850–70), 59

Majdanek: a German concentration camp, 123

Makhachkala: part of the Terek Peoples' SSR (1918–19), 104; Germans fail to reach (1941–43), 128

Makhno, Nestor Ivanovich: controls large area of southern Russia (1918–20), 95

Maklakovo: and the Northern Sea Route administration, 112

Malaya Vishera: Nicholas II's train halted at (1917), 86; Germans occupy (1941), 126

Poti: battles of (1809, 1829), 46; annexed by Russia (1804), 48; strikes in (before 1905), 68; Turks advance on (1917), 85; occupied by the Germans (1918), 104, 146; Germans fail to reach (1941–43), 128

Potsdam (Germany): conference at (1945), 113

Povorotnyi, Cape: Chinese territory, annexed by Russia (1860), 60

Prague: in the Holy Roman Empire, 20; Lenin in exile in (1912), 73; communist propaganda disseminated in, 108; communism established in (1948), 113; within Greater Germany (1939–45), 117; and the defeat of Germany (1944–45), 130; anti-Soviet revolt in (1968), 134

Predvinsk: shipbuilding at (after 1937), 112

Preslav: a Slav town in the Balkans, 12; within the area paying tribute to Kievan Russia, 13

Preslavets: a town paying tribute to Kievan Russia, 13

Pribilov Islands: Russian, sold to the United States (1867), 44

Prince Albert (Canada): Ukrainians at, 99

Prinkipo (Turkey): Trotsky in exile at, 113

Pripet Marshes: early Slav settlements in, 1, 4; controlled by the Goths, 5; controlled by the Huns, 6; controlled by the Slavs, 7; controlled by the Avars, 8; Slavs re-establish their control of, 9, 10; within Kievan Russia, 14; Polish, annexed by Russia (1793 and 1795), 42, 43; Germans hope to extend their territory towards (1914), 79; Polish army advances to (1920), 97; Russian army occupies Polish part of (1939), 114; occupied by the Germans (1941), 118, 119; Soviet army reaches (1944), 129

Prostitutes: exiled to Siberia, 54

Proudhon, Pierre Joseph: 'Property is theft', 55

Provedeniya Bay: on the Northern Sea Route, 112

Provinces of Russia: the boundaries, as established by Peter the Great, 38; as redrawn by Catherine the Great, 41; in 1900 (74)

Prussia: a Roman Catholic region, 24; Catherine the Great gives Russia a common frontier with, 41; a party to three partitions of Poland (1772, 1793, 1795), 42; Russia allies with, against Sweden (1714), 47; helps Russia suppress Polish revolt (1860), 53

Pruth, River: a highway of trade in Kievan Russia, 14; Russians fail to drive Turks from (1711), 37

Przemysl (Peremyshl): a town conquered by Kievan Russia, 13; a Polish town, Jews murdered in (1648–52), 31; annexed by Austria (1772), 43; Russians occupy (1914), 81; 81; Russians driven from (1915), 82; part of the West Ukrainian Republic (1918), 97; Polish (since 1921), annexed by the Soviet Union (1939), 114, 116; annexed by Germany (1941), 123

Pskov: a town in Kievan Russia, 13; Orthodox monastery established at, 16; frequently attacked by Teutonic Knights, 18, 20; conquered by the Principality of Moscow, 25; uprising in (1648–50), 32; peasant uprising in province of (1826–27), 51; peasant discontent and serfdom in the Province of (by 1860), 58; political assassinations in, 72; Bolsheviks active in, 73; agricultural workers strike in Province of (1905), 75; Nicholas II put under arrest at (1917), 86; occupied by German troops (1918), 91; occupied by the Germans (1941), 118, 119, 123, 126; Soviet partisans active near (1941–42), 127

Pskov, Lake of: western shore of reached by the Teutonic Knights, 20; Soviet partisans active against the Germans along eastern shore of (1941–42), 127

Pudozhskoi: a town in the Republic of Novgorod, 18

Pushkin, Alexander Sergeevich: urges the Siberian exile, 'keep your patience proud', 54

Pushkinskiye Gori: Soviet partisans near (1941–42), 127

Pustozersk: town founded by the Republic of Novgorod, 19; and the river systems of European Russia, 27

Putilov works (near Petrograd): strike in, suppressed by the army (1916), 84; further strike at (1917), 86

Qatar: comes under British control (1892), 61

Radek, Karl: in Switzerland at the time of the revolution (1917), 88

Radimichians: an eastern Slav tribe, 12

Radishchev, Alexander Nikolaevich: exiled to Siberia, 54

Radomsk: a centre of Polish revolt against Russia (1860), 53

Rakovsky, Christian: in Rumania at the time of the revolution (1917), 88

Razin, Stenka: leads peasants' revolt (1670–71), 32; peasants' flee eastwards across Urals after failure of revolt of, 33

Regina (Canada): Ukrainians at, 99

Republic of Novgorod: a Russian Principality, 17; styled 'Sovereign Great Novgorod', 18; unconquered by the Mongols, 21, 22; unconquered by the Lithuanians, 23; conquered by the Principality of Moscow, 25

Resht: Persian town, annexed by Russia (1723–25), 37

Reval (Tallin): and German eastward expansion (by 1500), 20; Roman Catholic control in, 24; taken by Russia from Sweden (1721), 36, 37, 47, 145; industrial growth of (after 1860), 56; strikes at (1905), 76; Germans hope to annex (1914), 79; Bolshevik influence in (1917), 89; United States famine relief arrives at (1921), 102; annexed by the Soviet Union (1939), 115, 116; a German plan for (1941), 122; German SS headquarters in, 123; reincorporated into the Soviet Union (1945), 133

Revolution of 1905: prelude to (1894–1904), 68; 75, 76, 77

Revolution of 1917: 86, 87, 88, 89, 90, 91

Rezhitsa: Tsarist troops move on Petrograd from (1917), 86

Rhine, River: within the Roman Empire, 4; Germanic tribes control eastern bank of, 5; controlled by the Huns, 6

Riabaya Mogila: battle of (1770), 46

Riazan: conquered by Kievan Russia, 13; conquered by the Principality of Moscow, 25; an industrial centre (by 1800), 34; in the most heavily populated area of Russia (in 1724), 38; industrial growth in the region of (by 1860), 56; peasant discontent in the Province of (1827–60), 57; serfdom in (by 1860), 58; peasant poverty in Province of (by 1904), 68; peasant uprising in Province of (1905), 75; a German plan for (1941), 122

Riga: and German eastward expansion (by 1500), 20; and Russian exports of timber and grain from (by 1800), 34; taken by Russia from Sweden (1721), 36, 37, 47, 145; large German community in (by 1914), 39; Napoleon advances towards (1812), 49; anarchists active in (1905–06), 55; an industrial centre (by 1860), 56; strikes in (before 1905), 68; Jewish political activity in, 70; industry in (by 1900), 71; Bolshevik activity in (1903–14), 73; revolution in (1905), 76; Germans hope to annex (1914), 79, 80; German army fails to reach (1915), 82; Tsarist troops move on Petrograd from (1917), 86; Bolshevik influence in (1917), 89; occupied by German troops (1918), 91; Treaty of (March 1921), 96; United States famine relief arrives at (1921), 102; annexed by the Soviet Union (1939), 116; occupied by the Germans (1941), 118, 119; a German plan for (1941), 122; Jewish uprising against the Germans in, 123; Germans driven from (1944), 130; reincorporated into the Soviet Union (1945), 133; over half a million inhabitants (1959), 138

Rochester (USA): Ukrainians at, 99

Roman Catholicism: established in western Europe, 15; extends its control eastwards, 24

Roman Empire: extends its rule to western shore of the Caspian Sea, 4

Romanov: uprising in (1648–50), 32

Romanovs: rule Russia (1613–1917), 29

Rosenberg, Alfred: draws up plan for partition of the Soviet Union (1941), 122

Rostock: a Hansa town on the Baltic, 20; under communist control (since 1945), 36; anti-communist revolt in (1953), 134

Rostov (Old Rostov): within Kievan Russia, 13; Orthodox monastery established at, 16

Rostov-on-Don: anti-Jewish violence in, 69; Bolsheviks in (1903–14), 73; revolution in (1905), 76; occupied by German troops (1918), 91; occupied by anti-Bolshevik forces (1919), 92, 146; claimed as part of the Ukraine, 97; Soviet aid to Republican Spain leaves from (1936–39), 101; famine in (1921), 102; occupied by the Germans (1941), 118, 120, 121, 123, 124, 128; a German plan for (1941), 122; Germans driven from